WORKBOOK FOR

BEING A NURSING ASSISTANT

FOURTH EDITION

Rose B. Schniedman, R.N., M.S. Ed., C.N.A.
Susan S. Lambert, M.A. Ed.

A BRADY BOOK, Prentice-Hall, Englewood Cliffs, New Jersey 07632

DEDICATION

To Della, who motivated and inspired us, with all our love, respect and admiration.

To Marty, Alan, Barbara, Barry, Stephen, and Luci who sustain us with their love.

To Carrie, Joey, Robert, Carly, and Felicia who are our future, whom we all love.

Schniedman, Rose B. and Lambert, Susan S.
Workbook for Being a Nursing Assistant, Fourth Edition.

©1986 by Brady Communications Company, A division of Simon & Schuster, Inc., Englewood Cliffs, New Jersey 07632.

For information, address Prentice-Hall, Englewood Cliffs, NJ 07632

ISBN 0-89303-593-9   01

Prentice-Hall of Australia, Pty., Ltd., Sydney
Prentice-Hall Canada, Inc., Scarborough, Ontario
Prentice-Hall Hispanoamericana, S.A., Mexico
Prentice-Hall of India Private Limited, New Delhi
Prentice-Hall International (UK) Limited, London
Prentice-Hall of Japan, Inc., Tokyo
Prentice-Hall Southeast Asia, Pte. Ltd., Singapore
Editora Prentice-Hall Do Brasil LTDA., Rio de Janeiro
Whitehall Books, Limited, Petone, New Zealand

Printed in the United States of America

10 9 8 7 6 5 4 3 2 1

CONTENTS

PREFACE

This workbook has been written to motivate interest, to instruct, to evaluate, and to involve you, the student, actively in the learning process. We asked you to:

* Locate, recall, and recognize information

* Change information into different forms, such as from pictures to words

* Discover relationships among facts, definitions, rules, procedures, and skills

* Find solutions to lifelike situations

* Learn by doing

A variety of exercises from crossword puzzles to flashcards have been included in an effort to meet your individual learning needs and to provide an effective learning experience that is compatible with your learning style. The knowledge and skill you gain will help you face the new experiences on the job as a nursing assistant.

This workbook is not intended to be used alone. It is totally dependent and coordinated with the textbook, Being a Nursing Assistant, Fourth Edition. It is planned to guide you through the textbook page by page and procedure by procedure. It is absolutely essential to read the textbook as you do each assignment. If you read something that puzzles you, ask your instructor to explain it.

This is not a book of tests. With the exception of the chapter quizzes and the final examination, we encourage you to keep your textbook open as you do each assignment. The questions in this workbook were not written to stump, trick, or fool you. They were written to help you learn to do all the nursing tasks and procedures you will be reading about and studying in your textbook. The answers to the questions can be found in the back of the book.

You can also use the workbook to review your classroom and clinical learning experiences. By completing these assignments, you can fix the procedures and key ideas firmly in your mind. If you are willing to be an active participant in the learning experiences, this workbook can help you with words to remember and can be an effective learning tool.

The more you read, review, and practice, the easier it will be for you to take the step from being a student to being a nursing assistant.

CHAPTER 1   BEING A NURSING ASSISTANT

SECTION 1

WORKBOOK ASSIGNMENT #1, CHAPTER 1, SECTION 1
THE HEALTH CARE INSTITUTION

In your text, find the list of objectives for this section. Next to each objective, write the page numbers where you can find information to help you meet these objectives.

WORKBOOK ASSIGNMENT #2, CHAPTER 1, SECTION 1
HEALTH CARE INSTITUTIONS

Read the chart titled "Five Basic Functions and Purposes of Health Care Institutions" in your textbook. Use the words listed below to fill in the blanks.

sciences   ill   prevent
education   community

1. To provide care for _____ and/or injured.

2. To _____ disease.

3. To promote individual and _____ health.

4. To promote facilities for the _____ of health care workers.

5. To promote research in the _____ of medicine and nursing.

WORKBOOK ASSIGNMENT #3, CHAPTER 1, SECTION 1
THE NURSING ASSISTANT: PART OF A TEAM

Read the information in your textbook titled "The Nursing Assistant: Part of a Team."

Circle the letter of the correct answer.

1. As a nursing assistant, you are a:

    A. Professional giver of health care
    B. Member of a health care team
    C. Task-oriented person
    D. Leader of the nursing service staff
    E. A and B.

2. You will work under the supervision of a:

    A. Professional nurse
    B. Licensed practical nurse
    C. Ward clerk or health unit coordinator
    D. Doctor
    E. Nursing assistant.

3. The nursing health care team in your institution may be organized in which of the following ways?

   A. Individual nursing
   B. Team nursing
   C. Primary nursing
   D. Functional nursing
   E. B, C, and D.

4. In functional (direct assignment) nursing, the head nurse assigns and directs:

   A. All patients to their patient care unit
   B. All meal trays to the correct patients
   C. All patient care responsibilities for the nursing staff
   D. All medical responsibilities
   E. C and D.

5. In primary nursing, the professional nurse is responsible for:

   A. Assessing the patient's needs
   B. Planning, implementing, and evaluating the patient's nursing care
   C. Discharge planning for her patient
   D. Patient education and family teaching
   E. All of the above.

WORKBOOK ASSIGNMENT #4, CHAPTER 1, SECTION 1
TEAM NURSING

In your textbook, read the information titled "Team Nursing."

Use the words listed below to fill in the blank spaces.

teams	done	Nursing Assistant (N.A.)
team	leader	Licensed Practical Nurses (L.P.N.)
task	advisor	assignments
group	members	Registered Nurses (R.N.)

The head nurse divides her staff into (A)_____. Each team has a (B)_____. The head nurse assigns a (C)_____ of patients to each team. The team leader then makes out patient care (D)_____ for members of her (E)_____. Team members may be (F)_____ _____ _____, (G)_____ _____ _____, or (H)_____ _____. The team leader is teacher (I)_____ and helper to all of her team (J)_____. This system is (K)_____ oriented. This means that nursing care is arranged according to what must be (L)_____.

WORKBOOK ASSIGNMENT #5, CHAPTER 1, SECTION 1
PRIMARY NURSING

In your textbook, read the information titled "Primary Nursing."

2

Use the words listed below to fill in the blank spaces.

responsibilities   needs   evaluating   nursing
care   patient   individual   delivery
accountable   professional   work   patient

Primary nursing is a method of patient care (A)_____ in which the
(B)_____ nurse is responsible and (C)_____ for the entire
(D)_____ care of the patient. She is responsible for assessing the
patient's (E)_____ and for planning, implementing, and (F)_____
the patient's nursing (G)_____. The purpose is to ensure that the
professional nurse (H)_____ directly with the (I)_____. In
addition, her (J)_____ include family teaching, patient education,
discharge planning, and community agencies recruiting to assist the patient after
discharge. This system is (K)_____ oriented. This means that nursing
care is arranged according to the total needs of the (L)_____ patient
sometimes called "Total Nursing Care."

SECTION 2

WORKBOOK ASSIGNMENT #6, CHAPTER 1, SECTION 2
WORKING WITH PEOPLE IN THE HEALTH CARE INSTITUTION

Find the list of objectives for this section. Next to each objective, write the
page numbers where you can find information to help you meet these objectives.

WORKBOOK ASSIGNMENT #7, CHAPTER 1, SECTION 2
WORKING WITH PEOPLE IN THE HEALTH CARE INSTITUTION

In your textbook, read "Key Ideas: Working With People in the Health Care
Institution." Fill in the empty circles provided below with the five major
groups of patients you will care for.

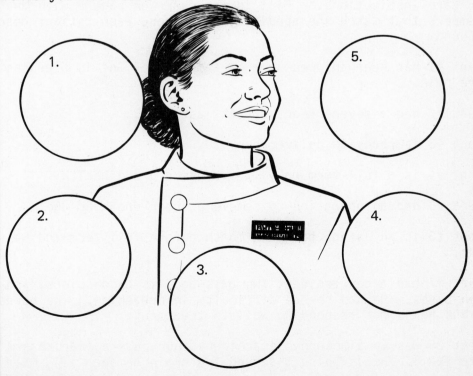

3

WORKBOOK ASSIGNMENT #8, CHAPTER 1, SECTION 2
WORKING WITH CHRONICALLY ILL OR ACUTELY ILL MEDICAL/SURGICAL PATIENTS

Read the information on "Working with Chronically Ill or Acutely Ill Medical/
Surgical Patients" in your textbook before filling in the blanks below.

1. _____ illness continues over years or a lifetime.

2. _____ illness comes on suddenly and runs its course within a few
   days.

3. Medical-surgical patients are those who have an (A)_____ or
   (B)_____ illness that is treated with medical or surgical
   intervention.

4. A _____ patient usually has to get used to, or adapt to, changes
   in the form of his or her body functions, as it may be necessary to repair
   or remove a part of the body that has been injured by illness or physical
   accident. Two examples of this are amputation and colostomy.

5. Surgical patients can be divided into three groups.

   A) _____ (before an operation).
   B) Those in the process of having an _____.
   C) _____ (after the operation).

WORKBOOK ASSIGNMENT #9, CHAPTER 1, SECTION 2
SPECIALTY AREAS

In your textbook, read the information titled "Patients in the Specialty Areas of
the Health Care Institutions." Fill in the chart on page 5 with an "X" under the
patient numbers that match the specialty area where each patient described below
would be found.

   Patient #1 has been injured in a car accident. She is bleeding and in
   severe pain.

   Patient #2 had a severe heart attack last week.

   Patient #3 is ready to deliver her baby.

   Patient #4 is a full-term baby, two hours old and healthy.

   Patient #5 had an operation to remove a tumor one hour ago.

   Patient #6 is an infant born one month before full term and weighs four
   pounds.

   Patient #7 had a car accident two days ago, is unconscious, and has many
   broken bones. He had severe difficulty in breathing. The bones have been
   set, but he is not responding well to treatment.

   Patient #8 was in a motorcycle accident four days ago and has a fracture
   of the skull. He is being observed for brain damage.

Patient #9 had her gallbladder removed in surgery an hour ago.

Patient #10 has been shot and had surgery to remove the bullet less than 1/2 hour ago.

Patient #11 fell out of a tree and has many bruises.

Patient #12 has had two heart attacks in the past year and now has pain in the left arm and in the chest. The doctor thinks he is starting to have another heart attack.

Patient #13 is having a bad reaction to an insect bite and is covered with red marks. This happened 1/2 hour ago.

Patient #14 was born four hours ago by cesarean section. The neonate is fine and appears normal and healthy.

PATIENT NUMBERS

	1	2	3	4	5	6	7	8	9	10	11	12	13	14
Labor & Delivery														
Newborn Nursery														
Premature Nursery														
Intensive Care- Critical Care Unit														
Coronary/Cardiac Care Unit														
Postoperative Recovery Room														
Emergency Department														

WORKBOOK ASSIGNMENT #10, CHAPTER 1, SECTION 3
YOUR JOB AS A NURSING ASSISTANT

Find the list of objectives for this section. Next to each objective, write the page numbers where you can find information to help you meet these objectives.

WORKBOOK ASSIGNMENT #11, CHAPTER 1, SECTION 3
TASK CHECK LIST

The following task check list will enable you or your instructor to keep a dated record of your experience in performing the procedures and tasks included in your textbook. When your instructor shows you how to do the procedure or task, write the date in the Date Demonstrated column. When you perform the procedure or task under direct supervision of your instructor, write the date in the Date Return Demonstrated column. Some institutions will have the instructor date and initial the form, but the instructor will not initial it until you do the procedure or task in a satisfactory manner. A copy of this task check list should be kept by the nursing assistant for future use. This completed task check list is a profile of what you are capable of doing and performing as a nursing assistant.

TASK CHECK LIST

Task or Procedure	Date Demonstrated	Date Return Demonstrated
Handwashing technique		
Using the face mask		
Double bagging		
Wearing the isolation gown		
Removing the isolation gown		
Making the closed empty bed		
Making the open empty bed (fan-folded)		
Making the occupied bed		
Making the operating room (O.R.) stretcher bed		
Lifting an object		
Locking arms with the patient		
Moving the non-ambulatory patient up in bed		

TASK CHECK LIST

Task or Procedure	Date Demonstrated	Date Return Demonstrated
Moving a patient up in bed with his help		
Moving the mattress up in bed with the patient's help		
Moving the helpless patient to one side of the bed on his back		
Log rolling		
Turning a patient on his side toward and away from you		
Helping a non-ambulatory patient from bed to wheelchair or armchair and back		
Helping the ambulatory patient back to bed from chair or wheelchair		
Using the portable mechanical patient lift		
Moving a patient from a bed to a stretcher and back		
Performing range-of-motion exercises		
Assisting the patient with oral hygiene		
Cleaning dentures		
Giving oral hygiene to the unconscious patient (special mouth care)		
Giving the complete bed bath		
Givng the partial bed bath		
Giving the tub bath		
Assisting with the shower		
Giving the patient a back rub		
Changing the patient's gown		
Shampooing the patient's hair		
Combing the patient's hair		
Shaving the patient's beard		
Offering the bedpan or urinal or bedside commode		
Assisting the patient to use the portable bedside commode		
Preparing the patient and serving a meal		

TASK CHECK LIST

Task or Procedure	Date Demonstrated	Date Return Demonstrated
Serving the food		
Feeding the handicapped patient		
Serving between-meal nourishments		
Passing drinking water		
Measuring the capacity of serving containers		
Determining amounts consumed		
Measuring urinary output		
Emptying urine from an indwelling catheter container		
Collecting a routine urine specimen		
Collecting a midstream clean-catch urine specimen		
Collecting a 24-hour urine specimen		
Collecting a sputum specimen		
Collecting a stool specimen		
Collecting a routine urine specimen from an infant		
Straining the urine		
Giving the cleansing enema		
Giving the ready-to-use cleansing enema		
Giving the ready-to-use oil retention enema		
Giving the Harris flush/return flow enema		
Using the disposable rectal tube with connected flatus bag		
Inserting a rectal suppository		
Giving perineal care		
Giving daily indwelling catheter care		
Giving the vaginal douche/nonsterile irrigation		

8

TASK CHECK LIST

Task or Procedure	Date Demonstrated	Date Return Demonstrated
Caring for the artificial eye		
Caring for the hearing aid		
Shaking down the glass thermometer		
Reading a Fahrenheit thermometer		
Reading a Centigrade thermometer		
Measuring an oral temperature		
Measuring a rectal temperature		
Measuring an axillary temperature		
Using a battery-operated thermometer to measure oral, rectal, and axillary temperatures		
Measuring the radial pulse		
Measuring the apical pulse		
Measuring the apical/radial pulse deficit		
Measuring blood pressure		
Admitting the patient		
Weighing and measuring the patient's height		
Caring for the patient's valuables		
Transferring the patient		
Discharging the patient		
Preparing the patient for a physical examination		
Changing a patient's gown with an intravenous		
Applying the warm compress		
Applying the cold compress		
Applying the cold soak		
Applying the warm soak		

TASK CHECK LIST

Task or Procedure	Date Demonstrated	Date Return Demonstrated
Applying the warm water bottle		
Applying the ice bag, cap, or collar		
Applying the commercial unit cold pack		
Applying the commercial unit warm pack		
Applying the heat lamp		
Applying the aquamatic K-pad		
Using the disposable sitz bath		
Using the portable chair-type or built-in sitz bath		
Giving the alcohol sponge bath		
Shaving a patient in preparation for surgery		
Assisting the patient with deep-breathing exercises		
Caring for an ostomy		
Applying elastic bandages		
Applying a triangle sling bandage		
Preventing decubitus ulcers		
Bowel and bladder training/rehabilitation of the incontinent patient		
Giving special back care		
Collecting a fresh urine specimen		
Collecting a fresh urine specimen from a closed urinary drainage system		
Testing the urine for sugar with the clinitest and clinistix test		
Testing the urine for acetone with the acetest		
Testing the urine for ketones with the ketostix strip test		
Turning the patient on a manually operated turning frame		
Sterilizing baby bottles		

10

Task or Procedure	Date Demonstrated	Date Return Demonstrated
Giving the infant a bath		
Giving postmortem care		

WORKBOOK ASSIGNMENT #12, CHAPTER 1, SECTION 3
THE NURSING ASSISTANT: AN IMPORTANT PERSON

In your textbook, read the information titled "The Nursing Assistant: An Important Person." Match the beginning of each sentence in Column A with the endings in Column B to form complete sentences. Write the correct letter in the space provided.

Column A

_____1. Being a nursing assistant

_____2. There are so many things to learn

_____3. Yours is a

_____4. Making mistakes can cause

_____5. Doing a good job

_____6. You will be helping sick people

Column B

A. extra pain and suffering for patients, even death.

B. is not just another job.

C. so many things to do.

D. serious occupation.

E. and making their stay in the health care institution easier.

F. is something to be proud of.

WORKBOOK ASSIGNMENT #13, CHAPTER 1, SECTION 3
ETHICAL BEHAVIOR

Read "Key Ideas: Ethical Behavior" in your textbook. Match the beginning of each statement of the "Code of Ethics" in Column A with the correct ending of the statement in Column B. Write the correct letter in the space provided.

	Column A		Column B
_____1.	Be conscientious in the performance of your duties	A.	your patients and your fellow workers.
_____2.	Be generous in helping	B.	beliefs and opinions that might be different from yours.
_____3.	Faithfully carry out the instructions	C.	always show that the patient's well-being is of the utmost importance to you.
_____4.	Respect the right of all patients to have		
_____5.	Let the patient know that it is	D.	you are given by your head nurse.
_____6.	Try to demonstrate that you are sincere in your involvement in the care of a human being	E.	not just your job to assist him.

WORKBOOK ASSIGNMENT #14, CHAPTER 1, SECTION 3
ETHICAL BEHAVIOR

Read "Key Ideas: Ethical Behavior" in your textbook. Circle the correct answer in the multiple choice questions below.

1. Your absence may cause:

    A. A patient to be deprived of the care he needs
    B. Your fellow workers to have an overload of work
    C. The nursing office to take a day off, too
    D. All of the above
    E. A and B.

2. If you do not understand something:

    A. Ask another nursing assistant to explain it to you
    B. Go to the library and try to look it up
    C. Ask your head nurse or team leader to explain it again
    D. Try to do your best anyway
    E. Talk it over with a patient.

3. One of the patients, Mr. Stone, has upset you by saying that "he didn't care if he ever got better, that he never wanted to go home." Being upset, you feel that you need to discuss this problem with someone. You should discuss this matter with:

    A. Another patient you have become friendly with
    B. Your family when you get home from work
    C. Your head nurse or team leader
    D. Relatives and friends of the patients
    E. Another nursing assistant.

4. Miss Blake, nursing assistant, reported to her head nurse or team leader for work at 3 P.M., exactly on time. While on duty, Miss Blake was caring for several patients. When she measured her patient's vital signs, she recorded them accurately on the proper form. When a call light went on, she responded quickly and was always polite. All of her co-workers liked her because she was pleasant and performed her job well. Miss Blake is an example of which of the following:

   A. Accuracy
   B. Dependability
   C. Cleanliness
   D. Ethical behavior
   E. Malpractice
   F. A and B.

WORKBOOK ASSIGNMENT #15, CHAPTER 1, SECTION 3
LEGAL ASPECTS

Read "Key Ideas: Legal Aspects" in your textbook.

Circle the letter T if the statement below is true, F if it is false.

T or F   1. "Negligence is the commission of an act or failure to perform an act where the respective performance or nonperformance would deviate from that which should have been done by a reasonably prudent person under the same or similar conditions."

T or F   2. "Malpractice is negligence when applied to the performance of a professional."

T or F   3. The following is an example of negligence. A nursing assistant performs procedures not included in her job description or for which she has not been trained.

T or F   4. The following is an example of negligence. A nursing assistant fails to fasten the safety strap over a patient on a stretcher and, as a result, the patient falls.

WORKBOOK ASSIGNMENT #16, CHAPTER 1
WORDS TO REMEMBER/GLOSSARY

Read the definition carefully and fill in the blanks with the correct vocabulary word.

1. _____ is the quality of being exact or correct, exact conformity to truth or rules, free from error or defects.

2. To work or act together jointly, to unite in producing an effect, or to share an activity for mutual benefit is to _____.

3. _____ means coming to work every day on time and doing what is asked at the proper time and in the proper way.

4. To keep promises and do what you ought to do, to act in accordance with the rules or standards for the right conduct or practice, is _____ _____.

5. _____ is the science that deals with the preservation of health. When used to describe an object or a person, it means clean and sanitary.

6. Any unusual event, such as an accident or a condition that is likely to cause an accident, is an _____.

7. The fundamental nursing task and procedures you, the nursing assistant, will be accountable for in your work, will be found in the _____ _____ given to you by your employing health care institution or agency.

RATIONALE FOR CHAPTER QUIZZES

This is the first of a series of brief chapter quizzes at the end of each chapter. Most of the time you will work on these quizzes yourself. Sometimes, however, your instructor may work on them with you. These chapter quizzes are designed to help you remember the important points in the chapter you just finished.

If you do not understand the question, ask your instructor for help. However, if you review the information in the workbook assignments and read the chapter in the textbook, you should find the answers to the questions easily. If you are not sure of your answers, after you have tried for yourself, ask your instructor for help.

These chapter quizzes will help you remember the things you are learning so you will be able to perform all of the tasks and procedures correctly as you are being taught. These quizzes will also be a way to review for the final examination at the end of the workbook when you have finished your training.

CHAPTER 1 QUIZ

Circle the letter of the correct answer for each question.

1. If you are confused about something you were told, you should:

    A. Do the best job you can and do not bother others with your problem.
    B. Ask another nursing assistant what to do.
    C. Ask your head nurse or team leader to explain what you are to do again, as you are a little confused by her instructions.
    D. Find the patient's doctor and ask him for help.
    E. Ask the medication nurse what to do.

2. A patient tells you in strict confidence that she cannot live on her hospital diet. She then offers you a box of candy as a gift. What should you do?

    A. Thank her for the gift, and keep her secret in confidence.
    B. Tell her that you are not allowed to accept the gift, but you will keep her secret in confidence anyway.
    C. Thank the patient and refuse the gift. Report to the head nurse or team leader that the patient is unable to live on her hospital diet.
    D. Thank the patient, keep the gift and her secret since she told you this in confidence and you want her to like you.
    E. Ignore the entire situation.

3. Which of the following statements are always true?

    A. A dependable person is quiet and keeps to herself.
    B. Dependability means more than coming to work every day on time.
    C. A dependable person keeps promises.
    D. Doing an assigned task as well as you can and finishing it quickly, quietly, and efficiently.
    E. B, C, and D.

4. The code for ethical behavior includes which of the following statements?

    A. Be conscientious in the performance of your duties. This means do the best you can.
    B. Be generous in helping your patients and your fellow workers.
    C. Respect the right of all patients to have beliefs and opinions that might be different than yours.
    D. Let the patient know that it is your pleasure to help him or her.
    E. All of the above.

5. Which of the following tasks and/or procedures are found on the nursing assistant's job description?

    A. Perform bedmaking techniques.
    B. Assist with transporting patients.
    C. Assist with safety measures.
    D. Assist with positioning the patients.
    E. All of the above.

6. Which of the following are part of the nursing health care team?

   A. Registered Nurses (RNs)
   B. Licensed Practical Nurses (LPNs)
   C. Nursing Assistants
   D. Ward Clerks or Health Unit Coordinators
   E. All of the above.

7. A nursing assistant should never discuss patient information with:

   A. One patient about another patient
   B. Relatives of the patient
   C. The news media
   D. The hospital volunteers
   E. All of the above.

8. Before every procedure, the nursing assistant checks the patient's identification bracelet to:

   A. Be sure the procedure is being done for the right patient
   B. Become familiar with the patient's middle name
   C. Let the patient think you are efficient
   D. None of the above
   E. All of the above.

9. A nursing assistant tries never to make a mistake; however, when a mistake occurs, the nursing assistant must report it to:

   A. The patient's doctor
   B. The head nurse or team leader
   C. The patient's family
   D. The other nursing assistants
   E. All of the above.

10. Examples of malpractice and/or negligence are:

   A. If the nursing assistant fails to fasten the safety straps on a patient in a wheelchair and the patient falls
   B. When a nursing assistant performs procedures which she has never been trained to do
   C. When a regular diet is served to the diabetic patient
   D. When the nursing assistant forgets to wash her hands after contact with a patient, and then goes to another patient
   E. All of the above.

CHAPTER 2   COMMUNICATION IN THE HEALTH CARE SETTING

SECTION 1

WORKBOOK ASSIGNMENT #1, CHAPTER 2, SECTION 1
COMMUNICATION AND HUMAN RELATIONS

Find the list of objectives for this section. Next to each objective, write the
page numbers where you can find information to help you meet these objectives.

WORKBOOK ASSIGNMENT #2, CHAPTER 2, SECTION 1
COMMUNICATION: RELATING TO PEOPLE

Read "Key Ideas: Communication--Relating to People" in your textbook. Read the
following situations and circle the letter of the answer that seems most
correct:

1. You have raised the bedside rails on the bed of a newly admitted woman
    who is 70 years old. She says, "What are you trying to do, put me in a
    crib?" The nursing assistant should respond by saying:

    A. "It is the hospital's policy to have the bedside rails up for all
        patients over the age of 65."
    B. "I'm just doing what the head nurse told me to do."
    C. "Does it seem like a crib to you?"
    D. "Don't you want them up?"
    E. "It may seem like a crib to you but it is really because we do not
        want you to fall. Our beds are high and probably narrower than you
        are used to."

2. A patient rings his call bell at mealtime. The nursing assistant answers
    the signal and the patient angrily says, "What's wrong with this place? I
    have no fork and my coffee is cold!" The nursing assistant should respond by
    saying:

    A. "I'll do something about it."
    B. "I'll see that you get a fork and hot coffee as soon as I can."
    C. "The dietary department must have a lot of new help."
    D. "That is an error I will correct immediately. I will get you a fork
        and hot coffee right now."
    E. "Well, that's the way it is around here."

3. A patient signals by ringing the call bell every 15 to 20 minutes. The
    nursing assistant responds and notices that the patient is making a lot of
    small requests, such as: "Please raise the window shade;" "Please lower
    the window shade;" "Please turn on the radio;" "Please turn my pillow." The
    nursing assistant should respond by:

    A. Telling the patient politely not to ring so often
    B. Deliberately delaying in answering the call signal or neglecting to
        answer it at all
    C. Explaining to the patient that she has other work to do
    D. Reporting to the head nurse or team leader, asking what to do, how to
        handle the situation, and asking the nurse to visit the patient, as
        something is obviously wrong
    E. Asking another nursing assistant to answer the patient's call signals.

17

4. Mrs. White, a nursing assistant, finished her assignment and is walking down the hall toward the nurse's lounge when another nursing assistant comes up to her and says, "Please get Mrs. Smalling in 203-B back to bed for me now. Her doctor is on the nursing unit in another room and wants to examine her. Thank you, Mrs. White, as I have to go and get the dressing cart for the head nurse so the doctor can change my patient's bandages." The nursing assistant on her way to the lounge should respond by saying:

A. "That's not my job, since it is not my patient."
B. "Do it yourself, I am going to the nurse's lounge for a cigarette."
C. "I will do this right away. By the time you get to Mrs. Smalling's room, she will be in bed."
D. "I am going to complain to the head nurse that you are always asking me to do your work."
E. "I am tired from my own assignment, and if this hospital wants me to do two jobs, let them pay me two salaries."

5. The nursing assistant has just been told by the team leader that walking to the linen closet five times during one patient's bed bath is bad technique, time consuming, and not acceptable. One trip should be made and all the linen needed for one patient must be brought into the room at one time. The nursing assistant should respond by saying:

A. "Thank you for taking the time to teach me. I will try your suggestion now that I understand that what I have been doing is not acceptable. I am sure that my feet will feel better if I do not do so much walking."
B. "How dare you criticize me!"
C. "I went to school to learn how to be a nursing assistant, and you have no right to tell me how to do anything."
D. "Well, my teacher at the school I attended told me all about you lazy team leaders, who do none of the work but like to tell other people how to act."
E. "You always manage to think of something else I do that you do not like; this is the fourth time this morning you have told me that I am doing something wrong."

6. Miss Smith, nursing assistant, is told to go to 201-A bed to give the patient, Mrs. Joseph, a message from her family. Miss Smith has never met this patient and even though other staff members refer to all of the patients by room and bed number, she does not feel this is right. What would be the right way for Miss Smith to greet the patient?

A. "Are you 201-A bed? Your husband called...."
B. "How do you do, Mrs. Joseph, I am Miss Smith, a nursing assistant, may I check your identification bracelet? Thank you. The head nurse asked me to give you this message...."
C. "Hi, your husband called...."
D. "Hi, are you the diabetic patient? Well, I have a message for you...."
E. "I was told to give you this message...."

WORKBOOK ASSIGNMENT #3, CHAPTER 2, SECTION 1
COMMUNICATING WITH PATIENTS

Read the information titled "Communicating with Patients" in your textbook.

Write the word "DO" or "DON'T" next to each statement.

1. _____ use a shrill or loud voice.

2. _____ speak clearly and slowly.

3. _____ speak in a harsh manner.

4. _____ use medical terms and abbreviations when talking with patients.

5. _____ use good manners.

6. _____ let the patient think you are too busy to listen.

7. _____ respect the patient's moods.

8. _____ show an interest in what the patient is saying.

9. _____ use slang words.

10. _____ speak using a pleasant tone of voice.

SECTION 2

WORKBOOK ASSIGNMENT #4, CHAPTER 2, SECTION 2
OBSERVING THE PATIENT

Find the list of objectives for this section. Next to each objective, write the page numbers where you can find information to help you meet these objectives.

WORKBOOK ASSIGNMENT #5, CHAPTER 2, SECTION 2
OBSERVING THE PATIENT

Read "Key Ideas: Observing the Patient" in your textbook. Read the following situations and circle the letter of the correct choice.

1. You have been taking care of Mrs. Jones, 101-A bed, for the last two days. Mrs. Jones has been able to get out of bed and brush her teeth in the bathroom; however, today she says to you, "I will brush my teeth later. I don't feel so good today. I am going to stay in bed. Don't bring me any breakfast." Your response should be:

   A. "Stay in bed and later you can get out and brush."
   B. "Are you comfortable? Would you like another blanket? I will be back in half an hour to see how you are feeling." The nursing assistant then goes to the head nurse or team leader to report this change in the patient's condition.
   C. "If you don't brush for one day, it will not hurt you."
   D. "When you give in to feeling sick, you will become very sick."
   E. "I am going to report to the doctor that you are dirty person."

2. Mr. Murray, the patient in room 209-C bed, had four bowel movements in the last two hours. The last time he wasn't able to wait for the bedpan and soiled the bed. Yesterday, he had one bowel movement the entire day. After you have cleaned the patient and changed his bed, what should you do next?

    A. Do nothing, this is part of your job.
    B. Report this to your head nurse or team leader as this is a definite change in the patient's condition.
    C. Tell the patient he is awful for dirtying the bed.
    D. Tell the doctor that the patient has moved his bowels in bed.
    E. Tell the patient's visitors so they can tell the patient never to dirty the bed again.

3. Mrs. Hernandez, the patient in room 103-A bed, is receiving a blood transfusion that has been running for the past hour. As you are making her bed, you notice that the color of her face is changing. She now has very red cheeks. Mrs. Hernandez cannot speak English and you cannot converse with her. You then notice that Mrs. Hernandez is scratching her arms and legs and seems very agitated. Your immediate response should be:

    A. Tell the doctor that Mrs. Hernandez is scratching her arms and legs.
    B. Tell the patient's visitors to tell her to stop scratching.
    C. Use body language so that Mrs. Hernandez will understand and stop scratching.
    D. Use the emergency signal to call for help. Report on the intercom to the head nurse or team leader that Mrs. Hernandez seems to be having a reaction to her treatment, and you need help with this patient.
    E. Ignore the whole thing; if the nurse wants to know what is going on with her patients, she would visit the patients often.

WORKBOOK ASSIGNMENT #6, CHAPTER 2, SECTION 2
EXAMPLES OF OBJECTIVE AND SUBJECTIVE REPORTING

Read the information titled "Subjective and Objective Reporting" in your textbook. The following are examples of objective and subjective reporting. Next to each statement place an "O" for objective reporting or an "S" for subjective reporting.

_____1. "Mr. Jones, in 101-A bed, picked up his selective menu but could not read it. He asked me to read it for him."

_____2. "Mrs. Adams, in 119-C bed, said she did not want to get out of bed."

_____3. "Mr. Cass, in 103-D, is in pain; he hasn't had his medication in three hours."

_____4. "Mrs. Williams, in 204-B bed, is getting better. It must be because her children visited her yesterday."

_____5. "Miss Johnson, in 406-B bed, has an elevated temperature of 101.2°F and is breathing rapidly 24 times per minute."

WORKBOOK ASSIGNMENT #7, CHAPTER 2
WORDS TO REMEMBER/GLOSSARY

Read the definition carefully and fill in the blanks with the correct vocabulary word.

1. Continues over many years or a lifetime, referred to as a _____ illness.

2. The term means born with or from birth. It refers to a physical or mental characteristic present in a baby at birth. Sometimes referred to as a birth defect. The word is _____.

3. When the skin looks blue or has a gray cast because there is not enough oxygen in the blood, it is called _____. This is usually seen in the patient's lips and nail beds.

4. Abnormal swelling of a part of the body caused by fluid collecting in that area is referred to as _____.

5. Characteristics that are passed down from parent to child. An example is the color of your eyes. Certain diseases can be _____. An example is diabetes.

6. Gathering information about the patient by noticing any change in his condition is called _____.

1. Circle the letter <u>T</u> if the statement below is true, <u>F</u> if it is false.

    T or F   a. When answering a patient's call signal, do whatever the patient requests, no matter what.

    T or F   b. If a patient uses the call signal too much, leave it out of his reach.

    T or F   c. When you use a telephone or intercom device, always speak clearly and slowly.

    T or F   d. When a patient is blind or deaf, you must teach him how to use the call signal.

    T or F   e. Some medical disorders could cause a loss of sight, hearing, speech, taste, or smell.

Circle the letter of the correct answer:

2. A patient complains to you that his "I.V. hurts." You look at the area on the patient's arm around the needle, and it appears red and swollen. You should:

    A. Do nothing. As a nursing assistant, this is not your job.
    B. Tell the patient to mention it to the nurse next time she comes in.
    C. Report this immediately to your head nurse or team leader. Although a nursing assistant does not regulate IV's, you still must be observant and report anything unusual.
    D. Tell the doctor.
    E. Tell another nursing assistant.

3. Because communication is basic to the mutual exchange of messages that make a connection between the nursing assistant and the patient, it is necessary to:

    A. Show an interest in what the patient is saying.
    B. Speak in a pleasant tone.
    C. Use good manners, courtesy, emotional control, sympathy, empathy and tact.
    D. Make your body movements look pleasing and energetic.
    E. All of the above.

4. When your patient appears to be very irritable, you should:

    A. Try to calm him down.
    B. Try to be an attentive, sympathetic listener.
    C. Report this excessive irritability to the head nurse or team leader.
    D. Be responsive to the patient's wishes.
    E. Answer the patient in the same irritable manner.

5. Mrs. Smith is a preoperative patient. She is scheduled to go to the operating room in the morning. You notice that when the head nurse or team leader is not around, Mrs. Smith drinks whiskey right from a bottle she keeps in her bedside table. You should:

    A. Tell the patient to stop drinking.
    B. Report this to your head nurse or team leader.
    C. Tell the patient's visitors that Mrs. Smith is drinking.
    D. Tell the doctor that the patient is drinking.
    E. Do nothing about it, as it is not your business.

6. Your patient has just been admitted to the health care insitution. The doctor ordered oxygen by face mask for this patient. You notice that as soon as the head nurse or team leader leaves the room, the patient takes the mask off. You should:

    A. Tell the doctor.
    B. Report this to the head nurse or team leader.
    C. Tell another nursing assistant.
    D. Call the pharmacy.
    E. Call the central service department.

7. Your patient is in the health care institution because of a diabetic condition. The doctor ordered a special therapeutic diet for her. You notice the patient eating a candy bar when she is alone. You should:

    A. Let her eat it; she really does not want to get well.
    B. Tell the patient she should not eat the candy without the head nurse's or team leader's permission.
    C. Report this incident to your head nurse or team leader who will tell you what to do.
    D. Ignore the whole thing.
    E. Tell the patient's visitors about the candy.

8. When objectively reporting your observations, you should:

    A. Tell the head nurse or team leader what you think is wrong with the patient.
    B. Tell the head nurse or team leader to give the patient some pills.
    C. Tell the head nurse or team leader exactly what you saw, smelled, felt, or what the patient said.
    D. Tell the head nurse or team leader to go to the patient at once, even though it is not an emergency.
    E. Tell the head nurse or team leader to observe the patient.

9. The head nurse or team leader has given you instructions to report exactly what the patient eats at mealtimes and not to give the patient anything between meals. However, during visiting hours, you notice that the patient is eating a hot dog that was brought in by a visitor. You should:

   A. Yell at the patient and take the food away.
   B. Call the visitors outside the room and yell at them.
   C. Call the doctor and tell him.
   D. Report this to the head nurse or team leader immediately.
   E. Ignore the whole situation.

10. Your patient was fine this morning and was able to get out of bed and walk around his room. However, after lunch, you notice that the patient is lying very quietly in his bed, does not answer when you talk to him, and his face is very red. You should:

    A. Yell at the patient to wake him.
    B. Call the visitors in to see the patient.
    C. Call the doctor.
    D. Report this to the head nurse or team leader immediately as this is a change in the patient's condition.
    E. Pay no attention to the situation, the nurse will see the patient for herself when she makes her afternoon rounds.

CHAPTER 3   INTRODUCTION TO MEDICAL TERMINOLOGY

SECTION 1

WORKBOOK ASSIGNMENT #1, CHAPTER 3, SECTION 1
INTRODUCTION TO MEDICAL TERMS AND ABBREVIATIONS

Find the list of objectives for this section. Next to each objective, write the page numbers where you can find information to help you meet these objectives.

WORKBOOK ASSIGNMENT #2, CHAPTER 3, SECTION 1
ABBREVIATIONS AND THEIR MEANINGS

Read the list of abbreviations and their meanings in your textbook. This is a big list, and there is a lot of important information here. It will be easier to remember what all the different abbreviations are if you try to learn them one at a time. One easy way to learn the list is to study from flash cards. Cut apart the cards on the pages 27 to 44. You will see that the name of the abbreviation is on one side and the meaning is on the other side. NOW YOU CAN TEST YOURSELF.

1. Arrange all the cards so the name of the abbreviation is facing up and the meaning is facing down.

2. Read the name of the first abbreviation in your stack.

3. Try to remember the meaning from studying the pages in your textbook.

4. Say the meaning out loud.

5. Turn the card over and read the meaning to see if you were right.

6. If you were correct, put the card in a pile on the left, and you are finished studying this card.

7. If you were wrong, put the card in a pile on the right, and you will study it later.

8. Repeat this for all the cards.

9. Now go back to the pile of cards on the right and study these.

10. Read each card front and back five times.

11. Close your eyes and try to say the name of the abbreviation and its meaning.

12. Open your eyes and see if you were correct.

13. Repeat this for all the cards that you originally put on the right side.

14. When you feel that you have learned them all, test yourself again.

15. Ask a friend or relative to test you by holding the first card up so you can see the name of the abbreviation and your friend or relative can see the meaning. You read the abbreviation and recite the meaning.

16. Your friend can read the meaning to know if you are correct.

17. Repeat this for all the cards.

18. Turn the stack upside down.

19. Now you must read the meaning and tell the name of the abbreviation.

20. Continue in this way over and over again, until you have learned all the abbreviations and their meanings.

aa	ABR	abd.
ac	AD	A&D
ad lib	ADL	Adm.
Adm. Spec.	A.M. or a.m. or am	amb.
Amt.	AP or A.P.	aqua
@	approx.	B&B or b&b
BM or B.M. or bm or b.m.	B.P. or BP	BR or br or B.R. or b.r.

Abdomen	Absolute Bed Rest	Of each; equal parts
Admission & Discharge	Admitting Diagnosis	Before Meals
Admission	Activities of Daily Living	As desired, if the patient so desires.
Ambulation - Walking - Ambulatory	Morning	Admission Urine Specimen
Water or H_2O	Appendectomy	Amount
Bowel and Bladder Training	Approximately	At
Bed Rest	Blood Pressure	Bowel Movement (feces)

BRP or B.R.P. or brp	BSC or bsc	C
$\overline{c}$ or c	Ca	Cath.
CBC or C.B.C.	cc or cc.	CCU or C.C.U.
CBR or C.B.R. or cbr	CO	C/O or c/o
CO_2	CS or cs or C.S. or c.s.	CSD or csd or C.S.D.
CSR or csr or C.S.R.	CVA or C.V.A.	CPR or C.P.R.
dc or d/c	Del. Rm. or d.r. or DR	Disch. or disch. or D/C

Centigrade or Celsius	Bedside Commode	Bathroom Privileges
Catheter	Cancer	With
Cardiac Care Unit	Cubic Centimeter	Complete Blood Count
Complaint of	Carbon Monoxide	Complete Bed Rest
Central Service Department	Central Supply	Carbon Dioxide
Cardiopulmonary Resuscitation	Cerebrovascular Accident or Stroke	Central Supply Room
Discharge	Delivery Room	Discontinue

D.&C. or D&C	drsg.	DOA or D.O.A.
Dr. or Dr	Dx	ECG or EKG
ED or E.D.	EEG or E.E.G.	EENT or E.E.N.T.
E. or E	ER or E.R.	F
F. or FE. or F or Fe	FBS or F.B.S.	FF or F.F.
ft	fx	gal
GI or G.I.	gt	gtt

Dead on Arrival	Dressing	Dilatation & Curettage
Electrocardiogram	Diagnosis	Doctor
Eyes, Ears, Nose & Throat	Electroencephalogram	Emergency Department
Fahrenheit	Emergency Room	Enema
Forced Fluids or Forced Feedings	Fasting Blood Sugar	Female
Gallon	Fractional Urine	Foot or Feet
Two or more drops	One drop	Gastrointestinal

GTT or G.T.T.	GU or G.U.	Gyn.
H_2O	hr	HS or hs
ht	hyper	hypo
HWB or hwb or HWB	ICU or I.C.U.	in. or in
I&O or I. & O.	irr	Isol. or isol.
IV or I.V.	L	Lab. or lab
lb	Liq or liq.	LPN or L.P.N.

Gynecology	Genitourinary	Glucose Tolerance Test
Bedtime or Hour of sleep	Hour	Water or aqua
Below or low	Above or high	Height
Inch	Intensive Care Unit	Hot water bottle
Isolation	Irregular	Intake & Output
Laboratory	Liter	Intravenous
Licensed Practical Nurse	Liquid or Liquor	Pound

LVN or L.V.N.	M	Mat
MD or M.D.	mess	mec
med	min	ml
noct	Mn or mn or M/n	N.A. or N/A
n/g or ng. or N.G.T.	NP	NPO or N.P.O.
Nsy	O_2	OB or O.B.
Obt or obt	OJ or O.J.	Ord.

Maternity	Male	Licensed Vocational Nurse
Meconium	Measure	Medical Doctor
Milliliter	Minute	Medicine
Nursing Assistant or Nursing Aide	Midnight	At night
Nothing by mouth	Neuropsychiatric or Nursing Procedure	Nasogastric tube
Obstetrics	Oxygen	Nursery
Orderly	Orange juice	Obtained

OOB or O.O.B.	OPD or O.P.D.	OR or O.R.
Ortho	OT or O.T.	oz
PAR or P.A.R.	pc	Ped or Peds
per	p.m. or P.M. or pm or PM	PMC or P.M.C.
PN or P.N.	po	post
postop or post op	post op spec	pp
PPBS	pre	prn or p.r.n.

Operating Room	Outpatient Department	Out of bed
Ounce	Occupational Therapy or Oral Temperature	Orthopedics
Pediatrics	After meals	Postanesthesia Room
Postmortem Care	Afternoon	By or through
After	By mouth	Pneumonia
Post Partum (after delivery)	After Surgery Urine Specimen	Postoperative
Whenever necessary; When required	Before	Postprandial Blood Sugar

preop or pre op	pre op spec	prep
PT or pt	PT or P.T.	q
qd	qh	q2h
q3h	q4h	QHS or qhs
qid or Q.I.D.	qam or q am or q.a.m.	qod or Q.O.D.
qs	qt	r or R
RM or rm	RN or R.N.	rom or R.O.M.

39

Prepare the patient for surgery by shaving the skin.	Urine specimen before surgery	Before surgery
Every	Physical Therapy	Patient or pint
Every two hours	Every hour	Every day
Every night at bedtime	Every four hours	Every three hours
Every other day	Every morning	Four times a day
Rectal temperature	Quart	Quantity sufficient
Range of motion	Registered Nurse	Room

RR or R Rm.	Rx	$\overline{s}$ or s
S & A	SOB	sos
SPD	Spec or spec	$\overline{ss}$ or ss
SSE or S.S.E.	stat	S & K
Surg	tid or T.I.D.	TLC or tlc
TPR	U/A or u/a	Ung.
WBC or W.B.C.	V.D. or vd	VDRL

Without	Prescription or treatment ordered by a physician	Recovery room
Whenever emergency arises; only if necessary	Shortness of breath	Sugar & Acetone test
One-half	Specimen	Special Purchasing Department
Sugar & Ketone Test	At once; immediately	Soapsuds enema
Tender Loving Care	Three times a day	Surgery
Ointment; unguent	Urine analysis	Temperature, Pulse, Respiration
Test for venereal disease (Syphilis)	Venereal Disease	White blood count

V.S. or VS	w/c	wc or W.C.
wt	$\overline{i}$	$\overline{ii}$
$\overline{iii}$	$\overline{iv}$	$\overline{v}$
$\overline{vi}$	$\overline{vii}$	$\overline{viii}$
$\overline{ix}$	$\overline{x}$	

Ward Clerk	Wheelchair	Vital signs
(Roman Numeral) two	(Roman Numeral) one	Weight
(Roman Numeral) five	(Roman Numeral) four	(Roman Numeral) three
(Roman Numeral) eight	(Roman Numeral) seven	(Roman Numeral) six
	(Roman Numeral) ten	(Roman Numeral) nine

CHAPTER 3   QUIZ

Write the abbreviations for the following terms.

1. Nothing by mouth _____

2. Oxygen _____

3. Intravenous _____

4. Before surgery _____

5. Every 2 hours _____.

Write the meaning of the following abbreviations:

6. R.N. _____ _____

7. Spec. _____

8. ADL _____

9. T.P.R. _____ _____ _____

10. C.S.R. _____ _____ _____.

CHAPTER 4   SAFETY AND FIRE PREVENTION

SECTION 1

WORKBOOK ASSIGNMENT #1, CHAPTER 4, SECTION 1
SAFETY AND FIRE PREVENTION

Find the list of objectives for this section. Next to each objective, write the
page numbers where you can find information to help you meet these objectives.

WORKBOOK ASSIGNMENT #2, CHAPTER 4, SECTION 1
SAFETY AND FIRE PREVENTION

Read Chapter 5, "Safety and Fire Prevention," in your textbook, then answer the
following questions.

1. Circle any unsafe conditions you can find in the picture below.

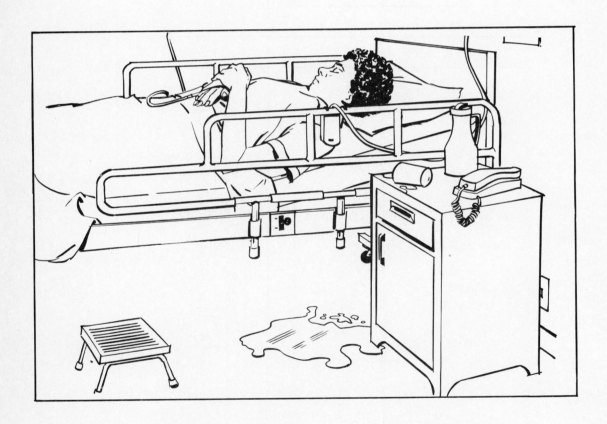

2. What should you do about the unsafe conditions you found in the picture? Circle the letter of the correct answer.

    A. Report this to your head nurse or team leader.
    B. Notify the housekeeping department.
    C. Wipe it up immediately.
    D. All of the above.

3. Circle any unsafe conditions you can find in the picture below.

4. What should you do about unsafe conditions you found in the picture? Circle the letter of the correct answer.

    A. Raise the side rail and lock it in place.
    B. Move the patient to the center of the bed.
    C. Always ask another nursing assistant to help you when making an occupied bed.
    D. All of the above.

5. Circle the name of the patient below who is not permitted to smoke.

MR. FALCON   MRS. ROBERTS

6. Why is the patient in the picture not permitted to smoke? Circle the letter of the correct answer.

   A. He is sleeping.
   B. He is receiving oxygen.
   C. She is reading.
   D. All of the above.

7. Circle any unsafe conditions you can find in the picture below.

48

8. What should you do about the unsafe conditions you found in the picture? Circle the letter of the correct answer.

    A. The razor is the patient's personal property. Therefore, you are not responsible for its condition, and cannot do anything about it.
    B. Have the patient turn off the razor and report this to your head nurse or team leader immediately.
    C. Take the razor away from the patient, and give it to your head nurse or team leader immediately.
    D. All of the above.

9. Circle any unsafe conditions you can find in this picture.

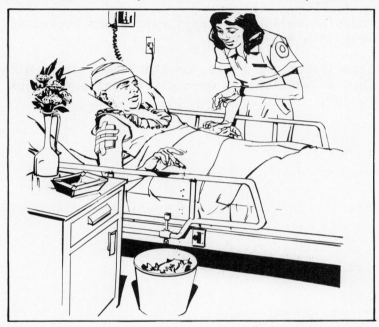

10. What should you do about the unsafe condition in this picture? Circle the letter of the correct answer.

    A. Empty the ashes into the proper container--usually a metal container filled with sand or water.
    B. Explain the danger to the patient and ask her to discard smoking material into the ashtray in the future.
    C. Report this to your head nurse or team leader.
    D. All of the above.

WORKBOOK ASSIGNMENT #3, CHAPTER 4
WORDS TO REMEMBER/GLOSSARY

Fill in the blanks with the vocabulary word to remember after reading the definition carefully.

1. A word used to mean any of the kinds of tubes that can be inserted into one of the body cavities. A _____ may be used for oxygen.

2. A colorless, odorless gas making up about one-fifth of the volume of the air is called _____. It is essential for human life.

3. A piece of equipment used in the health care institution to provide large amounts of extra oxygen for a patient is called an _____ _____.

CHAPTER 4 QUIZ

Circle the letter <u>T</u> if the statement below is true, <u>F</u> if it statement is false.

T   or   F   1.   Electrical appliances never cause safety hazards while oxygen
                  is in use.

T   or   F   2.   A wastebasket is a good place to empty ashtrays.

T   or   F   3.   You should always make sure the patient can reach his signal
                  cord before you leave his unit.

T   or   F   4.   The bedside rails are always raised and locked in place when the
                  patient is a small child.

T   or   F   5.   Be sure to set the brakes on the wheels of stretchers, examining
                  tables, or wheelchairs when moving patients on or off such
                  equipment.

CHAPTER 5   INFECTION CONTROL

SECTION 1

WORKBOOK ASSIGNMENT #1, CHAPTER 5, SECTION 1
MEDICAL ASEPSIS

Find the list of objectives for this section. Next to each objective, write the page numbers where you can find information to help you meet these objectives.

WORKBOOK ASSIGNMENT #2, CHAPTER 5, SECTION 1
MICROORGANISMS

Read "Key Ideas: Microorganisms" in your textbook. Pay particular attention to the illustration titled "Microorganisms are Everywhere."

Circle the letter beside those places where microorganisms can be found.

A. On the ground

B. In the air

C. On faucet handles

D. In human wastes

E. On our bodies

F. On animals

G. In flower vases

H. On the floor

I. In our bodies

J. On our clothing

K. On dishes

L. On bed linens

M. In liquids

N. In food

O. On a bedpan

P. All of the above

WORKBOOK ASSIGNMENT #3, CHAPTER 5, SECTION 1
WAYS THAT MICROORGANISMS ARE SPREAD

Read the chart titled "Ways that Microorganisms are Spread" in your textbook.

Circle the letter T if the statement below is true, F if it is false.

T or F   1. Microorganisms can be spread by touching the patient.

T or F   2. Microorganisms can be spread by washing your hands.

T or F   3. Microorganisms can be spread by talking.

T or F   4. Microorganisms can be spread by touching the patient's dishes.

T or F   5. Microorganisms can be spread by looking at the patient.

WORKBOOK ASSIGNMENT #4, CHAPTER 5, SECTION 1
DISINFECTION AND STERILIZATION

Read the information titled "Disinfection and Sterilization" in your textbook.
Circle the letter of the correct answer for each question.

1. What is the machine in the illustration above called?

    A. Sterilizer
    B. Autoclave
    C. Pasteurizer
    D. Wheelchair
    E. Suction machine.

2. The autoclave sterilizes or completely destroys microorganisms by combining
    _____.

    A. Soap with hot water under pressure
    B. Acid with steam
    C. Ammonia with steam under pressure
    D. Heat with steam under pressure
    E. Water and bleach under pressure.

3. Why is an autoclave used?

    A. To prevent the spread of disease or infection
    B. To sterilize without burning the article itself
    C. To sterilize at lower temperatures
    D. To completely destroy microorganisms
    E. All of the above.

<u>WORKBOOK ASSIGNMENT #5, CHAPTER 5, SECTION 1</u>
<u>HANDWASHING</u>

Read the information titled "Handwashing" in your textbook. Circle the letter
below when it is a time that is important to wash your hands.

A. After every contact with a patient

B. After using the toilet

C. Before every contact with a patient

D. After reporting to your head nurse or team leader

E. Before you handle a food tray

F. After using your handkerchief

G. Before answering the patient's call signal

H. Before eating or drinking

I. After answering a visitor's question

J. After touching each flower arrangement to change the water in the vase.

<u>WORKBOOK ASSIGNMENT #6, CHAPTER 5, SECTION 1</u>
<u>HANDWASHING</u>

Read "Rules to Follow: Handwashing" in your textbook. Study the following
picture. What is the nursing assistant doing wrong?

WORKBOOK ASSIGNMENT #7, CHAPTER 5, SECTION 2
THE PATIENT IN ISOLATION

Find the list of objectives for this section. Next to each objective, write the page numbers where you can find information to help you meet these objectives.

WORKBOOK ASSIGNMENT #8, CHAPTER 5, SECTION 2
CLEAN AND DIRTY

Read the information titled "Clean and Dirty" in your textbook.

Label each item described below by writing the word "CLEAN" or "DIRTY" in the blank spaces after each statement.

1. A freshly laundered sheet that has been placed on the chair beside a patient's bed. _____

2. Ice which is in the ice machine. _____

3. The linen on the shelf of the linen closet. _____

4. The toilet paper inside the patient's bedside table near the bedpan. _____

5. Left-over food on the patient's lunch tray. _____

6. A breakfast tray that has not yet been delivered to the patient's room. _____

WORKBOOK ASSIGNMENT #9, CHAPTER 5, SECTION 2
ISOLATION TECHNIQUE

Read "Key Ideas: Isolation Technique" in your textbook.

Circle the letter of the correct response for each question.

1. When a barrier isolation card is on the patient's door it means:

    A. No visitors.
    B. Family may visit.
    C. The patient is on isolation/protective care.
    D. The patient may have as many visitors as he desires.
    E. The patient is not on isolation.

2. To identify the type of isolation the patient is on, the nursing assistant must:

    A. Ask the head nurse.
    B. Ask the team leader.
    C. Read the isolation barrier card on the door.
    D. Call the doctor.
    E. Ask the patient.

3. The instructions the nursing assistant should follow are:

    A. Written on the order sheet
    B. Written on the isolation barrier card hanging on the patient's door
    C. On the patient's chart
    D. On the head nurse's desk
    E. Found in the nursing office.

WORKBOOK ASSIGNMENT #10, CHAPTER 5, SECTION 2
FACE MASKS

Read the information titled "Face Masks" and the "Procedure: Mask Technique" in
your textbook. In the illustration below, which sequence of pictures is correct?
Circle the letter for the one you choose.

WORKBOOK ASSIGNMENT #11, CHAPTER 5, SECTION 2
ISOLATION GOWNS

Read "Key Ideas: Isolation Gowns" and the "Procedure: Putting on an Isolation
Gown in the Hall Before Entering the Patient's Room" in your textbook.

Circle the letter <u>T</u> if the statement below is true, <u>F</u> if it is false.

T or F   1. Put on a clean gown in the hall before you enter the patient's
               room.

T or F   2. Take off dirty gown in the patient's room before leaving the
               unit.

T or F   3. To be effective, the isolation gown must cover your uniform
               completely.

T or F   4.   Individual gown technique means that a gown should be used only once.

T or F   5.   Disposable paper gowns are thrown away after one use.

WORKBOOK ASSIGNMENT #12, CHAPTER 5, SECTION 2
DOUBLE BAGGING TECHNIQUE

Read the information titled "Soiled, Contaminated Linen, Double-Bagging Technique" and study the illustration in your textbook carefully.

Circle the letter of the correct response for each question below.

1.   The nursing assistants in the illustration below are performing an isolation technique called _____ _____.

    A.   Contaminated linen
    B.   Bagging
    C.   Double-bagging
    D.   Isolation technique
    E.   Linen removing.

2.   This technique should be applied when removing _____.

    A.   Specimens
    B.   Linen
    C.   Trash
    D.   Contaminated articles
    E.   All of the above.

3. Place linen in the laundry bag _____ and seal the bag.

    A. Inside the isolation unit
    B. Outside the isolation unit
    C. In the clean utility room
    D. In the hall
    E. In the dirty utility room.

4. Place the sealed bag _____ outside the isolation unit.

    A. In the linen hamper
    B. In the hall
    C. In the housekeeping department
    D. Inside another bag
    E. In the utility room.

WORKBOOK ASSIGNMENT #13, CHAPTER 5, SECTION 2
CARE OF THE ISOLATED PATIENT

Read "Key Ideas: Personal Care of the Patient in Isolation" and study the
illustration "When leaving the patient's room" in your textbook.

Mrs. Smith, nursing assistant, is finished giving morning care to her patient,
Tom Green. She is ready to leave the isolation unit. The pictures below show
the things Mrs. Smith must remember to do before leaving the isolation unit;
however, the order has been scrambled. Number each picture in the correct order,
1 through 5.

A. _____

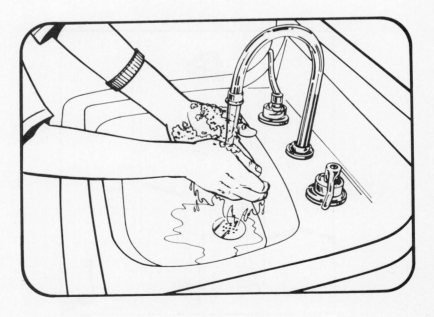

B. _____

C. _____

D. _____

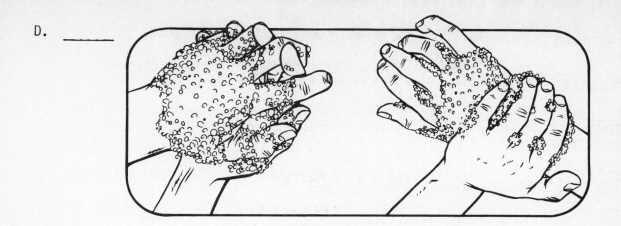

E. _____

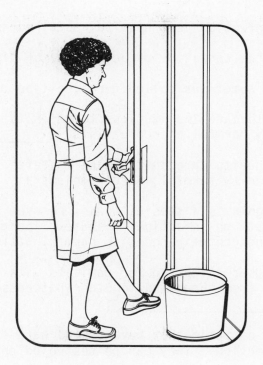

WORKBOOK ASSIGNMENT #14, CHAPTER 5
WORDS TO REMEMBER/GLOSSARY

Fill in the blanks with the vocabulary word to remember after reading the definition carefully.

1. An _____ is a piece of equipment used to sterilize instruments and other articles in the health care institution.

2. A _____ _____ _____ disease is one that is easily spread from one person to another.

3. _____ is the rubbing of one surface against another.

4. An _____ is a condition in body tissue in which germs or pathogens have multiplied and destroyed many cells.

5. _____ _____ is a special practice and procedure for cleanliness to decrease the chances for disease-causing bacteria to live and spread.

6. A _____ is a living thing so small it cannot be seen with the naked eye, but only through a microscope.

7. Disease-causing microorganisms are _____.

8. The process of destroying all microorganisms, including spores, is called _____.

9. A _____ infection is a hospital-acquired infection.

10. _____ is the condition of being free of disease-causing organisms.

11. _____ are sometimes called germs, a type of microorganisms.

12. A term used in health care institutions to refer to an object or area that is uncontaminated by harmful microorganisms is _____.

13. A term used in the health care institution to refer to an object or areas as being contaminated by harmful microorganisms is _____.

14. An _____ gown is a special gown worn over a uniform when in the room of a patient with an infectious disease. The gown helps protect the uniform from becoming contaminated with harmful bacteria.

15. Special procedures used in caring for patients with infectious diseases to prevent the disease from spreading to other patients and workers are called _____ _____.

16. _____ are bacteria that have formed hard shells around themselves for protection. They can be destroyed only by sterilization.

17. A _____ is a microscopic living parasite that can cause an infectious disease.

WORKBOOK ASSIGNMENT #15, CHAPTER 5
LEARNING BY DOING

As you study the procedures in this chapter, read every step carefully. Think
about the action words, the words that tell you what to do. Look at the pictures
closely and read the captions. You will be able to remember what to do more
easily if you try to do it after you have read about it. Learning by doing
involves your whole body in the learning process, not just your eyes and ears.
It is one of the most effective ways to learn.

Ask a fellow student or, if you are practicing at home, ask a friend or relative
to play the part of the patient. Actually do all of the steps of the procedure
several times, pretending you are a nursing assistant caring for several
patients. Work slowly at first. Look at the textbook whenever you are not sure
about what to do next. Practice in this way many times until you can work
quickly and you no longer need to look at the textbook.

Switch roles with your partner and take several turns at being the patient. Not
only will this give your partner a chance to learn the procedure, but you will
benefit as well. By putting yourself in the patient's place, you will begin to
understand how it feels to be a patient, and you will be able to treat real
patients as you yourself would like to be treated.

CHAPTER 5 QUIZ

Circle the letter T if the statement below is true, F if it is false.

T or F   1. Some bacteria are helpful to people.

T or F   2. Medical asepsis means preventing conditions that allow disease-producing bacteria to live and spread.

T or F   3. You should wash your hands before removing your face mask.

T or F   4. Bacteria may be killed in an autoclave.

T or F   5. An infected patient must be protected from getting infections from other patients.

T or F   6. Your hands are more likely to get bacteria on them than any other parts of your body.

T or F   7. Food that has not been eaten but was in the patient's isolation unit is considered to be contaminated (dirty).

T or F   8. A patient in isolation needs the same personal care as any other patient.

T or F   9. The thermometer used for a patient in isolation is kept inside the unit.

T or F   10. Your hands are considered to be contaminated as soon as they touch the patient or anything in his unit.

CHAPTER 6   YOUR WORKING ENVIRONMENT

SECTION 1

WORKBOOK ASSIGNMENT #1, CHAPTER 6, SECTION 1
THE PATIENT'S UNIT AND EQUIPMENT

Find the list of objectives for this section. Next to each objective, write the page numbers where you can find information to help you meet these objectives.

WORKBOOK ASSIGNMENT #2, CHAPTER 6, SECTION 1
THE PATIENT'S UNIT AND EQUIPMENT

Read the information titled "The Patient's Unit and Equipment" in your textbook. The following list is a sample equipment check list for the unit. Fill out the check list by writing an "X" beside each piece of equipment you can find in this picture. Be sure to fill in the missing equipment.

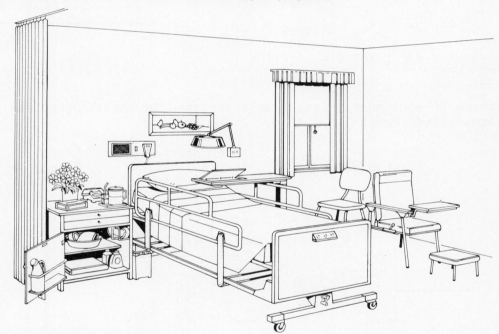

SAMPLE EQUIPMENT CHECK LIST

Unit # _____   Date: _____   Checked by: _____

Room # _____

Large equipment	Small equipment	Condition of unit
___bed	___urinal	Bed made:
___bed rails (2)	___bedpan	___closed
___overbed table	___blanket	___open
___lamp	___basin	___occupied
___straight chair	___emesis basin	___postoperative
___geriatric chair	___waste basket	___unit clean
___tray for chair	___powder	___unit not clean
___ottoman	___skin lotion	Equipment missing:
___screening curtain	___water pitcher	_____
___call signal	___cups	Equipment needing repair: _____
___bedside table	___straws	_____
	___tissues	_____

WORKBOOK ASSIGNMENT #3, CHAPTER 6, SECTION 1
DISPOSABLE EQUIPMENT

Label each piece of equipment in the blanks provided in the illustration below, using the terms listed here.

Emesis basin   Cups   Water pitcher   Urinal
Bedpan   Plastic gloves   Tissues   Tongue depressors
                                                                     Specimen containers

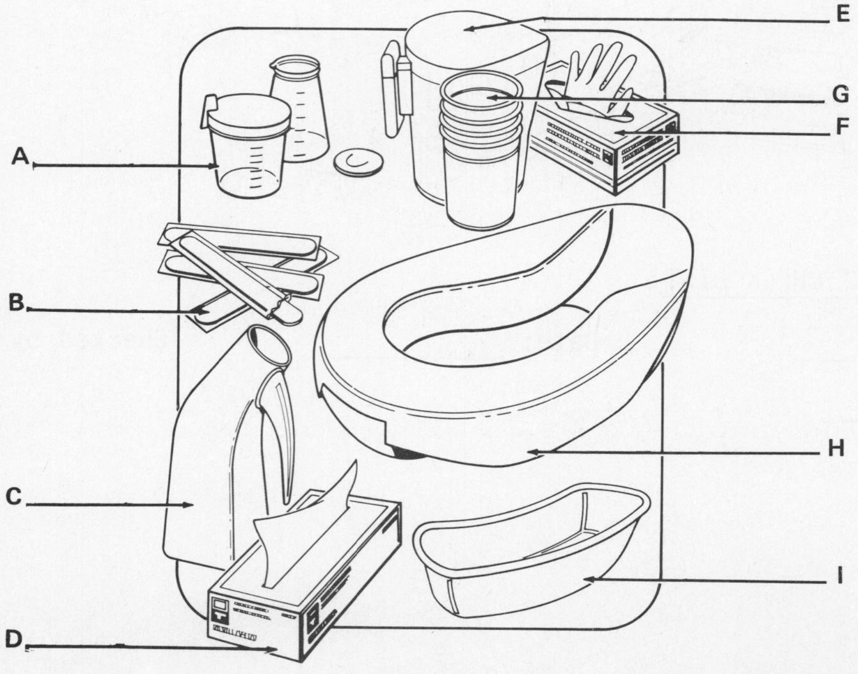

WORKBOOK ASSIGNMENT #4, CHAPTER 6, SECTION 1
REUSABLE EQUIPMENT

Label each piece of equipment in the blanks provided in the illustration below, using the terms listed here.

Folding screen	Patient lift	Stretcher	Supply table
Bed cradle	Walker	Intravenous pole	Wheelchair

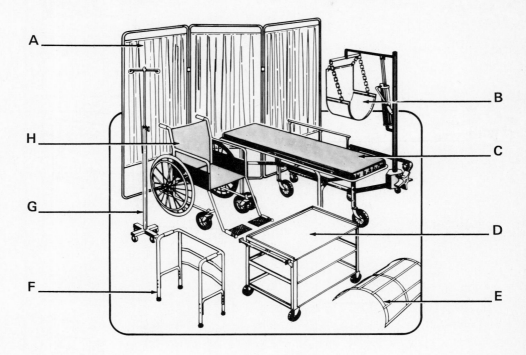

SECTION 2

WORKBOOK ASSIGNMENT #5, CHAPTER 6, SECTION 2
BEDMAKING

Find the list of objectives for this section. Next to each objective, write the page numbers where you can find information to help you meet these objectives.

WORKBOOK ASSIGNMENT #6, CHAPTER 6, SECTION 2
BEDMAKING

Read "Key Ideas: Bedmaking" in your textbook. Use the list below to correctly identify the type of bed and label the illustrations on the next page.

Closed bed	Postoperative bed
Open bed	Occupied bed

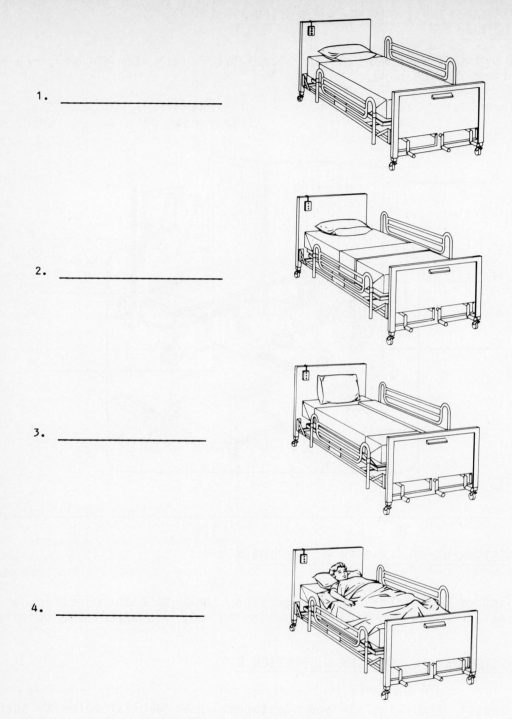

1. _____

2. _____

3. _____

4. _____

<u>WORKBOOK ASSIGNMENT #7, CHAPTER 6, SECTION 2</u>
<u>BEDMAKING</u>

Read "Key Ideas: Bedmaking" and "Rules to Follow: Bedmaking" in your textbook.
Use the following terms to fill in the space provided after each statement.

Closed bed   Occupied bed
Open bed   Postoperative bed

1. Mr. Striker was discharged early this morning. Environmental Service
    personnel cleaned the unit, and the head nurse has asked you to make the
    bed. Which type of bed will you make? _____

2. At the end of your shift, the head nurse tells you that Mr. Fine will be
    admitted shortly. She asks you to check the unit and make the bed. Which
    type of bed will you make? _____

3. The next morning you are assigned to give morning care to Mr. Fine. On
    the record of activities of daily living, you see that the notation C.B.R.,
    meaning complete bed rest, has been written. Which type of bed will you
    make for Mr. Fine? _____

4. The following morning the head nurse asks you to help prepare Mr. Fine for
    surgery. After you transport Mr. Fine to the operating room, you are
    responsible for preparing his unit for his return. Which type of bed
    will you make? _____

WORKBOOK ASSIGNMENT #8, CHAPTER 6, SECTION 2
BEDMAKING

Read "Key Ideas: Bedmaking" and "Rules to Follow: Bedmaking" in your textbook.

Use the list of words below to complete the following statements. Use these
answers to fill in the puzzle spaces that correspond to the number beside each
statement in the illustration.

pin	bedspread	wrinkles
fan-fold	floor	chair
uniform	side	draw
CBR	pin	ulcers
bottom	top	remove
mitered	mattress	fitted
hems	draw	torn
hamper	contaminated	extra
cotton	blanket	bags
plastic	shake	repair box

ACROSS

1. A _____ makes it easy for the patient to get back into his bed.

3. The _____ of the bed refers to the mattress pad, the bottom
    sheet, and the draw sheets.

7. In most health care institutions, the linen _____ is in the dirty
    utility room.

8. Many health care institutions make the bed without the blanket or _____.

9. Do not _____ the bed linen.

67

11. Never allow any linen to touch your _____.

12. The _____ draw sheet is about the size of half a regular sheet.

17. First make as much of the bed as possible on one _____ before going on to the other side.

18. The abbreviation for complete bed rest is _____.

19. Never use a _____ on any item of linen.

20. The plastic draw sheet and the disposable bed protector protect the _____.

23. A _____ corner is also called a hospital corner.

25. Some health care institutions use melt-away plastic _____ for laundry bags.

26. When using a folded sheet for a draw sheet, the fold must always be placed toward the head of the bed and the _____ toward the foot of the bed.

DOWN

1. Dirty linen should never be put on the _____.

2. Some health care institutions today use _____ bottom sheets.

3. Leave a folded _____ at the foot of the bed.

4. The _____ of the bed refers to the top sheet, blanket, and bedspread.

5. Return torn linen to a _____ in the linen closet.

6. Stack the bedmaking linen items on the _____ in the order that you will use them.

10. Never use bed _____ for any purpose other than that which it was intended.

11. Wrinkles in the sheets can cause painful decubitus _____.

12. As soon as you bring linen into the room, it is considered _____ and cannot be used elsewhere.

13. Never use a _____ piece of linen.

14. _____ should never touch the patient's skin.

15. Report to the head nurse or team leader if you see patients or visitors trying to _____ articles of linen from the unit for any reason.

16. Nursing assistants make beds without any _____ in the sheets.

21. Never bring _____ linen into a patient unit.

22. The bottom sheets must be firm and _____ under the patient.

24. When cotton _____ sheets are not available, a large sheet can be folded in half to cover the draw sheet.

WORKBOOK ASSIGNMENT #9, CHAPTER 6, SECTION 2
BEDMAKING

Read "Rules to Follow: Bedmaking" in your textbook. Write the word <u>DO</u>
or <u>DON'T</u> next to each of the following statements:

1. _____ report to the head nurse or team leader if you see patients
or visitors trying to remove articles of linen from the unit
for any reason.

2. _____ use bed linen for any purpose other than that for which it was
intended.

3. _____ shake the bed linen. Shaking would spread germs to everything
and everyone in the room, including you.

4. _____ allow any linen to touch your uniform.

5. _____ return torn linen to a "repair box" in the linen closet for
repair. Never use a torn piece of linen.

6. _____ use a pin on any item of linen.

7. _____ bring extra linen into a patient unit. If you do, it will
be considered contaminated (dirty) and cannot be used
elsewhere.

8. _____ put dirty linen on the floor.

WORKBOOK ASSIGNMENT #10, CHAPTER 6
WORDS TO REMEMBER/GLOSSARY

Fill in the blanks with the vocabulary word to remember after reading the
definition carefully.

1. When in place over a body area such as a foot or arm, the _____
holds the bedclothes (sheets and blankets) away from the patient so that
they do not touch that body part.

2. A _____ _____ is a small sheet made of plastic, rubber,
or cotton. It is placed crosswise on the middle of the bed over the
bottom sheet to help protect the bedding from a patient's discharges.

3. A pan used for catching material that a patient spits out, vomits or
expectorates is called an _____ _____.

LEARNING BY DOING

As you study the procedures in this chapter, read every step carefully. Think
about the action words, the words that tell you what to do. Look at the pictures
closely and read the captions. You will be able to remember what to do more
easily if you try to do it after you have read about it. Learning by doing
involves your whole body in the learning process, not just your eyes or ears. It
is one of the most effective ways to learn.

Ask a fellow student or, if you are practicing at home, ask a friend or relative
to play the part of the patient. Actually do all of the steps of the procedure
several times, pretending you are a nursing assistant caring for several
patients. Work slowly at first. Look at the textbook whenever you are not sure
about what to do next. Practice in this way many times until you can work
quickly, and you no longer need to look at the textbook.

Switch roles with your partner, and you take several turns at being the patient.
Not only will this give your partner a chance to learn the procedure, but you
will benefit as well. By putting yourself in the patient's place, you will begin
to understand how it feels to be a patient, and you will be able to treat real
patients as you yourself would like to be treated.

CHAPTER 6 QUIZ

Circle the letter <u>T</u> if the statement below is true, <u>F</u> if it is false.

T or F   1. Wrinkles in the bed linens can cause bedsores.

T or F   2. A patient's unit consists of the bed and bedside table.

T or F   3. All disposable equipment must be washed, disinfected, and
                sterilized.

T or F   4. The open bed is made exactly like the closed bed except for
                one thing--the top bedding is opened so that the patient can
                get into bed easily.

T or F   5. The cuff is made at the foot of the bed.

SECTION 1

WORKBOOK ASSIGNMENT #1, CHAPTER 7, SECTION 1
DAILY CARE OF THE PATIENT

Find the list of objectives for this section. Next to each objective, write the page numbers where you can find information to help you meet these objectives.

WORKBOOK ASSIGNMENT #2, CHAPTER 7, SECTION 1
SCHEDULE OF DAILY CARE - 24 HOUR NEEDS OF THE PATIENT

Read "Key Ideas: Schedule of Daily Care" in your textbook. Match the terms for daily care in Column A with the events of the day in Column B by drawing lines between the two columns. Write the correct letter in the space provided.

Column A	Column B
____1. Early morning care	A. After breakfast
____2. Morning care	B. After supper/before bedtime
____3. Afternoon care	C. Before breakfast
____4. Evening care	D. After lunch/before visiting

WORKBOOK ASSIGNMENT #3, CHAPTER 7, SECTION 1
SCHEDULE OF DAILY CARE

Read "Key Ideas: Schedule of Daily Care" in your textbook. Keep your book open. Read the following four situations and answer the questions that follow:

1. Mrs. Murphy, nursing assistant, is responsible for giving early morning care to Mrs. Paul. After greeting the patient and introducing herself, Mrs. Murphy offered Mrs. Paul the bedpan. Then she helped Mrs. Paul to wash her hands and face. Mrs. Murphy filled Mrs. Paul's pitcher with fresh drinking water and cleaned off the overbed table. Since Mrs. Paul was permitted to sit up, Mrs. Murphy raised the head of the bed. Feeling that Mrs. Paul was now ready for breakfast, Mrs. Murphy told Mrs. Paul that she would be back soon with the breakfast tray, and she left the room to give early morning care to her next patient.

    What did Mrs. Murphy forget to do for Mrs. Paul? _____

    _____

2. After breakfast was finished and the trays were taken away, Mrs. Murphy was ready to give morning care to Mrs. Paul. As she entered the room, she cheerfully chatted with Mrs. Paul about breakfast and the weather and then offered the bedpan. She assisted Mrs. Paul with oral hygiene and then gave her a partial bed bath. She gave Mrs. Paul a back rub and then helped her into a clean gown. She helped Mrs. Paul comb her hair and then straightened the unit. After checking to be sure Mrs. Paul was as comfortable as possible, Mrs. Murphy went on to her next patient.

   What did Mrs. Murphy forget to do for Mrs. Paul? _____

   _____

3. After lunch, but before visiting hours began, Mrs. Murphy started afternoon care for Mrs. Paul. She listened attentively as Mrs. Paul told her all about her oldest son who was coming in for a visit in just half an hour. As she listened, she changed Mrs. Paul's gown and straightened the unit, making appropriate comments now and again to show interest in Mrs. Paul's son. She offered the bedpan, assisted with oral hygiene and helped Mrs. Paul to wash her hands and face. Then she told Mrs. Paul that she would be leaving soon and Miss Bradley, another nursing assistant, would be in later to give evening care. She asked if there was anything else she could do for Mrs. Paul before she left. As she was leaving the room, she wished Mrs. Paul a pleasant visit with her son.

   What did Mrs. Murphy forget to do? _____

   _____

4. Later that evening, after supper, Miss Bradley, nursing assistant, entered the room, greeted Mrs. Paul and introduced herself. She explained to Mrs. Paul that she wanted to help her get clean and comfortable for a good night's rest. She offered the bedpan and assisted Mrs. Paul with oral hygiene. Next, Miss Bradley gave Mrs. Paul a back rub. Then she changed the draw sheet and smoothed and tightened all the sheets. She offered Mrs. Paul an extra blanket, which was gratefully accepted. After she filled Mrs. Paul's pitcher with fresh drinking water, she offered Mrs. Paul a drink. She wished Mrs. Paul a good night's sleep and asked if there was anything else she could do to make her comfortable before she went on to her next patient.

   What did Miss Bradley forget to do for Mrs. Paul? _____

   _____

WORKBOOK ASSIGNMENT #4, CHAPTER 7, SECTION 1
ORAL HYGIENE

Read "Key Ideas: Oral Hygiene" in your textbook. Fill in the blank spaces with the words listed below.

teeth	care	coating	daily
sick	clean	mouth	taste
oral hygiene	mouth	fuzzy	tongue
appetite			

A person's mouth and (A)_____ need even more care when a person is
(B)_____ than when he is well. This care is called (C)_____.
A sick person's mouth often has a bad (D)_____. Sometimes the
(E)_____ feels (F)_____ because of an illness. The
(G)_____ may be covered with a (H)_____ that spoils the
(I)_____. On the other hand, with good (J)_____, the
patient's (K)_____ will feel fresh and (L)_____. Cleaning
the patient's teeth and mouth, that is, giving (M)_____ is an essential
part of (N)_____ patient care.

WORKBOOK ASSIGNMENT #5, CHAPTER 7, SECTION 1
ORAL HYGIENE

Read "Key Ideas: Oral Hygiene" in your textbook.

Circle the letter T if the statement below is true, F if it is false.

T or F   1. Teeth should be brushed every morning, every evening, and after
                each meal.

T or F   2. In your work you will be giving oral hygiene to conscious and
                unconscious patients.

T or F   3. Patients are expected to clean their own dentures.

T or F   4. Oral hygiene is given to unconscious patients and patients who
                are N.P.O. every hour.

T or F   5. The purpose of oral hygiene is to keep oral tissues clean.

T or F   6. Unless this is done, tissues tend to dry out and develop a mucous
                coating much more rapidly.

WORKBOOK ASSIGNMENT #6, CHAPTER 7, SECTION 1
ORAL HYGIENE

Read the "Procedure: Oral Hygiene, Cleaning Dentures, and Oral Hygiene for the
Unconscious Patient" in your textbook.

Label the pictures on the next page with the letter of the procedure they are
illustrating.

A. Oral hygiene

B. Cleaning dentures

C. Oral hygiene for the unconscious patient

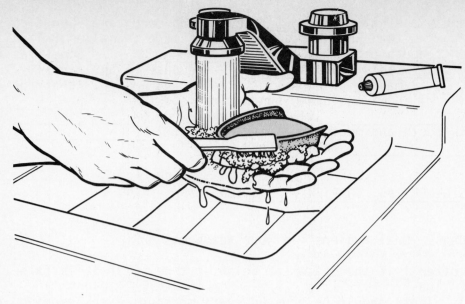

1 _____.

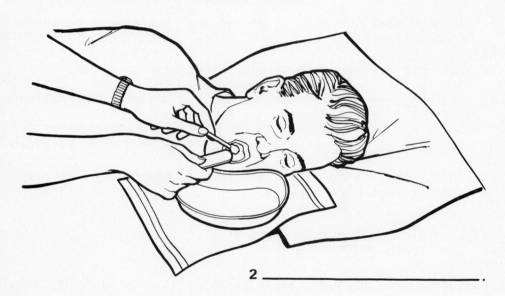

2 _____.

3 _____.

WORKBOOK ASSIGNMENT #7, CHAPTER 7, SECTION 1
TYPES OF BATH

Read the information titled "Types of Baths" in your textbook. A patient may be bathed in one of four ways, depending on his condition. Here is a list of the four ways for a patient to be bathed. Read the following questions and fill in the blank spaces with the correct answers.

Complete bed bath   Tub bath   Partial bed bath   Shower

1. Which type of bath is given to the helpless patient? _____

2. Which type of bath is often given for therapeutic reasons? _____

3. Which type of bath is given to the patient who is able to take care of most of his own bathing needs? _____

4. Which type of bath may be permitted for convalescent patients? _____

5. Which type of bath is given to a patient who is on complete bed rest? _____

6. Which type of bath is given to a patient who has been judged by his doctor to be strong enough to get out of bed and walk around? _____

7. In which type of bath do you bathe only the areas that are hard for the patient to reach? _____

8. In giving which type of bath will you get little or no help from the patient? _____

WORKBOOK ASSIGNMENT #8, CHAPTER 7, SECTION 1
BATHING THE PATIENT

Read "Key Ideas: Helping the Patient to Bathe" and "Rules to Follow: Bathing the Patient" in your textbook.

Circle the letter T if the statement below is true, F if it is false.

T or F   1. It is not necessary to always cover the patient with a bath blanket before giving the complete bed bath.

T or F   2. When giving a bed bath use good body mechanics, keep your feet separated, stand firmly, bend your knees, and keep your back straight.

T or F   3. Soap has a moisturing effect on the skin.

T or F   4. Only one part of the body is washed at a time. Wash, rinse, and dry each part or area very well then cover it right away with the bath blanket.

T or F   5. Putting the patient's hands and feet into the water makes him feel relaxed.

T or F   6. A nursing assistant may trim a patient's toenails if the patient requests this.

T or F   7. During the bath, the nursing assistant should be observing the patient's skin. Report any redness, rashes, broken skin, or tender places you see on the patient's body to your head nurse or team leader.

T or F   8. A bed bath stimulates circulation and helps prevent bedsores.

WORKBOOK ASSIGNMENT #9, CHAPTER 7, SECTION 1
THE TUB BATH

Read the "Procedure: The Tub Bath" in your textbook. Circle the letter of the correct answer for each question.

1. After telling your patient that you are going to help him to take a tub bath, you pull the curtains around the bed for privacy and help the patient out of bed. Which of the following three tasks should you do next?

   A. For safety, remove all electrical appliances from the room with the bathtub.
   B. Wash the bathtub with the disinfectant solution.
   C. Get the patient into a bathrobe and slippers and to the room with the bathtub, either walking or by wheelchair.

2. You have checked the room for electrical appliances and found a heat lamp on the counter. You took it out of the room and put it in its proper storage place. You placed a chair next to the bathtub and assisted your patient into the chair. What should you do next?

   A. Wash the bathtub with the disinfectant solution.
   B. Assist the patient to get undressed and into the bathtub.
   C. Fill the bathtub 1/2 full of water at 105°F (40.5°C). Test the temperature with a bath thermometer.

3. After filling the tub and placing a towel in the tub for the patient to sit on and a towel on the floor where the patient will step out of the tub, you assisted the patient to get undressed and into the bathtub. What should you do next?

   A. Let the patient stay in the bathtub as long as permitted, according to your instructions.
   B. Let the patient stay in the tub for 15 minutes.
   C. Help the patient wash himself, if help is needed.

4. You have helped the patient to wash himself and placed one towel across the chair. You then helped the patient out of the bathtub and seated him on the towel-covered chair. What should you do next?

   A. Help the patient return to his home and into bed.
   B. Wash the bathtub with the disinfectant solution.
   C. Dry the patient well by patting gently with a towel. Help him put on pajamas or a gown, bathrobe, and slippers.

5. After returning the patient to his room and helping him into bed, you made him comfortable. What should you do next?

   A. Return to the tub room. Clean the bathtub with disinfectant solution.
   B. Report to your head nurse or team leader:
      -- That you have given the patient a tub bath
      -- Your observations of anything unusual.
   C. Remove all used linens. Put them in the dirty linen hamper in the utility room.

WORKBOOK ASSIGNMENT #10, CHAPTER 7, SECTION 1
THE BACK RUB

Read the "Procedure: Giving the Patient a Back Rub" in your textbook.

Circle the letter T if the statement below is true, F if it is false.

T or F   1. Lotion should be warmed by placing the container in a basin of warm water.

T or F   2. Pour a small amount of lotion on the patient's back.

T or F   3. Rub your hands together using friction to warm the lotion.

T or F   4. Exert firm pressure as you stroke upward from the buttocks toward the shoulders.

T or F   5. Use all your strength as you stroke downward from shoulders to buttocks.

T or F   6. Use circular motion on each soft area.

T or F   7. This rhythmic rubbing motion should be continued from 1-1/2 to 3 minutes.

T or F   8. Dry the patient's back by rubbing gently with a towel.

WORKBOOK ASSIGNMENT #11, CHAPTER 7, SECTION 1
BATHING THE PATIENT

Read "Key Ideas: Helping the Patient to Bathe" in your textbook.

Circle the letter T if the statement below is true, F if it is false.

T or F 1. Bathing gets rid of dirt on the patient's body.

T or F 2. Bathing prevents cavities.

T or F 3. Bathing eliminates body odors.

T or F 4. Bathing eliminates body hair.

T or F 5. Bathing stimulates circulation.

T or F 6. Bathing helps to prevent bedsores.

T or F 7. Bathing requires body movement.

T or F 8. Bathing helps to prevent dandruff.

T or F 9. Bathing requires the patient's legs and arms to be lifted.

T or F 10. Bathing requires the patient's head and torso to be turned.

T or F 11. Bathing exercises muscles that might otherwise remain unused.

T or F 12. Bathing creates the opportunity for the nursing assistant to observe the patient's body carefully.

WORKBOOK ASSIGNMENT #12, CHAPTER 7, SECTION 1
SHAMPOOING THE PATIENT'S HAIR

Read the "Procedure: Shampooing the Patient's Hair" in your textbook. The following group of questions refers to Step 15 from the procedure. Find Step 15 and read it once again. Making a trough is a simple thing to do but if you have never done it before it may seem tricky. After answering these questions, actually make a trough from a plastic sheet. Check your work by pouring water through it. If the water runs from the top, where the patient's head would be, through the trough, and into the large basin on the chair, you have succeeded in making a trough.

Fill in the blank spaces with the words listed below.

plastic   head   basin   three
open   chair   channel

1. A trough can be made by rolling up the sides of a sheet made of _____.

2. You must roll _____ sides of the sheet.

3. Roll each side over three times to make the _____.

4. Put the short rolled end under the patient's _____.

5. Hang the _____ end over the side of the bed.

6. This unrolled free or open end of the plastic sheet should be put into the large _____.

7. The large basin should be on the _____.

WORKBOOK ASSIGNMENT #13, CHAPTER 7, SECTION 2
BEDPAN; URINAL; BEDSIDE COMMODE

Find the list of objectives for this section. Next to each objective, write the page numbers where you can find information to help you meet these objectives.

WORKBOOK ASSIGNMENT #14, CHAPTER 7, SECTION 2
EQUIPMENT

Read "Section 2: Bedpan; Urinal; Bedside Commode" in your textbook. Fill in the blanks with the names of the pieces of equipment pictured here.

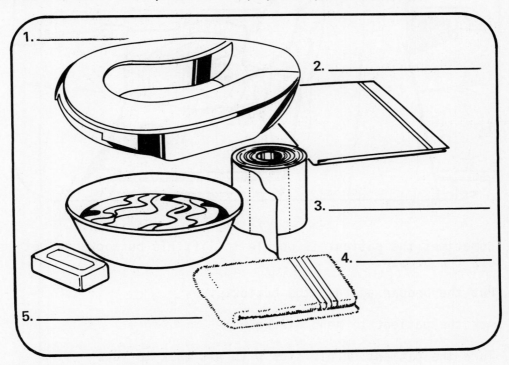

1. _____
2. _____
3. _____
4. _____
5. _____

WORKBOOK ASSIGNMENT #15, CHAPTER 7, SECTION 2
THE BEDPAN

Read the "Procedure: Offering the Bedpan" in your textbook. This procedure describes two methods for helping the patient onto the bedpan (see steps 10 and 11 in your textbook). Read each of the following statements. If the statement goes with picture "A," write the letter "A" in the blank beside the statement. If the statements goes with the picture "B," write the letter "B" in the blank beside the statement.

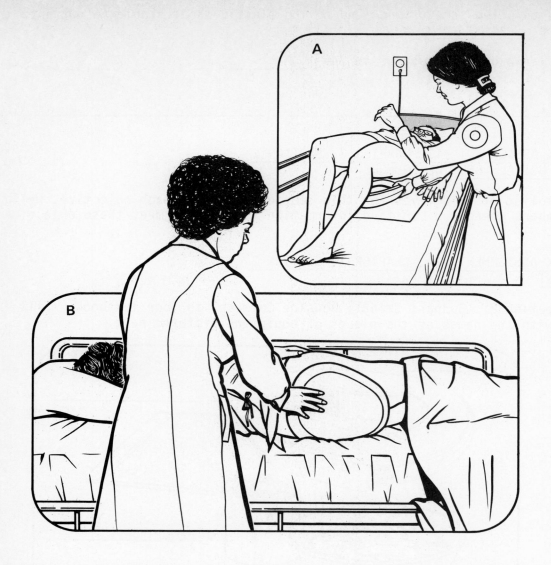

_____ 1. Sometimes the patient is unable to lift his buttocks to get on or off the bedpan.

_____ 2. Put the bedpan against the buttocks.

_____ 3. Ask the patient to bend his knees.

_____ 4. Turn the patient on his side with his back to you.

_____ 5. Place the bedpan in position with the seat of the bedpan under his buttocks.

_____ 6. Ask the patient to raise his hips.

_____ 7. If necessary, help the patient to raise his buttocks by slipping your hand under the lower part of his back.

_____ 8. Then turn the patient back onto the bedpan.

82

WORKBOOK ASSIGNMENT #16, CHAPTER 7, SECTION 2
THE URINAL

Read the "Procedure: Offering the Urinal" in your textbook. Circle BEFORE or AFTER in each statement.

1. Pull the curtain around the bed for privacy BEFORE or AFTER you give the urinal to the patient.

2. Leave the room to give the patient privacy BEFORE or AFTER you wash your hands.

3. Return to the room and wash your hands BEFORE or AFTER the patient signals.

4. Cover the urinal and take it to the patient's bathroom BEFORE or AFTER you check the urine for abnormal (unusual) appearance.

5. Empty the urinal into the toilet BEFORE or AFTER you rinse it with cold water.

WORKBOOK ASSIGNMENT #17, CHAPTER 7, SECTION 2
THE BEDSIDE COMMODE

Read the "Procedure: The Portable Bedside Commode" in your textbook.

Circle the letter T if the statement below is true, F if it is false.

T or F   1. Put the commode next to the patient's bathroom.

T or F   2. Leave the room to give the patient privacy.

T or F   3. Help the patient if he is unable to clean himself.

T or F   4. Help the patient to wash his hands in the bathroom sink.

T or F   5. Remove the bedpan from under the commode. Cover it and carry it to the dirty utility room.

WORKBOOK ASSIGNMENT #18, CHAPTER 7
WORDS TO REMEMBER/GLOSSARY

Fill in the blanks with the vocabulary word to remember after reading the definition carefully.

1. _____ are artificial teeth. They replace some or all of a person's teeth and are described as being partial or complete, and upper or lower.

2. _____ refers to anything to do with the mouth.

3. Cleanliness of the mouth is _____ _____.

<u>WORKBOOK ASSIGNMENT #19, CHAPTER 7</u>
<u>LEARNING BY DOING</u>

As you study the procedures in this chapter, read every step carefully. Think about the action words, the words that tell you what to do. Look at the pictures closely and read the captions. You will be able to remember what to do more easily if you try to do it after you have read about it. Learning by doing involves your whole body in the learning process, not just your eyes or ears. It is one of the most effective ways to learn.

Ask a fellow student or, if you are practicing at home, ask a friend or relative to play the part of the patient. Actually do all of the steps of the procedure several times, pretending you are a nursing assistant caring for several patients. Work slowly at first. Look at the textbook whenever you are not sure about what to do next. Practice in this way many times until you can work quickly, and you no longer need to look at the textbook.

Switch roles with your partner, and you take several turns at being the patient. Not only will this give your partner a chance to learn the procedure, but you will benefit as well. By putting yourself in the patient's place, you will begin to understand how it feels to be a patient, and you will be able to treat real patients as you yourself would like to be treated.

CHAPTER 7 QUIZ

Here is a list of 10 of the procedures taught in this chapter. Write the number of the procedure that is the correct response in the blank that follows the question.

A. Oral hygiene
B. Cleaning dentures
C. The complete bed bath
D. The tub bath
E. Giving the patient a back rub

F. Changing the patient's gown
G. Shampooing the patient's hair
H. Combing the patient's hair
I. Shaving the patient's beard
J. Offering the bedpan

1. Which procedure involves the use of a razor? _____

2. Which procedure involves making a trough? _____

3. Which procedure involves cleaning the patient's teeth and mouth? _____

4. Which procedure involves parting the hair down the middle to make it easier to comb? _____

5. Which procedure involves washing a bathtub with disinfectant solution? _____

6. Which procedure involves cleaning the patient's false teeth? _____

7. Which procedure involves checking the excreta for abnormal appearance? _____

8. Which procedure involves stimulating the patient's circulation in order to prevent decubitus ulcers? _____

9. Which procedure involves making a mitten with a washcloth? _____

10. Which procedure involves taking off one sleeve at a time, leaving the old gown in place on the patient? _____

CHAPTER 8   HUMAN ANATOMY AND PHYSIOLOGY

WORKBOOK ASSIGNMENT #1
HUMAN ANATOMY AND PHYSIOLOGY

Find the list of objectives for this section. Next to each objective, write the page numbers where you can find information to help you meet these objectives.

WORKBOOK ASSIGNMENT #2
CELLS TO TISSUES TO ORGANS TO SYSTEMS TO MAN

Read "Key Ideas: The Cell" in your textbook before answering the following questions. Choose the correct word from the list below to complete each sentence.

tissues	systems	cell membrane
cytoplasm	nucleus	microscopic
bodily	division	structure

1. Anatomy is the study of the _____ of the body.

2. Physiology is the study of the _____ functions.

3. Cells are _____ in size.

4. Cells consist of three main parts. One is the _____, where the activities of the cell take place. The second is _____, which directs cellular activities. The third is the _____, which keeps the living substances of a cell, called the protoplasm, within bounds and allows materials to pass in and out of the cell.

5. Cells reproduce by _____.

6. Groups of cells of the same type that do a particular kind of work are called _____.

7. Tissues are grouped together to form _____, such as the heart, lungs, and liver.

8. Organs that work together to perform similar tasks make up _____.

WORKBOOK ASSIGNMENT #3
HUMAN ANATOMY AND PHYSIOLOGY

Read Chapter 8, "Human Anatomy and Physiology," in your textbook. Fill in the blank spaces with the words listed below to complete each statement.

organs	systems
tissues	cell

1. Groups of organs acting together to carry out body functions are called _____.

2. The _____ is the basic building unit of all living matter.

3. Two or more kinds of tissue grouped together to make up body parts are called _____.

4. Groups of cells of the same kind form _____.

WORKBOOK ASSIGNMENT #4
HUMAN ANATOMY AND PHYSIOLOGY

1. Underline the names of the two systems that work in close harmony to supply all the cells with oxygen.

   A. Skeletal system   F. Reproductive system
   B. Muscular system   G. Respiratory system
   C. Gastrointestinal system   H. Circulatory system
   D. Nervous system   I. Endocrine system
   E. Excretory system   J. Integumentary system

2. Draw squares around the letters of the two systems that work in close harmony to supply all the cells with the basic nutrients needed for energy and growth.

   A. Skeletal system   F. Reproductive system
   B. Muscular system   G. Respiratory system
   C. Gastrointestinal system   H. Circulatory system
   D. Nervous system   I. Endocrine system
   E. Excretory system   J. Integumentary system

3. Mark an "X" beside the letters of the five systems that remove or eliminate body wastes.

   A. Skeletal system   F. Reproductive system
   B. Muscular system   G. Respiratory system
   C. Gastrointestinal system   H. Circulatory system
   D. Nervous system   I. Endocrine system
   E. Excretory system   J. Integumentary system

4. Draw a triangle around the letter of the body system that controls the functioning of all the other systems as well as every activity of the person.

   A. Skeletal system   F. Reproductive system
   B. Muscular system   G. Respiratory system
   C. Gastrointestinal system   H. Circulatory system
   D. Nervous system   I. Endocrine system
   E. Excretory system   J. Integumentary system

WORKBOOK ASSIGNMENT #5
ORGANS AND SYSTEMS

Read Chapter 8, "Human Anatomy and Physiology," in your textbook before answering the following questions. On the blank line next to each organ, write the letter of the body system of which it is a part.

87

Choose from the following list of body systems.

A.	Integumentary	F.	Gastrointestinal
B.	Respiratory	G.	Nervous
C.	Reproductive	H.	Excretory
D.	Endocrine	I.	Muscular
E.	Circulatory	J.	Skeletal

1. Brain _____
2. Skin _____
3. Esophagus _____
4. Bones _____
5. Spinal cord _____
6. Hair _____
7. Muscles _____
8. Mouth _____
9. Nerves _____
10. Joints _____
11. Appendix _____
12. Sweat glands _____
13. Oil glands _____
14. Bladder _____
15. Uterus _____
16. Tendons _____
17. Gallbladder _____
18. Lungs _____
19. Vagina _____
20. Teeth _____
21. Heart _____
22. Urethra _____
23. Rectum _____

24. Ovaries _____
25. Salivary glands _____
26. Bronchi _____
27. Blood _____
28. Stomach _____
29. Kidneys _____
30. Testes _____
31. Duodenum _____
32. Larynx _____
33. Breasts _____
34. Ureters _____
35. Intestines _____
36. Scrotum _____
37. Thyroid glands _____
38. Veins _____
39. Nose _____
40. Pineal gland _____
41. Liver _____
42. Parathyroid gland _____
43. Arteries _____
44. Adrenal glands _____
45. Penis _____
46. Colon _____

47. Pharynx _____

48. Thymus _____

49. Lymph nodes _____

50. Anus _____

51. Trachea _____

52. Fallopian tubes _____

53. Pituitary gland _____

54. Capillaries _____

55. Lymph _____

56. Ligaments _____

57. Spleen _____

WORKBOOK ASSIGNMENT #6
NAMES FOR BODY AREAS

Read "Key Ideas: Names for Body Areas" in your textbook before answering the following questions. Write the letters of the body locations from Column A in the space next to their matching description in Column B.

Column A

A. Anterior

B. Deep

C. Ventral

D. Inferior

E. Posterior

F. Superficial

G. Superior

H. Dorsal

Column B

_____ 1. Toward the back

_____ 2. On or near the surface

_____ 3. Toward the front

_____ 4. Upper portion

_____ 5. On the back side

_____ 6. Lower portion

_____ 7. On the belly side

_____ 8. Distant from the surface.

WORKBOOK ASSIGNMENT #7
WORDS TO REMEMBER/GLOSSARY

Fill in the blanks with the vocabulary word to remember after reading the definition carefully.

1. The region of the body between the chest and the pelvis is called the _____.

2. _____ is the study of the structure of an organism, such as a plant, an animal, or a human being and any of its parts.

3. _____ are the fundamental building blocks of all living matter.

4. _____ is tissue that connects, supports, covers, ensheathes, lines, pads, or protects.

5. _____ is the tissue composing the skin. Also, the tissue lining the passages of the hollow organs of the respiratory, digestive, and urinary systems is epithelial tissue.

6. An _____ is part of the body made of several types of tissues grouped together to perform a certain function.

7. _____ are tough cords of connective tissue that bind muscles to body parts.

8. _____ is a group of cells of the same type that do a particular kind of work.

9. _____ _____ is a watery environment around each cell that acts as a place of exchange for gases, food, and waste products between cells and the blood.

10. A _____ is a growth in or on the body. There are two kinds:

    1. Benign tumors, which grow slowly and can usually be removed by surgery.
    2. Malignant tumors, which grow wildly and are sometimes called cancer. They often are a threat to a person's life.

11. _____ is the study of the functions of the body tissues and organs.

CHAPTER 8 QUIZ

Write the letters of the body systems from Column A in the spaces next to their matching descriptions in Column B.

Column A

A. Skeletal system
B. Muscular system
C. Digestive system
D. Nervous system
E. Excretory system

F. Integumentary system
G. Endocrine system
H. Circulatory system
I. Respiratory system
J. Reproductive system

Column B

_____1. Gives movement to the body

_____2. Takes in food, absorbs it, and converts it to energy

_____3. Supports and protects the body

_____4. Removes wastes

_____5. Secretes hormones into the blood

_____6. Controls the activities of the body

_____7. Provides the first line of defense against infection

_____8. Carries food, oxygen, and water to body cells

_____9. Gives the body air to supply oxygen to the cells

_____10. Allows a new human being to be born.

SECTION 1

WORKBOOK ASSIGNMENT #1, CHAPTER 9, SECTION 1
ANATOMY AND PHYSIOLOGY

Read "Section 1: Anatomy and Physiology" in your textbook. Study the diagram of
the skeleton and surface muscles. Use it as a guide when filling in the blanks
in the diagram below with the names of the bones and surface muscles.

SKELETON AND SURFACE MUSCLES

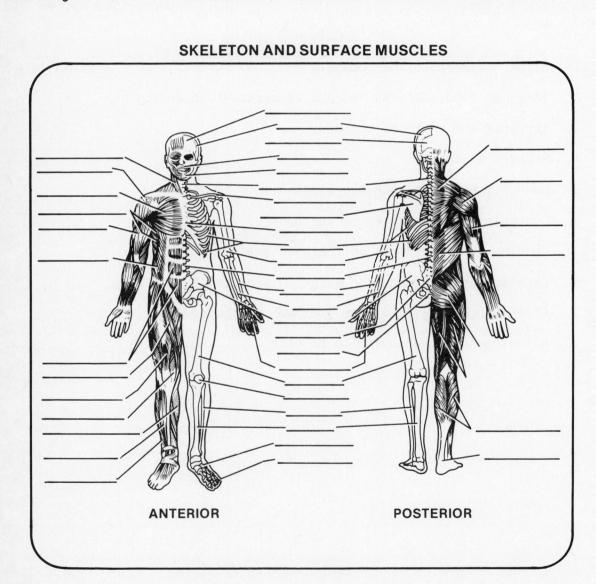

ANTERIOR   POSTERIOR

92

WORKBOOK ASSIGNMENT #2, CHAPTER 9, SECTION 2
BODY MECHANICS

Find the list of objectives for this section. Next to each objective, write the page numbers where you can find information to help you meet these objectives.

WORKBOOK ASSIGNMENT #3, CHAPTER 9, SECTION 2
BODY MECHANICS

Read "Key Ideas: Body Mechanics" in your textbook.

1. In the illustration below, circle the letter of the picture that illustrates correct lifting technique.

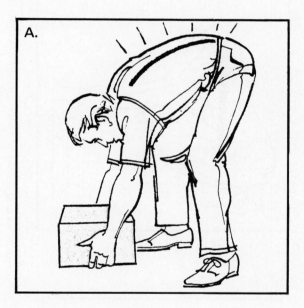

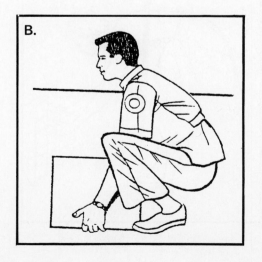

2. Try to lift a heavy object, such as a stack of books, in the same way as the nursing assistant in picture "A" above. Now, try to lift it again, but this time try to do it in the same way as the nursing assistant in picture "B." Which method placed less strain on your back? Which method placed the most strain on your legs? To avoid injury to your back, it is wise to keep your back in a vertical position while you squat, and actually lift the object by straightening your legs until you are in a standing position.

3. Stand in front of a bookcase. Remove a book from the bottom shelf by the method shown in picture C below. Remove another book by the method shown in picture D below. Which method placed the most strain on your back muscles? Try to let your legs do the work, not your back.

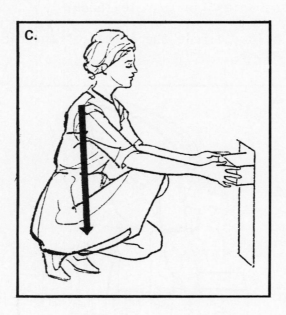

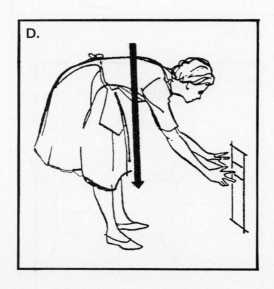

4. Try to lift a chair with one hand. Now try to lift the same chair using both hands. Which was easier? This is an example of distributing the workload over as many muscles as possible to avoid strain.

    Practice lifting a book or a cup in front of a mirror. Did you squat close to the book? Did you keep your back straight? Try this again with a heavier object. If you are practicing at home, you might use a shoe box filled with cans of food, a bag of groceries, or a bucket of water. Look in the mirror as you lift the object. Did you squat close to the load? Did you keep your back straight? Did you grip the object firmly? Did you hold the load close to your body? Did you lift by pushing up with the strong leg muscles? Practice again and again, until you feel comfortable moving and lifting in this way.

5. In the illustration below, circle the letter of the picture that illustrates the correct way to change the direction of movement.

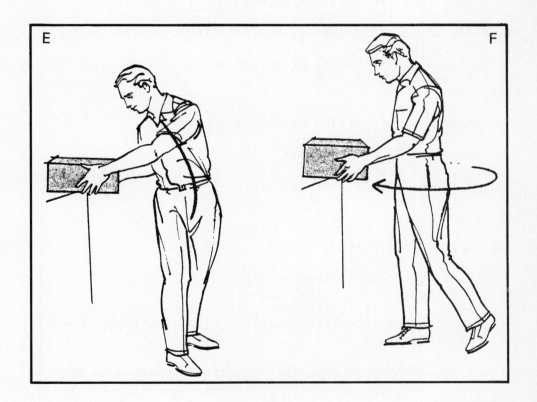

WORKBOOK ASSIGNMENT #4, CHAPTER 9, SECTION 2
BODY MECHANICS

Read "Key Ideas: Body Mechanics" in your textbook. Circle the letter of the correct response for each question.

1. The term body mechanics refers to _____.

    A. The correct positioning of the patient's body
    B. The bones and joints
    C. Special ways of standing and moving one's body
    D. Artificial arms or legs
    E. Rolling the patient like a log.

2. The purpose of good body mechanics is _____.

    A. To rest comfortably in a hospital bed
    B. To make the best use of strength and avoid fatigue
    C. To feel good while losing weight
    D. To avoid friction and irritation to the patient's skin
    E. To become stronger and more agile.

3. When an action requires physical effort _____.

    A. Get close to the load that is being lifted
    B. Use good posture
    C. Try to use as many muscles or groups of muscles as possible
    D. Ask a friend to do it
    E. A, B, and C.

4. For good balance, when lifting an object _____.

    A. Keep your feet 12 inches apart
    B. Avoid twisting your arms
    C. Arrange the patient's body correctly
    D. Keep your eyes open
    E. All of the above.

5. When you have to move a heavy object _____.

    A. It is better to push it than to lift it.
    B. It is best to pull it, rather than lift it.
    C. It is better to roll it than carry it.
    D. It is best to get help from another nursing assistant.
    E. All of the above.

6. The correct positioning of a patient's body is referred to as _____.

    A. Body mechanics
    B. Body alignment
    C. Body position
    D. Special patient care treatments
    E. Body arrangement.

WORKBOOK ASSIGNMENT #5, CHAPTER 9, SECTION 2
LIFTING AND MOVING PATIENTS

Read "Key Ideas: Lifting and Moving Patients" in your textbook.

Fill in the blank spaces with the words listed below.

friction   position   slide
draw sheet   irritation   role
folded   bed   grip

A pull sheet can help you move the patient in (1)_____ more easily. A
regular sheet (2)_____ over many times and placed (3)_____
the patient can be used as a pull sheet. The cotton (4)_____ can
also be used as a pull sheet. When moving the patient, (5)_____ the
pull sheet up tightly on each side next to the patient's body. (6)_____
the rolled portion to (7)_____ the patient into the desired
(8)_____. By using the pull sheet we avoid (9)_____ and
(10)_____ to the patient's skin that touches the bedding.

WORKBOOK ASSIGNMENT #6, CHAPTER 9, SECTION 2
LOCKING ARMS WITH THE PATIENT

Read the information titled "Procedure: Locking Arms with the Patient" in your
textbook.

ROLE-PLAY

Re-read each step of the above procedure carefully. Look at the picture closely.
Pay particular attention to the position of the nursing assistant's hands and the
patient's hands. Ask a fellow student, or if you are practicing at home, ask a
friend or relative to play the part of the patient. Pretend that your patient's
pillow needs to be rearranged. Actually do all 15 steps of the procedure several
times. Work slowly at first. Look at the textbook whenever you are not sure
about what to do next. Practice in this way many times until you can work more
quickly, until you no longer need to look at the textbook, and until you feel
comfortable using this technique.

Switch roles with your partner and you take several turns at being the patient.
Not only will this give your partner a chance to learn this technique, but you
will benefit as well. By putting yourself in the patient's place you will begin
to understand how it feels to be a patient, and you will be able to treat real
patients as you yourself would like to be treated.

WORKBOOK ASSIGNMENT #7, CHAPTER 9, SECTION 2
BODY MECHANICS

Read the "Procedure: Body Mechanics" in your textbook. Label each of the
pictures on the following pages with the letter in front of the procedure as
listed below.

A.   Turning a patient on his side away from you
B.   Moving the mattress to the head of the bed with the patient's help
C.   Moving a helpless patient to one side of the bed on his back
D.   Rolling the patient like a log
E.   Moving the non-ambulatory patient up in bed
F.   Turning a patient on his side toward you
G.   Moving a patient up in bed with his help.

1 _____

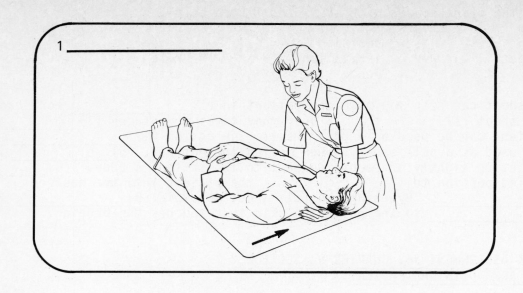

2 _____

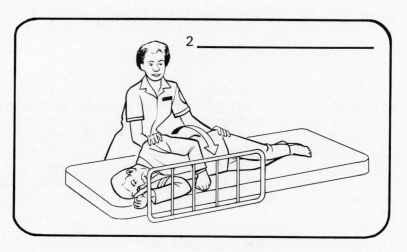

3 _____

98

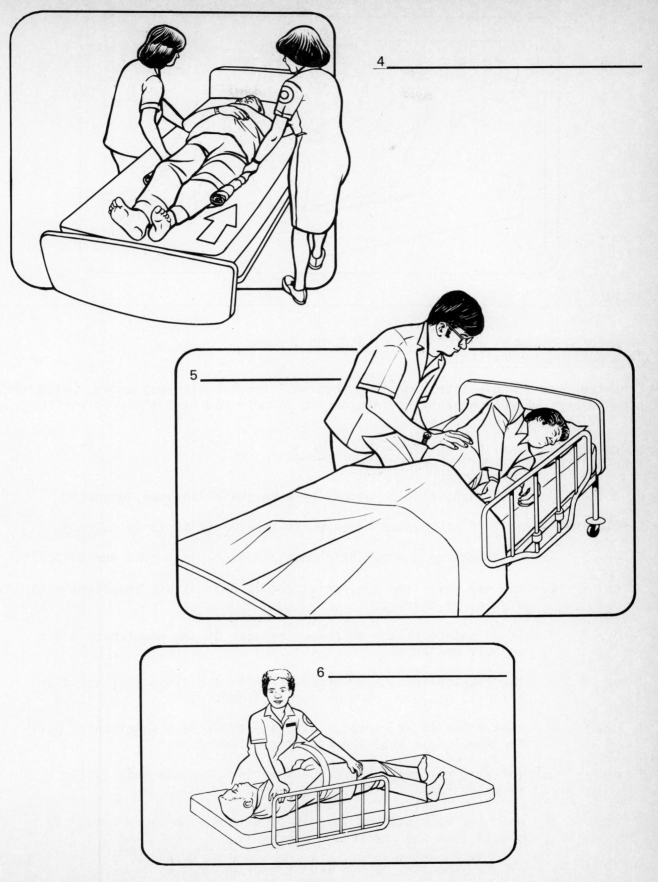

4 _____

5 _____

6 _____

99

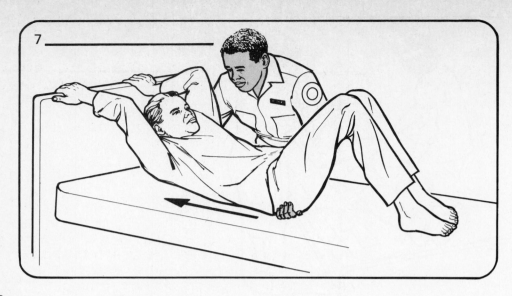

7 _____ _____

SECTION 3

WORKBOOK ASSIGNMENT #8, CHAPTER 9, SECTION 3
TRANSPORTING THE PATIENT

Find the list of objectives for this section. Next to each objective, write the page numbers where you can find information to help you meet these objectives.

WORKBOOK ASSIGNMENT #9, CHAPTER 9, SECTION 3
TRANSPORTING A PATIENT BY WHEELCHAIR

Read "Key Ideas: Transporting a Patient by Wheelchair" in your textbook.

Circle the letter T if the statement below is true, F if it is false.

T or F   1.   A patient in a wheelchair must always be in a robe and slippers.

T or F   2.   You may cover the patient's feet as well as his shoulders with a sheet or blanket.

T or F   3.   It is not necessary to cover the seat of the wheelchair under any circumstances.

T or F   4.   The wheelchair must be wiped off with a disinfectant solution after it has been used by each patient.

T or F   5.   When entering an elevator with a patient in a wheelchair, pull the wheelchair into the elevator backwards.

T or F   6.   There is no need to turn the wheelchair around once inside the elevator.

T or F   7.   When moving a patient in a wheelchair down a steep ramp, you should take the chair down backwards.

T or F   8. Always lock both wheels when the patient is getting in or out of the wheelchair.

T or F   9. It is necessary to lock the wheels of the chair whenever you must turn your back to the patient, even if it is for a moment.

WORKBOOK ASSIGNMENT #10, CHAPTER 9, SECTION 3
USING THE STRETCHER

Read "Key Ideas: Using a Stretcher" in your textbook.

Circle the letter T if the statement below is true, F if it is false.

T or F   1. A hospital stretcher is a wheeled cart on which patients remain lying down while they are moved from one place to another.

T or F   2. Litters and gurneys are the same as stretchers.

T or F   3. Whenever you are moving a stretcher, you should stand at the end where the patient's head is.

T or F   4. Push the stretcher so the patient's head is moving first.

T or F   5. Be careful to protect the patient's head at all times.

SECTION 4
_____

WORKBOOK ASSIGNMENT #11, CHAPTER 9, SECTION 4
CARE OF THE ORTHOPEDIC PATIENT

Find the list of objectives for this section. Next to each objective, write the page numbers where you can find information to help you meet these objectives.

WORKBOOK ASSIGNMENT #12, CHAPTER 9, SECTION 4
ORTHOPEDIC CARE

Read "Key Ideas: Scope of Orthopedics" in your textbook. Fill in the blanks with the words listed below.

casts   skin
position   support
                               weakness

1. Orthopedic equipment is designed to provide _____ for the injured part until it heals.

2. Orthopedic equipment is designed to prevent deformity and _____ in the injured muscles and joints.

3. Besides routine nursing care, the orthopedic patient needs special _____ care.

4. Patients in a plaster _____ often suffer feelings of restriction and fatigue.

5. The turning frame is a hospital bed designed to provide a variety of _____.

WORKBOOK ASSIGNMENT #13, CHAPTER 9, SECTION 4
TRACTION AND PLASTER CASTS

Read the information concerning the care of the patient in "Traction and Plaster Casts" in your textbook.

Write NEVER or ALWAYS in the blank bedside each statement.

1. _____ move the sand bags used with the traction without permission from the head nurse or team leader.

2. _____ check the traction apparatus and report any defect to the head nurse or team leader.

3. _____ check the position of the ropes and weights and report any condition that should not exist.

4. _____ change the patient's body position without permission from the head nurse or team leader.

5. _____ report to your head nurse or team leader if you notice that the patient has slid down in bed.

6. _____ check the skin on the body part where the cast ends to see if it is cold, blue, or irritated.

7. _____ report any complaints of pain to your head nurse or team leader.

8. _____ ask the patient if he feels tingling or numbness.

9. _____ allow the cast to become soiled while bedpans and urinals are being used, if possible.

10. _____ report any unusuasl odor to your head nurse or team leader.

WORKBOOK ASSIGNMENT #14, CHAPTER 9
WORDS TO REMEMBER/GLOSSARY

Fill in the blanks with the vocabulary word to remember after reading the definition carefully.

1. To be able to walk about, not bed-ridden, is to be _____.

2. _____ _____ refers to the arrangement of the body in a straight line, the placing of portions of the body in the correct anatomical position.

3. A _____ is a part of the body where two bones come together.

4. A break in a bone is known as a _____.

5. The equipment known as a _____ device is for pulling and stretching parts of the patient's body by using pulleys and weights. Traction is used to keep broken bones properly lined up while they are healing.

6. The equipment known as a _____ is a metal bar suspended over the bed and is used by the patient to help him raise or move his body more easily.

7. Reversible beds used in the care of the patients with certain orthopedic conditions are known as _____ _____.

WORKBOOK ASSIGNMENT #15, CHAPTER 9
LEARNING BY DOING

As you study the procedures in this chapter, read every step carefully. Think about the action words, the words that tell you what to do. Look at the pictures closely and read the captions. You will be able to remember what to do more easily if you try to do it after you have read about it. Learning by doing involves your whole body in the learning process, not just your eyes or ears. It is one of the most effective ways to learn.

Ask a fellow student or, if you are practicing at home, ask a friend or relative to play the part of the patient. Actually do all of the steps of the procedure several times, pretending you are a nursing assistant caring for several patients. Work slowly at first. Look at the textbook whenever you are not sure about what to do next. Practice in this way many times until you can work quickly, and you no longer need to look at the textbook.

Switch roles with your partners and you take several turns at being the patient. Not only will this give your partner a chance to learn the procedure, but you will benefit as well. By putting yourself in the patient's place, you will begin to understand how it feels to be a patient, and you will be able to treat real patients as you yourself would like to be treated.

CHAPTER 9 QUIZ

Circle the letter of the correct response.

1. You are going to pick up a heavy package from the floor. You should:

   A. Use only one hand for lifting.
   B. Keep your feet close together.
   C. Bend over at the waist.
   D. Bend your knees and squat down.
   E. All of the above.

2. You have helped a patient out of bed and into a wheelchair. The patient seems to be perspiring a lot. He looks pale and says he feels faint. What should you do next?

   A. Leave the patient and go immediately to the nursing station for help.
   B. Stay with the patient and ring the call bell for help.
   C. Stay with the patient and tell him he'll be all right.
   D. Hurry out of the room and ask the first doctor you see for help.
   E. All of the above.

3. To lift smoothly and to avoid strain _____.

   A. Always count "one-two-three" with the person you are working with.
   B. Say ready and go, so you work in unison with another nursing assistant.
   C. Say ready and go, so you work in unison with the patient.
   D. Work in bright light.
   E. A, B, C and D.

4. When you are moving a patient in a wheelchair out of an elevator:

   A. Ask everyone else to step out first.
   B. Turn the chair around and pull it out of the elevator backwards.
   C. Push the button marked "open" so the doors of the elevator will not close until you are out.
   D. All of the above.
   E. A and B only.

5. When working with the patient's help or with the help of another nursing assistant, always count "one, two, three" so you will both:

   A. Lift or move smoothly to avoid strain.
   B. Begin the motion at the same time.
   C. So you can see which of you moves fastest.
   D. All of the above.
   E. A and B only.

In the questions below, pick the correct thing to do out of the section marked ACTIONS. Put the letter for that correct action on the line after each situation described in WHAT DO YOU DO?

ACTIONS

A. Lock the wheels on the stretcher
B. Ask another person to help you
C. Tell your head nurse or team leader

WHAT DO YOU DO?

6. Before you change the position of a completely helpless patient?_____

7. Before you move a patient onto a stretcher? _____

8. After you lock the stretcher wheels, but before you move a patient from a stretcher to a bed? _____

9. When moving the non-ambulatory patient into a wheelchair from the bed? _____

10. When moving the helpless patient up in bed with a pull, draw, or turning sheet? _____

SECTION 1
***

WORKBOOK ASSIGNMENT #1, CHAPTER 10, SECTION 1
ANATOMY AND PHYSIOLOGY

Read "Section 1: Anatomy and Physiology" in your textbook. Study the diagram of
the magnified cross section of the skin and the parts of the skin. Use the
diagram as a guide when filling in the blanks in the illustration below with the
names of the parts of the skin.

MAGNIFIED CROSS SECTION OF THE SKIN

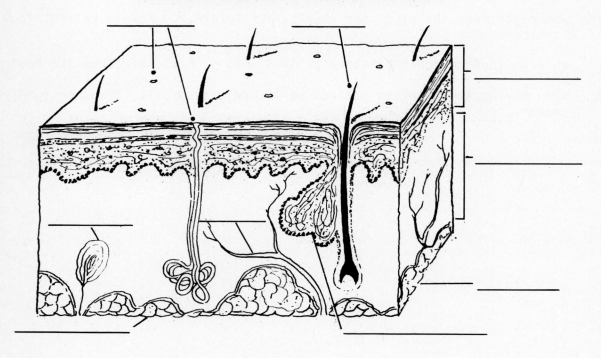

SECTION 2
***

WORKBOOK ASSIGNMENT #2, CHAPTER 10, SECTION 2
CARE OF THE PATIENT WITH POTENTIAL SKIN PROBLEMS

Find the list of objectives for this section. Next to each objective, write the
page numbers where you can find information to help you meet these objectives.

WORKBOOK ASSIGNMENT #3, CHAPTER 10, SECTION 2
DECUBITUS ULCERS

Read "Key Ideas: Decubitus Ulcers" and "Rules to Follow: Preventing Bedsores"
in your textbook.

Fill in the blanks with the words listed below.

bedpan	redness
bony	rim
dry	rub
friction	two
plastic	wrinkles

1. Even _____ in the bed linen can be a cause of decubitus ulcers.

2. Bedsores are most likely to occur on _____ areas.

3. Bedsores also occur where body parts rub against each other causing _____.

4. Signs of bedsores include heat, _____, tenderness, discomfort, and a feeling of burning.

5. You should change the position of the patient's body every _____ hours.

6. Covering the _____ with pads can reduce pressure.

7. Powdering the _____ of the bedpan will minimize friction.

8. Keep the patient's body as clean and _____ as possible.

9. If a part of the patient's body shows signs of developing a bedsore, gently _____ the area with skin lotion.

10. Be sure the _____ never touches the patient's skin.

WORKBOOK ASSIGNMENT #4, CHAPTER 10, SECTION 2
PREVENTING DECUBITUS ULCERS

Read the "Procedure: Preventing Decubitus Ulcers (Bedsores) in the Incontinent Patient" in your textbook. There are 22 steps in this procedure. Each step is an action--something for you to do. Find the key word or words in each step that tell you what to do. These are the words that show ACTION. They are "doing" words called verbs.

1. _____   8. _____

2. _____   9. _____

3. _____   10. _____

4. _____   11. _____

5. _____   12. _____

6. _____   13. _____

7. _____   14. _____

15. _____   19. _____

16. _____   20. _____

17. _____   21. _____

18. _____   22. _____

WORKBOOK ASSIGNMENT #5, CHAPTER 10
WORDS TO REMEMBER/GLOSSARY

1. _____ _____ are also called bedsores. These are areas
   on the skin that become broken and painful. They are caused by continuing
   pressure on a body part and usually occur when a patient is kept in bed for
   a long period of time.

2. _____ is the inability to control one's bladder or bowels.

3. _____ is the inner layer of skin.

4. _____ is the outer layer or surface of the skin.

WORKBOOK ASSIGNMENT #6, CHAPTER 10
LEARNING BY DOING

As you study the procedure in this chapter, read every step carefully. Think
about the action words, the words that tell you what to do. Look at the pictures
closely and read the captions. You will be able to remember what to do more
easily if you try to do it after you have read about it. Learning by doing
involves your whole body in the learning process, not just your eyes or ears. It
is one of the most effective ways to learn.

Ask a fellow student or, if you are practicing at home, ask a friend or relative
to play the part of the patient. Actually do all of the steps of the procedure
several times, pretending you are a nursing assistant caring for several
patients. Work slowly at first. Look at the textbook whenever you are not sure
about what to do next. Practice in this way many times until you can work
quickly, and you no longer need to look at the textbook.

Switch roles with your partner, and you take several turns at being the patient.
Not only will this give your partner a chance to learn the procedure, but you
will benefit as well. By putting yourself in the patient's place, you will begin
to understand how it feels to be a patient, and you will be able to treat real
patients as you yourself would like to be treated.

Write <u>YES</u> beside each statement that is a primary function of the skin and <u>NO</u> beside each statement that is not.

1. _____ The skin helps to regulate body temperature by controlling loss of heat from the body.

2. _____ The skin supports and protects the body.

3. _____ The skin gives movement to the body.

4. _____ The skin provides the first line of defense against infection.

Write <u>YES</u> beside each statement which is a rule to follow for preventing bedsores and <u>NO</u> beside each statement that is not.

5. _____ You should change the patient's position every two hours.

6. _____ Keep linen dry and wrinkle-free at all times.

7. _____ When you are doing work such as giving a back rub, making a corner on a bed, or moving the patient, work with the directions of your efforts, not against them.

8. _____ If the patient is incontinent, use a disposable bed protector.

Fill in the blanks below with the letter of the correct procedure.

A. Preventing bedsores in the incontinent patient
B. Giving the alcohol sponge bath
C. Special back care to prevent decubitus ulcers.

9. Which procedure involves washing the patient each time he/she voids or defecates? _____

10. In which procedure do you perform a rhythmic rubbing motion? _____

SECTION 1

WORKBOOK ASSIGNMENT #1, CHAPTER 11, SECTION 1
ANATOMY AND PHYSIOLOGY

Read "Section 1: Anatomy and Physiology" in your textbook. Study the diagrams
of the circulatory and respiratory systems. Use them as guides when filling in
the blanks in the illustrations below with the names of the organs included in
these systems.

THE HEART

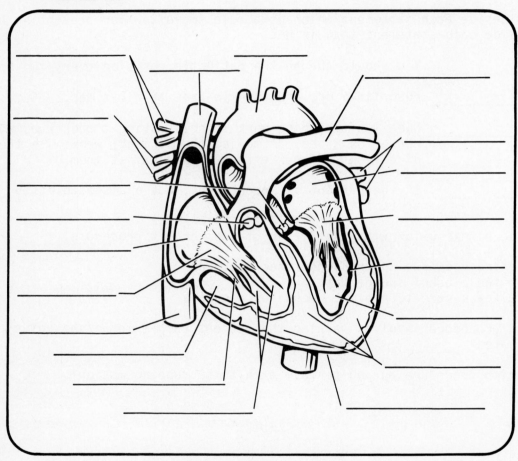

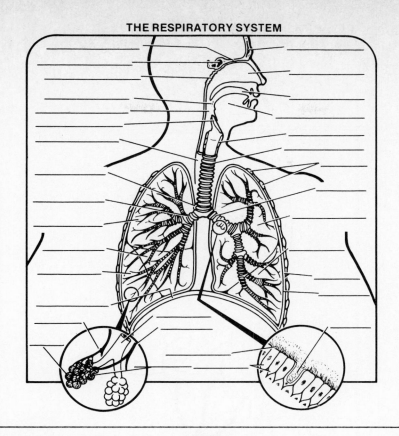

SECTION 2

WORKBOOK ASSIGNMENT #2, CHAPTER 11, SECTION 2
VITAL SIGNS

Find the list of objectives for this section. Next to each objective, write the page numbers where you can find information to help you meet these objectives.

WORKBOOK ASSIGNMENT #3, CHAPTER 11, SECTION 2
VITAL SIGNS

Read "Key Ideas: Vital Signs" in your textbook. There are 12 items below. Some are pictures; some are words. Look at each one carefully. Write the abbreviation for the vital sign it refers to in the blanks provided. Use the following abbreviations:

T--Temperature   P--Pulse   R--Respiration   B.P.--Blood pressure

1. _____

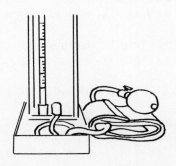

2. _____ How much heat is in the body
3. _____ How often a person breathes in and out and how the breathing sounds
4. _____ Respiration
5. _____ Blood pressure
6. _____ Temperature
7. _____ Pulse
8. _____

9. _____

10. _____

11. _____ How much effort the heart is exerting to circulate the blood
12. _____ How fast the heart beats.

WORKBOOK ASSIGNMENT #4, CHAPTER 11, SECTION 2
VITAL SIGNS

Read "Key Ideas: Vital Signs" in your textbook. Circle the letter of the correct answer.

1. When your head nurse or team leader asks you to take <u>temps</u>, you should:

   A. Measure and record the patient's temperature, pulse, and respiration.
   B. Measure and record the patient's blood pressure, pulse, and respiration.
   C. Measure and record the patient's temperature, pulse, respiration, and blood pressure.
   D. Measure and record the patient's temperature.
   E. Measure and record the patient's blood pressure.

2. When your head nurse or team leader ask you to take <u>vital signs</u>, you should:

   A. Measure and record the patient's temperature, pulse, and respiration.
   B. Measure and record the patient's blood pressure, pulse, and respiration.
   C. Measure and record the patient's temperature, pulse, respiration, and blood pressure.
   D. Measure and record the patient's temperature.
   E. Measure and record the patient's blood pressure.

3. When your head nurse or team leader asks you to take <u>blood pressure</u>, you should:

    A. Measure and record the patient's temperature, pulse and respiration.
    B. Measure and record the patient's blood pressure, pulse, and respiration.
    C. Measure and record the patient's temperature, pulse, respiration, and blood pressure.
    D. Measure and record the patient's temperature.
    E. Measure and record the patient's blood pressure.

SECTION 3

WORKBOOK ASSIGNMENT #5, CHAPTER 11, SECTION 3
MEASURING THE TEMPERATURE

Find the list of objectives for this section. Next to each objective write the page numbers where you can find information to help you meet these objectives.

WORKBOOK ASSIGNMENT #6, CHAPTER 11, SECTION 3
SHAKING DOWN THE GLASS THERMOMETER

Read the "Procedure: Shaking Down the Glass Thermometer" in your textbook. Write the word <u>DO</u> or <u>DON'T</u> beside each statement.

1. _____ wash your hands before touching the thermometer.

2. _____ use a thermometer that is cracked or chipped.

3. _____ hold the thermometer firmly between your fingers and your thumb at the bulb end, furthest from the stem.

4. _____ stand clear of any hard surfaces such as counters and tables.

5. _____ practice with your arm over a pillow or mattress.

6. _____ shake your hand loosely from the shoulder.

7. _____ snap your wrist again and again.

8. _____ shake down the mercury below the numbers and lines.

WORKBOOK ASSIGNMENT #7, CHAPTER 11, SECTION 3
READING A FAHRENHEIT THERMOMETER

Fill in the mercury on the Farenheit scales ·below. The first one is an example.

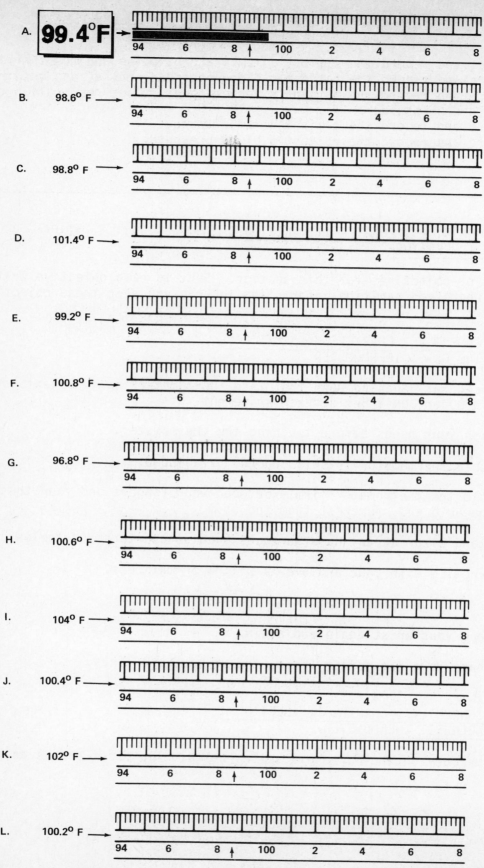

A. **99.4°F →**

94   6   8   100   2   4   6   8

B. 98.6° F →

94   6   8   100   2   4   6   8

C. 98.8° F →

94   6   8   100   2   4   6   8

D. 101.4° F →

94   6   8   100   2   4   6   8

E. 99.2° F →

94   6   8   100   2   4   6   8

F. 100.8° F →

94   6   8   100   2   4   6   8

G. 96.8° F →

94   6   8   100   2   4   6   8

H. 100.6° F →

94   6   8   100   2   4   6   8

I. 104° F →

94   6   8   100   2   4   6   8

J. 100.4° F →

94   6   8   100   2   4   6   8

K. 102° F →

94   6   8   100   2   4   6   8

L. 100.2° F →

94   6   8   100   2   4   6   8

114

WORKBOOK ASSIGNMENT #8, CHAPTER 11, SECTION 3
MEASURING AN ORAL TEMPERATURE

Read the "Procedure: Measuring an Oral Temperature" in your textbook.

Circle the letter of the correct response.

1. You are measuring Mr. Howard's temperature by mouth. You have just told
    him that you are going to measure his temperature. Which one of the
    three tasks should you do next?

    A. Ask all visitors to step out of the room if this is your hospital's
        policy.
    B. Shake the mercury down.
    C. Ask the patient if he has recently had hot or cold fluids or if he
        has been smoking.

2. Mr. Howard said that he has just finished a cup of tea. Which one of the
    following three tasks should you do next?

    A. Pull the curtain around the bed for privacy.
    B. Come back in 10 minutes.
    C. Wash your hands.

3. Ten minutes have passed, and you returned to Mr. Howard's room to find him
    sitting in a chair. Which one of the following three tasks should you do
    next?

    A. Take the thermometer out of its container.
    B. Shake the mercury down.
    C. Dry it with a paper towel.

4. You have just rinsed the thermometer with cool tap water. Which one of the
    following three tasks should you do next?

    A. Dry it with a paper tissue.
    B. Shake the mercury down.
    C. Gently put the bulb end in the patient's mouth.

5. You have just shaken the mercury down. Which one of the following three
    tasks should you do next?

    A. Ask the patient to keep his mouth and lips closed.
    B. Gently put the bulb end in the patient's mouth under the tongue.
    C. Read the thermometer.

6. The thermometer has been in the patient's mouth five minutes. Which one of
    the following three tasks should you do next in order to get the MOST
    ACCURATE READING?

    A. Take the thermometer out of the patient's mouth.
    B. Leave the thermometer in the patient's mouth three more minutes to
        total eight minutes.
    C. Hold the stem end and wipe the thermometer with the tissue.

115

7. You have just taken the thermometer out of Mr. Howard's mouth. Which one of the following three tasks should you do next?

    A. Hold the stem end and wipe the thermometer with the tissue.
    B. Read the thermometer.
    C. Shake the mercury down.

8. You have just read the thermometer. Which one of the following three tasks should you do next?

    A. Shake the mercury down.
    B. Replace the thermometer in its container.
    C. Record the temperature.

9. You have just recorded the temperature in the TPR book. Which one of the following three tasks should you do next?

    A. Shake the mercury down.
    B. Fill the container with disinfectant solution.
    C. Wash your hands.

WORKBOOK ASSIGNMENT #9, CHAPTER 11, SECTION 3
MEASURING RECTAL TEMPERATURE

Read "Key Ideas: Measuring Rectal Temperatures" in your textbook.

Write R for rectal in the blank beside each description if you would measure the patient's temperature by rectum. Write O for oral in the blank beside each description if you would measure that patient's temperature by mouth.

1. _____ The patient is five years old.
2. _____ The patient is sitting in a chair.
3. _____ The patient is having an ice pack applied to his neck.
4. _____ The patient has a nasogastric tube in place.
5. _____ The patient is getting oxygen by cannula.
6. _____ The patient has just had a baby.
7. _____ The patient's face is partially paralyzed.
8. _____ The patient is unconscious.

WORKBOOK ASSIGNMENT #10, CHAPTER 11, SECTION 3
MEASURING RECTAL TEMPERATURE

Read the "Procedure: Measuring Rectal Temperature" in your workbook.

Write DO or DON'T beside each statement.

1. _____ rinse the thermometer off with hot water after taking it out of its container.
2. _____ hold the thermometer by the bulb end.
3. _____ look closely for cracks or chips.
4. _____ put lubricating jelly on the thermometer directly from the tube.
5. _____ avoid overexposing the patient.
6. _____ with one hand, raise the upper buttock until you can see anus.

7. _____ hold the thermometer while it is in a child's rectum at all   times.
8. _____ leave a patient with a rectal thermometer inserted in the rectum.
9. _____ keep the thermometer in place three minutes.
10. _____ record the temperature immediately.

SECTION 4

WORKBOOK ASSIGNMENT #11, CHAPTER 11, SECTION 4
MEASURING THE PULSE

Find the list of objectives for this section. Next to each objective write the page numbers where you can find information to help you meet these objectives.

WORKBOOK ASSIGNMENT #12, CHAPTER 11, SECTION 4
PULSES

Read "Section 3: Measuring the Pulse" in your textbook. Label the pulses in the following diagram.

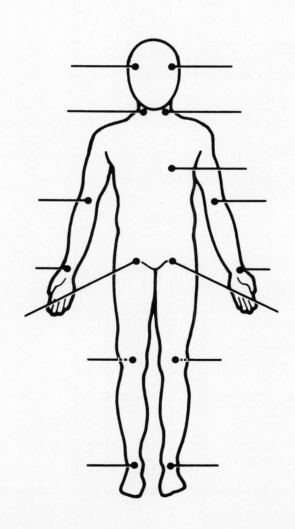

WORKBOOK ASSIGNMENT #13, CHAPTER 11, SECTION 4
THE PULSE

Read "Key Ideas: The Pulse" in your textbook.

Circle the letter of the best response in the multiple choice questions below.

1. You will need to report the number of pulse beats per minute. This is called the:

    A. Rate
    B. Rhythm
    C. Force of the beat.

2. You will need to report the regularity of the pulse beats, that is, whether or not the length of time between the beats is steady and regular. This is called the:

    A. Rate
    B. Rhythm
    C. Force of the beat.

3. You will need to report whether the pulse is weak or bounding. This is called the:

    A. Rate
    B. Rhythm
    C. Force of the beat.

4. The range of normal pulse rates for adults is from _____ to _____ beats per minute.

    A. 72 to 80
    B. 60 to 100
    C. 50 to 92.

5. Always report a pulse rate of under _____ and over _____ beats per minute.

    A. Under 72 and over 80
    B. Under 60 and over 100
    C. Under 50 and over 92.

WORKBOOK ASSIGNMENT #14, CHAPTER 11, SECTION 4
MEASURING THE RADIAL PULSE

Read the "Procedure: Measuring the Radial Pulse" in your textbook. Examine the pictures below carefully.

Circle the letter beside the picture that shows the correct technique for feeling the radial pulse.

A)

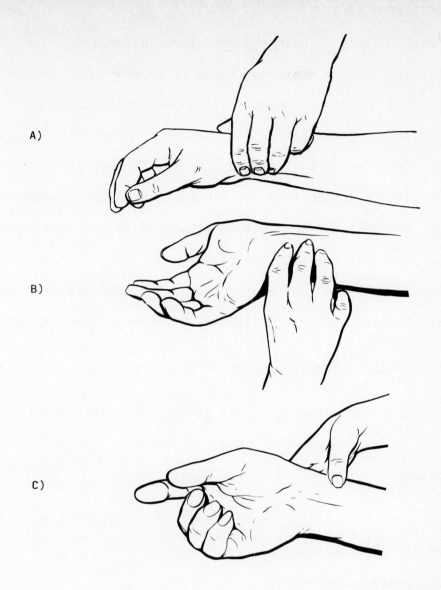

B)

C)

WORKBOOK ASSIGNMENT #15, CHAPTER 11, SECTION 5
MEASURING RESPIRATIONS

Find the list of objectives for this section. Next to each objective write the
page numbers where you can find information to help you meet these objectives.

WORKBOOK ASSIGNMENT #16, CHAPTER 11, SECTION 5
MEASURING RESPIRATIONS

Read "Key Ideas: Measuring Respirations" in your textbook.

Circle the letter T if the statement below is true, F if it is false.

T or F   1. The body needs oxygen to change food into energy.

T or F   2. Inhaling is part of the process of respiration.

T or F   3. Exhaling is part of the process of respiration.

T or F   4. Taking oxygen from the air is part of the process of respiration.

T or F   5. One respiration includes breathing in once and breathing out once.

T or F   6. Contract means to get bigger.

T or F   7. Tell the patient you are going to count his respirations.

T or F   8. Labored respiration is when a person is working hard to get his breath.

T or F   9. Adults normally breathe at a rate of from 16 to 20 times a minute.

T or F 10. A normal person breathes at the same rate regardless of what he is doing.

WORKBOOK ASSIGNMENT #17, CHAPTER 11, SECTION 5
ABNORMAL RESPIRATIONS

Here are the names of five types of abnormal respirations. Below the list are descriptions of these five types. In the blank beside each description, write the letter of the type that matches it.

A. Stertorous respiration
B. Abdominal respiration
C. Shallow respiration
D. Irregular respiration
E. Cheyne-Stokes respiration

1. _____ Breathing with only the upper part of the lungs

2. _____ Using mostly abdominal muscles for breathing

3. _____ A pattern where the breathing is slow and shallow, then faster and deeper to a peak, then slow and shallow again. The breathing may stop for 10 seconds before beginning the pattern again.

4. _____ Abnormal sounds, like snoring while breathing

5. _____ The depth and rate are not steady

WORKBOOK ASSIGNMENT #18, CHAPTER 11, SECTION 5
MEASURING RESPIRATIONS

Read the "Procedure: Measuring Respirations" in your textbook. Circle the letter of the correct response.

1. To be sure the patient will not know you are watching his breathing you should:

   A. Count respirations while taking his temperature.
   B. Hold the patient's wrist just as if you were taking his pulse.
   C. Distract him by talking about the weather.

2. What should you do if you cannot clearly see the chest rise and fall?

   A. Fold the patient's arm across his chest to feel his breathing as you hold his wrist.
   B. Place your hand on the upper part of the patient's chest to feel his breathing.
   C. Call the head nurse or team leader as this might be an emergency.

3. If you count the chest rising 15 times in one full minute, you would report:

   A. 30 respirations per minute
   B. 15 respirations per minute
   C. 7 respirations per minute.

4. If you count nine respirations in 30 seconds, you would report:

   A. 27 respirations per minute
   B. 9 respirations per minute
   C. 18 respirations per minute.

5. If you count 19 respirations in a full minute, you would report:

   A. 19 respirations per minute
   B. 38 respirations per minute
   C. 9 respirations per minute.

WORKBOOK ASSIGNMENT #19, CHAPTER 11, SECTIONS 1, 2, 3, 4 and 5
SAMPLE FORM FOR RECORDING VITAL SIGNS

Record the following information on the TPR form in the illustration on page 123.

1. Fill in the TPRs for 12 midnight:

A.	Mary Jones	98.6°F	88	20
B.	Wm. Smith	97.4°F	96	16
C.	Lil Carrie	98.2°F	72	14
D.	Pat Shiff	101.8°F	104	22
E.	Gale Joseph	99.8°F	92	20

2. Fill in the TPRs for 4 A.M.:

A.	Mary Jones	99.6°F	92	16
B.	Wm. Smith	98.2°F	78	18
C.	Lil Carrie	98.2°F	74	20
D.	Pat Shiff	102.8°F	112	24
E.	Gale Joseph	100.0°F	88	22

3. Fill in the TPRs for 8 A.M.:

A.	Mary Jones	98.8°F	80	16
B.	Wm. Smith	99.0°F	86	18
C.	Lil Carrie	97.8°F	88	16
D.	Pat Shiff	101.6°F	96	22
E.	Gale Joseph	99.6°F	82	18

4. Fill in the TPRs for 12 Noon:

A.	Mary Jones	98.8°F	80	16
B.	Wm. Smith	99.0°F	72	14
C.	Lil Carrie	98.0°F	76	18
D.	Pat Shiff	103.0°F	96	24
E.	Gale Joseph	98.8°F	72	18

5. Fill in the TPRs for 4 P.M.:

A.	Mary Jones	97.2°F	68	16
B.	Wm. Smith	100.8°F	88	18
C.	Lil Carrie	98.0°F	68	16
D.	Pat Shiff	104.8°F	104	26
E.	Gale Joseph	101.8°F	92	16

6. Fill in the TPRs for 8 P.M.:

A.	Mary Jones	98.2°F	80	18
B.	Wm. Smith	103.2°F	88	20
C.	Lil Carrie	98.4°F	72	16
D.	Pat Shiff	102.6°F	88	22
E.	Gale Joseph	99.6°F	86	18

7. Place an R in front of Pat Shiff's 4 P.M. temperature, because it was taken by rectum.

8. Place an A in front of Mary Jones' 4 P.M. temperature, because it was taken by axilla.

9. Circle all elevated temperatures.

		12M			4AM			8AM			12N			4PM			8PM		
Rm. #	Patient Name	T	P	R	T	P	R	T	P	R	T	P	R	T	P	R	T	P	R
404A	Mary Jones																		
404B	Lil Carrie																		
405A	Wm. Smith																		
405B																			
406A	Pat Shiff																		
406B	Gale Joseph																		

SECTION 6

WORKBOOK ASSIGNMENT #20, CHAPTER 11, SECTION 6
MEASURING THE BLOOD PRESSURE

Find the list of objectives for this section. Next to each objective, write the page numbers where you can find information to help you meet these objectives.

WORKBOOK ASSIGNMENT #21, CHAPTER 11, SECTION 6
BLOOD PRESSURE

Read "Key Ideas: Blood Pressure" in your textbook. Circle the letter of the correct answer.

1. You are measuring the force of the blood flowing through the arteries when you:

    A. Measure a patient's temperature
    B. Count a patient's respirations
    C. Measure a patient's blood pressure
    D. Count a patient's pulse
    E. Measure a patient's vital signs.

2. "mm" is the abbreviation for:

    A. Mercury
    B. Centimeters
    C. Millimeters
    D. Cubic centimeters
    E. Systolic.

123

3. "Hg" is the abbreviation for:

   A. Mercury
   B. Centimeters
   C. Millimeters
   D. Oxygen
   E. Diastolic.

4. When a patient's blood pressure is higher than the normal range for his age and condition, it is referred to as:

   A. Hypotension
   B. High blood pressure
   C. Diastolic pressure
   D. Millimeters mercury
   E. Low blood pressure.

5. When a patient's blood pressure is lower than the normal range for his age and condition, it is referred to as:

   A. Hypertension
   B. High blood pressure
   C. Diastolic pressure
   D. Millimeters mercury
   E. Low blood pressure.

6. High blood pressure is also called:

   A. Hypotension
   B. Hypertension
   C. Systolic pressure
   D. Diastolic pressure
   E. Cheyne-Stokes pressure.

7. Low blood pressure is also called:

   A. Systolic pressure
   B. Diastolic pressure
   C. Irregular pressure
   D. Hypotension
   E. Hypertension.

8. Use the following labels to label the four main parts of the aneroid sphygmomanometer on the next page--manometer, valve, cuff, and bulb.

ANEROID SPHYGMOMANOMETER

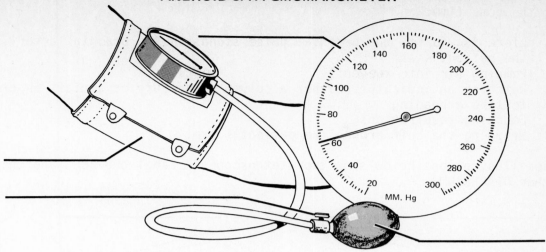

9. When you use a mercury sphygmomanometer, you will be:

   A. Watching the level of a column of mercury on a measuring scale
   B. Watching a pointer on a dial
   C. Counting respirations
   D. Watching a digital display
   E. Recharging the batteries.

10. When you use the aneroid sphygmomanometer, you will be:

   A. Watching the level of a column of mercury on a measuring scale
   B. Watching a pointer on a dial
   C. Counting respirations
   D. Watching a digital display
   E. Recharging the batteries.

11. The illustrations below show two sphygmomanometers. Correctly label one ANEROID and the other MERCURY.

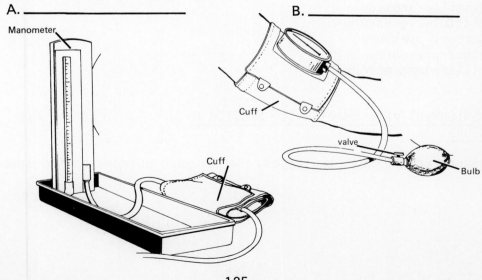

12. When taking a patient's blood pressure, which two things will you be doing at the same time:

    A. Listening to how the brachial pulse sounds in the brachial artery in the patient's arm
    B. Pumping air into the cuff
    C. Watching an indicator (either a column of mercury or a dial) in order to take a reading
    D. Counting respirations
    E. Wrapping the cuff around the patient's arm.

13. The illustrations below show two stethoscopes. Label one BELL and the other DIAPHRAGM.

    A. _____   B. _____

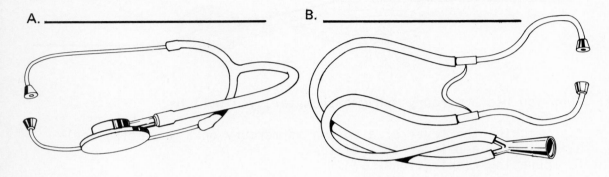

14. When recording blood pressure you should write it 120/80 or $\frac{120}{80}$. The top number stands for the:

    A. Systolic pressure
    B. Diastolic pressure
    C. Mercury pressure
    D. Blood pressure
    E. Millimeters mercury.

15. The bottom number of a recorded blood pressure stands for the:

    A. Systolic pressure
    B. Diastolic pressure
    C. Mercury pressure
    D. Blood pressure
    E. Millimeters mercury.

WORKBOOK ASSIGNMENT #22, CHAPTER 11, SECTION 6
BLOOD PRESSURE

Read the gauges on the next two pages. Write your answers on the space provided.

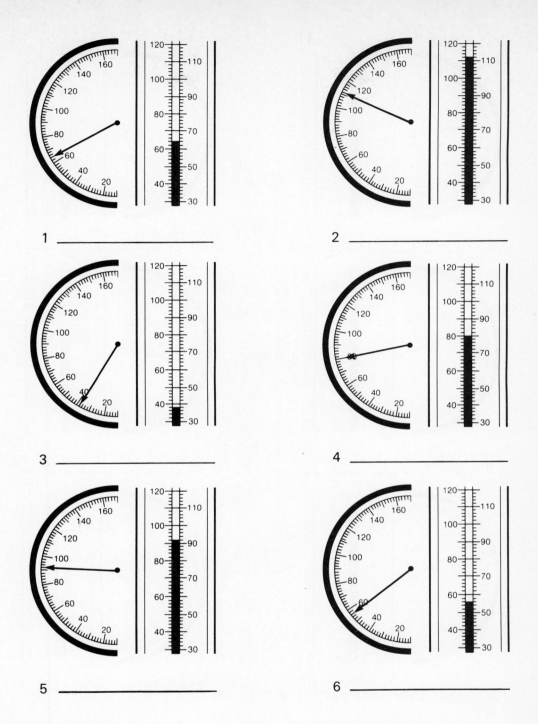

1 _____

2 _____

3 _____

4 _____

5 _____

6 _____

127

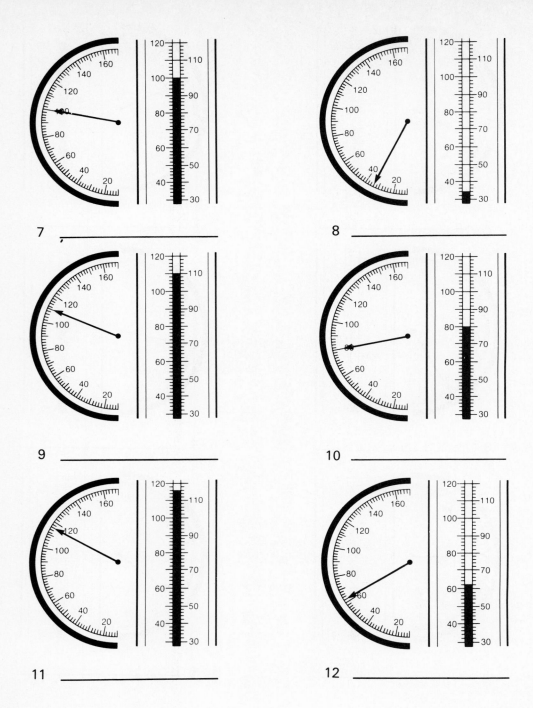

7 ,

8 _____

9 _____

10 _____

11 _____

12 _____

128

WORKBOOK ASSIGNMENT #23, CHAPTER 11
WORDS TO REMEMBER/GLOSSARY

Fill in the blanks with the vocabulary word to remember after carefully reading
the definition.

1. The area under the arms, the armpit, is called the _____ area.

2. The force of the blood on the inner walls of the blood vessels as it flows
   through them is known as the _____ _____.

3. A measurement of temperature using a scale divided into 100 units or degrees.
   This system in which the freezing temperature of water is 0° is often
   referred to as celsius or _____.

4. In taking a patient's blood pressure, one records the bottom number as the
   reading for the _____ blood pressure. This is the relaxing phase
   of the heartbeat.

5. The name of a system for measuring temperature. In the _____
   system the temperature of water at boiling is 212°. At freezing, it is 32°.
   These temperatures are written 212°F and 32°F.

6. The rhythmic expansion and contraction of the arteries caused by the beating
   of the heart. The expansion and contraction show how fast, how regular, and
   with what force the heart is beating. This is called the _____.

7. The body process of breathing, inhaling, and exhaling is called _____.

8. The force with which blood is pumped when the heart muscle is contracting.
   When taking a patient's blood pressure, the top number is the _____
   blood pressure.

9. Temperature, pulse, respiration, and blood pressure are _____.

10. The fluid circulating through the heart, arteries, veins, and capillaries
    that carries nourishment and oxygen to the tissues and takes away waste
    matter and carbon dioxide is called _____.

11. _____ refers to the lungs.

WORKBOOK ASSIGNMENT #24, CHAPTER 11
LEARNING BY DOING

As you study the procedures in this chapter, read every step carefully. Think
about the action words, the words that tell you what to do. Look at the pictures
closely and read the captions. You will be able to remember what to do more
easily if you try to do it after you have read about it. Learning by doing
involves your whole body in the learning process, not just your eyes or ears. It
is one of the most effective ways to learn.

Ask a fellow student or, if you are practicing at home, ask a friend or relative to play the part of the patient. Actually do all of the steps of the procedure several times, pretending you are a nursing assistant caring for several patients. Work slowly at first. Look at the textbook whenever you are not sure about what to do next. Practice in this way many times until you can work quickly, and you no longer need to look at the textbook.

Switch roles with your partner, and you take several turns at being the patient. Not only will this give your partner a chance to learn the procedure, but you will benefit as well. By putting yourself in the patient's place, you will begin to understand how it feels to be a patient, and you will be able to treat real patients as you yourself would like to be treated.

CHAPTER 11 QUIZ

Here is a list of the procedures in this chapter.

A. Shaking down the glass thermometer
B. Reading a fahrenheit thermometer
C. Reading a centigrade thermometer
D. Measuring an oral temperature
E. Measuring a rectal temperature
F. Measuring axillary temperature
G. Using a battery-operated electronic oral thermometer
H. Using a battery-operated electronic rectal thermometer
I. Using a battery-operated electronic oral thermometer to measure axillary temperature
J. Measuring the radial pulse
K. Measuring the apical pulse
L. Measuring the apical pulse deficit
M. Measuring respirations
N. Measuring blood pressure

Fill in the blanks with the letters of the appropriate procedures:

1. Which procedure requires the use of a sphygmomanometer? _____

2. Which six procedures require the use of glass thermometers? _____ _____
   _____ _____
   _____ _____

3. Which two procedures could be used to get a measurement of R-100.4°F? _____ _____

4. In which three procedures would you observe the rate, rhythm, and force? _____ _____ _____

5. Which three procedures involve the use of a stethoscope? _____ _____ _____

6. For which procedure would the normal adult rate be from 16 to 20 times a minute? _____

7. Which procedure could involve two nursing assistants working together? _____

8. Which procedure involves counting by twos like this: 2, 4, 6, 8? _____

9. Which three procedures would you do if your head nurse or team leader said, "take blood pressure?" _____ _____ _____

10. Which two procedures could you use to measure temperature if the patient is receiving oxygen by cannula, catheter, face mask, or oxygen tent?
    _____ _____

SECTION 1

WORKBOOK ASSIGNMENT #1, CHAPTER 12, SECTION 1
ANATOMY AND PHYSIOLOGY

Read "Section 1: Anatomy and Physiology" in your textbook. Study the diagram of the gastrointestinal system. Use it as a guide when filling in the blanks in the illustration below with the names of the system organs included in this system.

THE DIGESTIVE SYSTEM

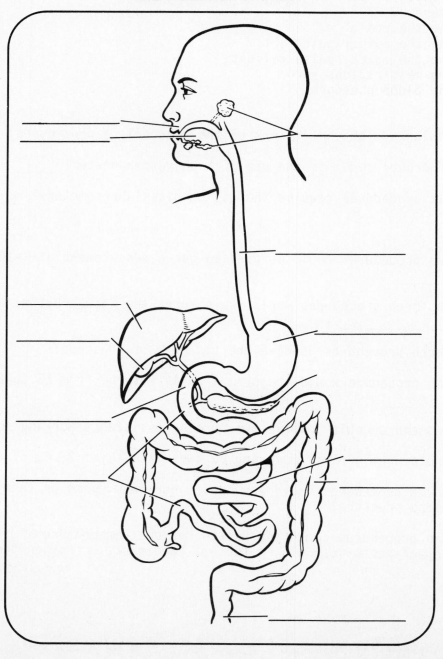

WORKBOOK ASSIGNMENT #2, CHAPTER 12, SECTION 2
THERAPEUTIC DIETS

Find the list of objectives for this section. Next to each objective, write the page numbers where you can find information to help you meet these objectives.

WORKBOOK ASSIGNMENT #3, CHAPTER 12, SECTION 2
A WELL-BALANCED DIET

Read "Key Ideas: A Well-Balanced Diet" and study the chart titled the "Four Basic Food Groups" in your textbook. Beside each food write the LETTER of the food group, listed below, to which it belongs:

A. Dairy products
B. Vegetables and fruits
C. Meat and meat substitutes
D. Breads, cereals, and potatoes

1. Peas _____

2. Onions _____

3. Milk _____

4. Macaroni _____

5. Broccoli _____

6. Rice _____

7. Bread _____

8. Dried beans _____

9. Yogurt _____

10. Cake _____

11. Nuts _____

12. Carrots _____

13. Potatoes _____

14. Cheese _____

WORKBOOK ASSIGNMENT #4, CHAPTER 12, SECTION 2
TYPES OF DIETS GIVEN TO PATIENTS

Read the chart titled "Types of Diets Given to Patients; What They are and Why They are Used?" in your textbook. It will be easier to remember what all the different diets are if you try to learn them one at a time. One easy way to learn the rest of the list is to study from flash cards. Cut apart the cards on page 135 and 136. You will see that the name of the diet is on one side and the description of the diet is on the other side. Now you can test yourself.

1. Arrange all 15 cards so the name of the diet is facing up and the description is facing down.
2. Read the name of the first diet in your stack.
3. Try to remember the description from your study of the chart.
4. Say the description out loud.
5. Turn the card over and read the description to see if you were right.
6. If you were correct, put the card in a pile on the left and you are finished studying this card.
7. If you were wrong, put the card in a pile on the right and you will study it later.
8. Repeat this for all the cards.

9. Now go back to the pile of cards on the right and study these.
10. Read each one, front and back, five times.
11. Close your eyes and try to say the name of the diet and its description.
12. Open your eyes and see if you were correct.
13. Repeat this for all the cards that you originally put on the right side.
14. When you feel that you have learned them all, test yourself again.
15. Ask a friend or relative to test you by holding the first card up so you can see the name of the diet and she or he can see the description.
16. You read the name and recite the description.
17. Your friend can read the description to check if you are correct.
18. Repeat this for all the cards.
19. Turn the stack upside down.
20. Now you read the description and tell the name of the diet.
21. Continue in this way over and over again until you have learned all the types of diets and their descriptions.

SECTION 3

WORKBOOK ASSIGNMENT #5, CHAPTER 12, SECTION 3
NUTRITION FOR THE PATIENT

Find the list of objectives for this section. Next to each objective write the page numbers where you can find information to help you meet these objectives.

WORKBOOK ASSIGNMENT #6, CHAPTER 12, SECTION 3
FEEDING THE HANDICAPPED PATIENT

Read "Key Ideas: Feeding the Handicapped Patient" and "Procedure: Feeding the Handicapped Patient or the Patient Who is Unable to Feed Himself" in your textbook.

Circle the letter T if the statement below is true, F if it is false.

T or F   1. Always use a spoon when feeding a handicapped patient.

T or F   2. Fill the spoon completely with food.

T or F   3. Give the food to the patient from the tip of the spoon, not the side.

T or F   4. Put the food in one side of the patient's mouth so he can chew it easily.

T or F   5. Feed a paralyzed patient on the side of his mouth that is not paralyzed.

Clear liquid (Hospital surgical)	Full liquid	Light or soft
Soft (mechanical)	Bland	Low residue
High calorie	Low calorie	Diabetic
High protein	Low fat	Low cholesterol
Low sodium (salt)	Salt free (sodium)	Tube feeding

Foods soft in consistency; no rich or strongly flavored food that could cause disease.	Broth, tea, coffee, ginger ale, gelatin, strained fruit juices, liquids, custard, junket, ice cream, sherbert, soft-cooked eggs.	Broth, tea, ginger ale, gelatin.
Foods low in bulk; omits food difficult to digest.	Foods mild in flavor and easy to digest; omits spicy foods.	Same foods as on a normal diet, but chopped or strained.
Precise balances of carbohydrates, protein, and fats devised according to the needs of individual patients.	Low in cream, butter, cereals, desserts, and fats.	Foods high in protein, minerals, and vitamins.
Low in eggs, whole milk, and meats.	Limited amounts of butter, cream, fats, and eggs.	Meals supplemented with high protein foods, such as meat, fish, cheese, milk, and eggs.
Milk formula or liquid forms of meat or vegetables given to the patient through a tube; follow with a glass of water.	Completely without salt.	Limited amount of foods containing sodium; no salt allowed on tray.

WORKBOOK ASSIGNMENT #7, CHAPTER 12, SECTION 3
PASSING DRINKING WATER

Read "Key Ideas: Passing Drinking Water" and the "Procedure: Passing Drinking Water" in your textbook. Write DO or DON'T next to each statement below.

1. _____ pass fresh drinking water to patients at regular intervals during the day.

2. _____ give ice to a patient whose pitcher is tagged omit ice.

3. _____ check to see which patients are N.P.O.

4. _____ check to see which patients are on restricted fluids.

5. _____ check to see which patients should get only tap water.

6. _____ replace the water pitcher on the same patient's table from which it was taken.

WORKBOOK ASSIGNMENT #8, CHAPTER 12, SECTION 3
SERVING THE FOOD

Read the "Procedure: Serving the Food" in your textbook.

Read question 1 below. Then read the list of actions. Decide which action is the best thing to do in that situation. Put the letter for that correct action on the line after situation 1. Choose the correct response for each situation in the same way.

ACTIONS: PICK THE RIGHT THING TO DO IN EACH SITUATION.

A. Check the tray yourself.
B. Check the tray card against the ID band.
C. Help any patient who needs it.
D. Record this on the daily activity sheet.
E. Correct anything that is wrong.

SITUATIONS: WHAT SHOULD YOU DO?

1. Before you give a tray to a patient? _____

2. To find out which tray goes to which patient? _____

3. If a patient cannot cut his meat? _____

4. If a patient tells you he didn't get a fork? _____

5. If the patient ate only half his food? _____

6. If a patient tells you he has the wrong tray? _____

7. If the patient refuses to accept the tray and actually eats nothing? _____

8. If some food spills? _____

9. If a patient seems too weak to pour his own coffee? _____

10. If a patient on a regular diet didn't get any sugar on his tray and he wants some? _____

11. If you see a coffee pot on the patient's tray but no cup? _____

12. To be sure everything is on the tray? _____

13. If a weak patient asks you to butter his bread? _____

14. If the patient ate all the food served to him? _____

15. If the patient tells you he didn't get any bread and butter and you see none? _____

SECTION 4

WORKBOOK ASSIGNMENT #9, CHAPTER 12, SECTION 4
NASOGASTRIC TUBES

Find the list of objectives for this section. Next to each objective write the page numbers where you can find information to help you meet these objectives.

WORKBOOK ASSIGNMENT #10, CHAPTER 12, SECTION 4
NASOGASTRIC TUBES

Read "Key Ideas: Nasogastric Tubes" in your textbook. Write the letters of the matching terms and phrases from Column B in the blanks next to the words in Column A that mean the same thing.

Column A	Column B
_____1. Nasogastric tube	A. Naso
_____2. Tube feeding	B. N.P.O.
_____3. Suction	C. Levine Tube
_____4. Nostrils	D. Stomach
_____5. Nasogastric feeding	E. Washing out
_____6. Gastric	F. To remove fluids
_____7. Nothing by mouth	G. Gavage
_____8. Lavage	H. Nasogastric feeding

WORKBOOK ASSIGNMENT #11, CHAPTER 12, SECTION 4
SUCTION

Read the information on "Suction" and "Rules to Follow: Suction (Vacuum Drainage)" in your textbook.

Circle the letter T if the statement below is true, F if it is false.

T or F   1. Suction is used to put fluids into the body.

T or F   2. Report to your head nurse or team leader immediately if you think there might be a leak in the tube and suction system.

T or F   3. When straightening the unit of a patient who has closed chest drainage, it is acceptable to store the clamp in the bathroom.

T or F   4. Never raise the drainage bottle or disconnect the tubing.

T or F   5. If you notice that the level of fluid in the container stops rising or rises very quickly, measure the fluid and take a specimen immediately.

WORKBOOK ASSIGNMENT #12, CHAPTER 12, SECTION 4
CARING FOR THE PATIENT WITH A NASOGASTRIC TUBE

Read "Rules to Follow: Caring for the Patient with a Nasogastric Tube" in your textbook.

Use the following letter of the correct response to fill in the blanks below.

A. Gag or vomit
B. Pull on the tube
C. Refasten the connecting tube
D. Clean and free from mucous deposits

1. Never _____ when moving the patient or changing his position.

2. Keep the tube _____ at the entrance to the nostrils.

3. Remember to _____ to the patient's clean gown after bathing him and changing his gown.

4. If the patient begins to _____ while the tube is in place, report this immediately to the head nurse or team leader.

SECTION 5

WORKBOOK ASSIGNMENT #13, CHAPTER 12, SECTION 5
RECTAL TREATMENTS

Find the list of objectives for this section. Next to each objective, write the page numbers where you can find information to help you meet these objectives.

RECTAL TREATMENTS

Read "Key Ideas: Rectal Treatments" and "Positioning the Patient for the Enema" in your textbook.

In the exercise below, circle the letter of the correct response.

1. Which type of enema inserts oil into the rectum to soften the stool?

    A. Cleansing enema
    B. Oil retention enema
    C. Paraplegic enema
    D. Flatus enema
    E. C and D only.

2. If the patient has any complaints before you start giving him an enema:

    A. Wait one-half hour and begin again.
    B. Report this to your head nurse or team leader.
    C. Do not go ahead with the enema until you are told to do so by your head nurse or team leader.
    D. Talk with the patient and explain the reasons for giving the enema, until you have his consent to go ahead.
    E. B and C only.

3. Occasionally, a patient may complain of a cramp-like pain after the enema has started. You should:

    A. Wait one-half hour and begin again.
    B. Report this to you head nurse or team leader.
    C. Do not go ahead with the enema until you are told to do so by your head nurse or team leader.
    D. Stop the flow of solution until the pain goes away, then start again.
    E. B and C only.

4. Which position is a patient in when he is on his left side with his right knee bent toward his chest?

    A. Paraplegic enema position
    B. Left Sims' position
    C. Anatomical position
    D. Rotating enema position
    E. Prone position.

5. Which position is a patient in when he lies on his back with his buttocks raised over the bedpan and his knees separated, to receive an enema?

    A. Paraplegic enema position
    B. Left Sims' position
    C. Anatomical position
    D. Rotating enema position
    E. Prone position.

WORKBOOK ASSIGNMENT #15, CHAPTER 12, SECTION 5
THE CLEANSING ENEMA

Read "Procedure: The Cleansing Enema" in your textbook.

In each statement below, underline BEFORE or AFTER. The first statement is done for you as an example:

1. Wash your hands BEFORE or AFTER you assemble your equipment.

2. Place the disposable bed protector under the patient's hips BEFORE or AFTER pulling the curtain around the bed for privacy.

3. Lubricate the enema tip BEFORE or AFTER you expose the patient's buttocks.

4. Raise the blanket in a triangle over the anal area BEFORE or AFTER putting on the gloves.

5. Tell the patient to take slow deep breaths BEFORE or AFTER opening the clamp and raising the enema bag 18 inches above the mattress or 12 inches above the anus.

6. Close the clamp BEFORE or AFTER removing the tubing from the patient's rectum.

7. Wrap the tubing in a paper towel BEFORE or AFTER placing the tubing in the enema container.

8. Help the patient onto the bedpan BEFORE or AFTER raising the back of the bed.

9. If the patient is permitted to go to the bathroom to expel the enema, assist him to the bathroom BEFORE or AFTER disposing of the enema equipment.

10. Add one package of enema soap BEFORE or AFTER filling the container with fluid.

WORKBOOK ASSIGNMENT #16, CHAPTER 12, SECTION 5
OBSERVING AND REPORTING THE RESULTS OF AN ENEMA

There are seven things that should be reported to your head nurse or team leader routinely after administering a cleansing enema. From the list below, circle the letters of the seven items that should be reported:

A. Your observations of anything unusual
B. If you used disposable gloves
C. The type of solution used
D. The results, color of stool, consistency, flatus (gas) expelled, and unusual material noted
E. Whether the enema was expelled into the bedpan or toilet
F. That you have given the patient a cleansing enema
G. Whether or not a specimen was obtained
H. How the patient tolerated the procedure
I. That you have disposed of the enema equipment
J. The time the enema was given
L. Where the enema was given.

WORKBOOK ASSIGNMENT #17, CHAPTER 12, SECTION 5
OBSERVING AND REPORTING THE RESULTS OF AN ENEMA

When observing the results of an enema, look for anything that does not appear normal. Circle the word REPORT beside each of the following observations that you would report to your head nurse or team leader. Circle the word SPECIMEN if, when making that observation, you would collect a specimen and then report to your head nurse or team leader:

1. If the stool has a very bad odor, you should REPORT this or collect a SPECIMEN.

2. If the stool is very hard, you should REPORT this or collect a SPECIMEN.

3. If the stool is small in amount, you should REPORT this or collect a SPECIMEN.

4. If the stool looks like perked coffee grounds, you should REPORT this or collect a SPECIMEN.

5. If the stool is completely black, you should REPORT this or collect a SPECIMEN.

6. If the stool is accompanied by flatus, you should REPORT this or collect a SPECIMEN.

7. If the stool is very soft, you should REPORT this or collect a SPECIMEN.

8. If the stool is streaked with red, white, yellow, or gray, you should REPORT this or collect a SPECIMEN.

9. If the stool is large in amount, you should REPORT this or collect a SPECIMEN.

WORKBOOK ASSIGNMENT #18, CHAPTER 12, SECTION 5
DISPOSABLE RECTAL TUBE WITH CONNECTED FLATUS BAG

Read "Key Ideas: Disposable Rectal Tube with Connected Flatus Bag" and the "Procedure: Disposable Rectal Tube with Connected Flatus Bag" in your textbook. There are 16 steps in this procedure. Each steps is an action--something for you to do. Find the key word or words in each step that tell you what to do. These are the words that show action. They are "doing" words called verbs. The first one is done for you as an example:

1. _Assemble_   7. _____

2. _____   8. _____ _____

3. _____   9. _____ _____ _____

4. _____   10. _____

5. _____   11. _____

6. _____   12. _____ _____

142

13. _____ _____ _____ _____

14. _____

15. _____

16. _____

WORKBOOK ASSIGNMENT #19, CHAPTER 12
WORDS TO REMEMBER/GLOSSARY

Read the definition carefully, then fill in the blanks below with the vocabulary word to remember.

1. A liquid that flows through a tube into a rectum to wash out its contents is called an _____.

2. Intestinal gas is also called _____.

3. A substance such as petroleum jelly, glycerine, or cold cream that is to make a surface smooth or moist is known as _____.

4. Washing out the rectum by injecting a stream of water, giving an enema, is also called _____ _____.

5. Units for measuring the energy produced when food is oxidized in the body are called _____.

6. The process of taking food into the body to maintain life is referred to as _____.

7. The posterior opening in the body through which feces is excreted is the _____.

8. The _____ extends from the large intestine to the anus.

9. The total of all the physical and chemical changes that take place in living organisms and cells is called _____.

10. The body area between the thighs, which includes the area of the anus and the external genital organs, is called the _____.

11. _____ is the movement of the intestines that pushes food along to the next part of the digestive system.

12. A substance that moistens food and helps in swallowing, which also contains an enzyme (chemical) that helps digest starches, is called _____.

13. The _____ is the part of the digestive tract between the esophagus and the duodenum.

14. _____ refers mainly to the treatment of disease; something that helps heal.

15. A diet containing a variety of foods from each of the basic food groups is called a _____ _____ _____.

143

WORKBOOK ASSIGNMENT #20, CHAPTER 12
LEARNING BY DOING

As you study the procedures in this chapter, read every step carefully. Think about the action words, the words that tell you what to do. Look at the pictures closely and read the captions. You will be able to remember what to do more easily if you try to do it after you have read about it. Learning by doing involves your whole body in the learning process, not just your eyes or ears. It is one of the most effective ways to learn.

Ask a fellow student or, if you are practicing at home, ask a friend or relative to play the part of the patient. Actually do all of the steps of the procedure several times, pretending you are a nursing assistant caring for several patients. Work slowly at first. Look at the textbook whenever you are not sure about what to do next. Practice in this way many times until you can work quickly, and you no longer need to look at the textbook.

Switch roles with your partner, and you take several turns being the patient. Not only will this give your partner a chance to learn the procedure, but you will benefit as well. By putting yourself in the patient's place, you will begin to understand how it feels to be a patient, and you will be able to treat real patients as you yourself would like to be treated.

Label each of the pictures below with the letter of the food group listed here that it represents:

GROUP A: DAIRY PRODUCTS
GROUP B: VEGETABLES AND FRUIT
GROUP C: MEAT AND FISH
GROUP D: BREADS, CEREALS AND POTATOES

1. _____

2. _____

3. _____

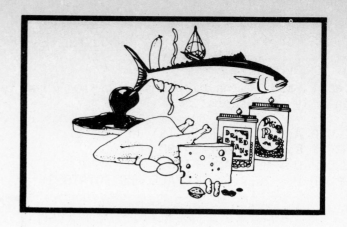

4. _____

5. Those patients who are unable to chew or swallow solid foods are likely to be on a:

   A. Light or soft diet
   B. High-calorie diet
   C. Low-sodium diet
   D. Full liquid diet
   E. Bland diet.

6. Those patients who have had surgery or are very ill are likely to be on a:

   A. Light or soft diet
   B. Clear liquid diet
   C. Low-calorie diet
   D. Full liquid diet
   E. High-protein diet.

7. You are serving a meal to a small child. How can you be sure you are giving him the right tray?

A. Ask him what his name is so you can check it with the tray card.
B. Ask some of the other nursing assistants if they know this child's name.
C. Compare the name on the tray card with the child's I.D. bracelet.
D. Make a guess and hope you are correct.
E. Ask his parents.

8. You are feeding a patient who needs help because he cannot see. It is important to:

A. Feed him as quickly as possible.
B. Let him hold a piece of buttered bread.
C. Check his name card on the tray.
D. Tell him what you are going to feed him and whether the food is hot or cold.
E. Be friendly and talkative.

9. When serving between-meal nourishments, your head nurse or team leader will give you a list of patients that will show:

A. Those who are not to be given anything
B. Those who are allowed to have certain nourishments, such as skim milk or tea
C. All of the above
D. None of the above.

10. Before you pass drinking water, be sure you know:

A. Which patients are N.P.O.
B. Which patients are on restricted fluids
C. For which patients you omit ice
D. Which patients may have ice water
E. All of the above.

Answer the following questions by filling in the blanks below with the letter of the appropriate procedure from the list.

A. The Cleansing Enema
B. Giving the Ready-to-Use Cleansing Enema
C. Giving the Ready-to-Use Oil Retention Enema
D. Giving the Harris Flush
E. Using the Disposable Rectal Tube with Connected Flatus Bag

11. Which type of enema is used frequently in the home as well as in the health care institution? _____

12. Which procedure involves clean water running into the rectum and gas and water running out of the rectum repeatedly for 10 minutes? _____

13. Which procedure is used to relieve the accumulation of intestinal gas in the lower bowel? _____

147

14. In which procedure is the patient expected to hold in the enema solution for 10 to 20 minutes? _____

15. For which procedure would you need instructions concerning whether to use a soapsuds solution, a saline solution, or tap water only? _____

SECTION 1

WORKBOOK ASSIGNMENT #1, CHAPTER 13, SECTION 1
ANATOMY AND PHYSIOLOGY

Read "Section 1: Anatomy and Physiology" in your textbook. Study the diagram of the excretory system. Use it as a guide when filling in the blanks in the diagram below with the names of the organs included in this system.

THE URINARY SYSTEM

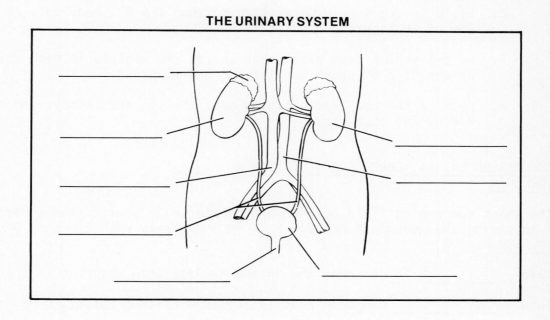

SECTION 2

WORKBOOK ASSIGNMENT #2, CHAPTER 13, SECTION 2
FLUID BALANCE

Find the list of objectives for this section. Next to each objective, write the page numbers where you can find information to help you meet these objectives.

WORKBOOK ASSIGNMENT #3, CHAPTER 13, SECTION 2
FLUID BALANCE

Read "Section 2: Fluid Balance" in your textbook.

Circle the letter T if the statement below is true, F if it is false.

T or F   1. Water is essential to human life.

T or F   2. Some fluid is lost from the body through perspiration.

T or F   3. Some body fluids are evaporated from the lungs in breathing.

T or F   4. Fluids may be lost from the body by vomiting, bleeding, severe diarrhea, or excessive sweating.

T or F   5. An "intake and output" record is kept for a full 24-hour period.

T or F   6. Fluid intake should be written on the "I & O" sheet only at the end of an eight-hour shift.

T or F   7. At the end of each eight-hour shift, the amounts in each column on the "I & O" sheet are totaled and recorded.

T or F   8. Most of the body waste fluids pass through the kidneys and are discharged as feces.

WORKBOOK ASSIGNMENT #4, CHAPTER 13, SECTION 2
FLUID BALANCE

Read the chart concerning fluid balance and imbalance in your textbook carefully before answering the questions below. Fill in the blanks with the word BALANCE or IMBALANCE.

1. Fluid _____ can mean the intake is less than output.

2. Fluid _____ can mean that intake is more than output.

3. Fluid _____ means that intake equals output.

4. Fluid _____ can result from not drinking or eating enough.

5. Fluid _____ can result from too much vomiting, bleeding, urinating, perspiring, or drainage.

SECTION 3

WORKBOOK ASSIGNMENT #5, CHAPTER 13, SECTION 3
FLUID INTAKE

Find the list of objectives for this section. Next to each objective write the page numbers where you can find information to help you meet these objectives.

WORKBOOK ASSIGNMENT #6, CHAPTER 13, SECTION 3
INTAKE AND OUTPUT

INTAKE AND OUTPUT SHEET

Hospital # ______________________ Patient Name ______________________

Date ______________________ Room # ______________________

INTAKE				OUTPUT			
				URINE		GASTRIC	
Time 7-3	BY MOUTH	TUBE	PARENTERAL	VOIDED	CATHETER	EMESIS	SUCTION
TOTAL							
Time 3-11							
TOTAL							
Time 11-7							
TOTAL							
24 HOUR TOTAL							
24 Hour Grand Total • Intake				24 Hour Grand Total • Output			

1. Write the numeral 1 in every space where you could enter intake and output if you were working between the hours of 3 P.M. and 11 P.M.

2. Write the numeral 2 in every space where you could enter intake by mouth.

3. Write the numeral 3 in every space where you could enter the amounts of urine voided.

4. Write the numeral 4 in every space where you could write the totals for intake, if you were working from 7 A.M. to 3 P.M.

5. Write the numeral 5 in every space where you could write a 24-hour total for output.

6. Write the numeral 6 in every space where the nurse could enter parenteral intake if she were working 11 P.M. to 7 A.M.

7. Write the numeral 7 in every space where you could enter gastric output by suction.

8. Write the numeral 8 in every space where you could enter the total urinary output by catheter.

9. Write the numeral 9 in every space where you could enter intake by tube feeding.

10. Write the numeral 10 in every space where you could enter the 24-hour grand total for intake.

WORKBOOK ASSIGNMENT #7, CHAPTER 13, SECTION 3
FLUID INTAKE

Read "Key Ideas: Fluid Intake" in your textbook. Beside each item in the following list of foods and drinks write FLUID if the item is considered liquid. Write NO if the item is not considered a fluid.

1. _____ Banana
2. _____ Gelatin
3. _____ Coffee
4. _____ Pizza
5. _____ Toast
6. _____ Water
7. _____ Peaches
8. _____ Tomato soup
9. _____ Milk
10. _____ Ice cream

11. _____ Fruit juice
12. _____ Carrots
13. _____ Chicken soup
14. _____ Tea
15. _____ Custard
16. _____ Cookies
17. _____ Soft drinks
18. _____ Hamburger
19. _____ Orange juice
20. _____ Cottage cheese

WORKBOOK ASSIGNMENT #8, CHAPTER 13, SECTION 3
FLUID INTAKE

Read "Key Ideas: Fluid Intake" in your textbook.

Circle the letter T if the statement below is true, F if it is false.

T or F 1. The abbreviation "cc" means a cubic centimeter.

T or F 2. A ml is the same measurement as a cc.

T or F 3. There are 30 cc in one ounce.

T or F 4. There are 30 ml in one ounce.

T or F 5. The abbreviation "ml" means milliliter.

WORKBOOK ASSIGNMENT #9, CHAPTER 13, SECTION 3
CALIBRATED GRADUATE

Read "Key Ideas: Fluid Intake" in your textbook.

In the blank space under each illustration below, write the number of ccs contained in the calibrated graduate, measuring cup, baby's bottle, and graduate.

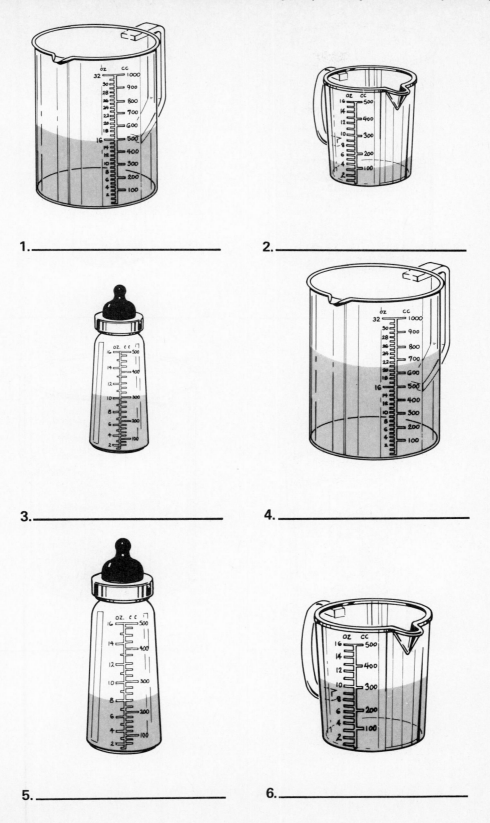

1._____

2._____

3._____

4._____

5._____

6._____

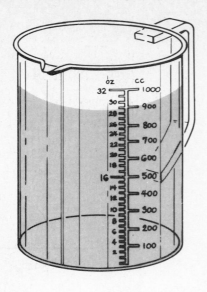

7. _____

8. _____

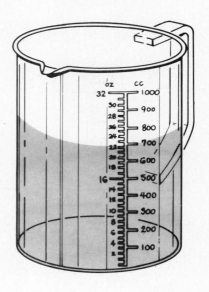

9. _____

10. _____

When measuring fluid intake, you will have to note the difference between the amount the patient actually drinks and the amount he leaves in the serving container. Read the "Procedure: Determining the Amounts Consumed" in your textbook.

SITUATION

Mr. Steller is on intake and output. He drank half a cup of tea. You are responsible for entering this information on his I&O sheet. From your list of the capacity of each serving container, you know that a full tea cup holds 180 cc. Fill in the blanks as we go through the procedure together to determine how much tea Mr. Steller actually drank.

1. Assemble your equipment on the _____ table.

   A. Graduate
   B. Pen and paper
   C. The leftover _____ in the tea cup.

2. Pour the leftover tea into the _____.

3. Look at the level and determine the _____ in cc (for the purpose of this example, let's say there are 80 cc of tea left in the graduate).

4. Determine the amount in the _____ serving container from the list. There are 180 cc in a full tea cup.

5. A) _____ the leftover amount, 80 cc, from the full container amount, 180.

   180 cc = container amount
   -80 cc = leftover amount

   B) _____ cc--this figure is the amount Mr. Steller actually
   C) _____. Immediately D) _____ this amount on the
   E) _____ side of the intake and output sheet.

6. Later Mr. Steller ate some chicken soup. You poured the leftover chicken soup into the graduate and found that he left more than 120 cc of soup. The full container amount of that bowl is 240 cc. How much fluid intake should you record on his I&O sheet?

   240 cc = full container
   -120 cc = leftover amount

   A) _____ cc = amount Mr. Steller consumed.

   You will record B) _____ on the C) _____ side of Mr. Steller's I&O sheet.

7. Mrs. Golden is also on intake and output. She drank some water. You poured the leftover water into the graduate and found that she left 270 cc of water in the glass. The full container amount for that glass is 300 cc. How much fluid intake should you record on her I&O sheet?

   300 cc = full container amount
   -270 cc = leftover amount

   A) _____ cc = amount Mrs. Golden consumed. You will record
   B) _____ cc on the intake side of Mrs. Golden's I&O sheet.

8. Mr. Trent is also on intake and output. He drank some milk from a small container. On the container it says that it contains 8 fluid ounces. Look at the chart titled "U.S. Customary Liquid Measure with Equivalent Metric Measurements" in your textbook to see how many cc equal 8 oz:

   8 oz. = A) _____ cc. Now you know the full container amount is 240 cc. Next you pour the leftover amount into a graduate and see that the leftover amount is 60 cc.

   240 cc = full container amount
   -60 cc = leftover amount

   B) _____ cc = amount Mr. Trent C)_____. You will record
   D) _____ cc on the I&O sheet for Mr. Trent.

9. Mrs. Jones is also on intake and output. She ate almost all her ice cream. You poured the leftover ice cream into a graduate and determined that she left only 30 cc. The full container amount for the bowl is 120 cc. How much fluid intake should you record on her I&O sheet?

   120 cc = full container amount
   -30 cc = leftover amount

   A) _____ cc = amount Mrs. Jones consumed. You will record
   B) _____ cc on the intake side of Mrs. Jones' intake and output sheet.

10. The nursing assistant must A) _____ the amount of B) _____ as soon as the patient drinks any fluids on the C) _____ side of the I&O D) _____ .

WORKBOOK ASSIGNMENT #11, CHAPTER 13, SECTION 3
MEASURING THE CAPACITY OF SERVING CONTAINERS

When measuring intake, you will need a complete list of the capacity of each dish, glass, bowl, or cup used by the patients. Read the procedure titled "Measuring the Capacity of Serving Containers" in your textbook. Try it at home. You can use a measuring cup for a graduate. How much soup does your soup bowl hold? How much coffee does your mug hold? How much orange juice does your glass hold? Practice by making a list of the capacity of each serving container in your kitchen.

Mrs. Morris is on intake and output. She drank a full glass of soda. You are responsible for entering this information on her I&O sheet. Fill in the blanks as we go through the procedure together to determine how much soda that glass holds.

1. Assemble your equipment in the utility room:

   A. In this case you will need the empty glass
   B. Graduate
   C. _____
   D. Pen and paper.

2. Fill the glass with _____.

3. Pour this water into the _____.

4. Look at the _____ of the water and determine the amount in cc (_____).

5. Write this information on the _____.

6. You now know how many _____ are in the glass.

SECTION 4

WORKBOOK ASSIGNMENT #12, CHAPTER 13, SECTION 4
FORCING AND RESTRICTING FLUIDS

Find the list of objectives for this section. Next to each objective write the page numbers where you can find information to help you meet these objectives.

WORKBOOK ASSIGNMENT #13, CHAPTER 13, SECTION 4
FORCING AND RESTRICTING FLUIDS

Read "Key Ideas: Force Fluids, Restrict Fluids, Nothing by Mouth" in your textbook.

1. A patient on force fluids needs encouragement to:

   A. Drink more
   B. Drink less
   C. Drink cold liquids only
   D. Eat more
   E. Eat less.

2. Restrict fluids means that:

   A. The patient should drink as much as possible
   B. The patient should drink as little as possible
   C. The patient should not drink anything
   D. The patient is limited to certain amounts of fluids
   E. All of the above.

3. Nothing by mouth means that:

    A. The patient should drink as much as possible.
    B. The patient should drink as little as possible.
    C. The patient cannot eat or drink anything at all.
    D. The patient is limited to certain amounts of fluid.
    E. The patient is limited to certain amounts of foods.

4. When a patient is on N.P.O. you should:

    A. Remove the water pitcher
    B. Not give him any food or drink
    C. Write N.P.O. on the intake side of the I&O sheet
    D. Place a sign stating N.P.O. on the bed or door
    E. All of the above.

5. When a patient is on force fluids, the nursing assistant can persuade the patient to drink more fluids by:

    A. Showing enthusiasm and being cheerful
    B. Providing different kinds of liquids that the patient prefers as permitted on his therapeutic diet
    C. Offering liquids without being asked
    D. Offering hot and cold drinks
    E. All of the above.

SECTION 5

___

WORKBOOK ASSIGNMENT #14, CHAPTER 13, SECTION 5
FLUID OUTPUT

Find the list of objectives for this section. Next to each objective write the page numbers where you can find information to help you meet these objectives.

WORKBOOK ASSIGNMENT #15, CHAPTER 13, SECTION 5
FLUID OUTPUT

Read "Key Ideas: Measuring Fluid Output" in your textbook.

Match the beginning of each sentence in Column A with its ending in Column B to form complete sentences about fluid output. Write the correct letter in the space provided.

Column A	Column B
_____1. Fluid output is the sum total of liquids	A. to void or to pass water.
_____2. To urinate means to	B. the fluid is lost in the air breathed out.
_____3. Other terms for urinate are	C. that come out of the body.
_____4. Insensible loss means that	D. discharge urine from the body.

158

	Column A		Column B

_____5.	Fluid is also discharged	D.	discharge urine from the body.
_____6.	Output also includes emesis or drainage from a wound	E.	or from the stomach and loss of blood.
_____7.	A patient who is on I&O	F.	from the body in feces.
_____8.	Every time the patient uses the urinal, emesis basin, or bedpan	G.	the urine and other liquids must be measured
		H.	and ask him to cooperate
_____9.	You should tell a patient his output is being measured	I.	must have his output as well as his intake measured and recorded.

WORKBOOK ASSIGNMENT #16, CHAPTER 13, SECTION 5
MEASURING URINARY OUTPUT

Read the "Procedure: Measuring Urinary Output" in your textbook. There are 11 steps in this procedure. Each step is an action--something for you to do. Find the key word or words in each step that tell you what to do. These are the words that show action--"doing" words called verbs. The first one is done for you as an example.

1. Assemble _____

2. _____

3. _____

4. _____

5. _____

6. _____

7. _____, _____

8. _____, _____

9. _____, _____

10. _____

11. _____

WORKBOOK ASSIGNMENT #17, CHAPTER 13, SECTION 5
URINARY CATHETERS

Read the information titled "Urinary Catheters" and the "Rules to Follow: Indwelling Urinary Catheters" in your textbook.

From the following three actions, choose the correct response for each situation.

A. Report this to your head nurse or team leader.
B. Correct what is wrong.
C. Hold the bag lower than the patient's urinary bladder.

<u>SITUATIONS</u>

1. _____ You notice that the patient is lying on the tubing.

2. _____ The level of urine in the container has been the same the last three times you checked it.

3. _____ The patient complains of burning or tenderness in the urethral area.

4. _____ The patient is ready to get out of bed for a short walk.

5. _____ You notice a kink in the tubing--it is bent in some way to prevent fluid from going through it.

6. _____ You notice the tape has come loose from the patient's thigh.

7. _____ The patient says he feels the need to urinate.

WORKBOOK ASSIGNMENT #18, CHAPTER 13, SECTION 5
DAILY INDWELLING CATHETER CARE

Read "Key Ideas: Daily Indwelling Catheter Care" in your textbook.

Circle the letter of the correct response below.

1. An indwelling catheter is inserted through the patient's urethra into the _____ by the head nurse or team leader.

   A. Rectum
   B. Bladder
   C. Anus
   D. Penis
   E. Vagina.

2. The indwelling catheter allows for:

   A. Bowel movement
   B. Vomitus
   C. Drainage of urine
   D. Expelling flatus
   E. Secreting stomach acid.

3. _____ technique should be used at all times when you are handling and caring for this equipment.

   A. Medical Asepsis
   B. Sterile
   C. Gown
   D. Enema
   E. Perineal.

4. The catheter is attached to tubing that should be _____ loosely to the inner side of the patient's thigh.

A. Tied
B. Stuck
C. Suctioned
D. Taped
E. Bound.

5. The container is kept lower than the level of the urinary _____.

A. Bag
B. Bladder
C. Catheter
D. Tube
E. Opening.

WORKBOOK ASSIGNMENT #19, CHAPTER 13, SECTION 5
GIVING DAILY INDWELLING CATHETER CARE

Read the "Procedure: Giving Daily Indwelling Catheter Care" in your textbook.

Circle the letter T if the statement below is true, F if it is false.

T or F   1. Washing the genital area or giving perineal care can be done
               after giving daily indwelling catheter care.

T or F   2. You will need plenty of light to observe effectively.

T or F   3. You will be observing for crusting, lesions, or anything
               abnormal.

T or F   4. Apply antiseptic solution on the entire area where the catheter
               enters the patient's body.

T or F   5. Apply antiseptic solution to the four inches of the tube furthest
               from the patient.

SECTION 6
_____

WORKBOOK ASSIGNMENT #20, CHAPTER 13, SECTION 6
SPECIMEN COLLECTION

Find the list of objectives for this chapter. Next to each objective write the
page numbers where you can find information to help you meet these objectives.

WORKBOOK ASSIGNMENT #21, CHAPTER 13, SECTION 6
SPECIMEN COLLECTION

Read "Key Ideas: Specimen Collection" in your textbook.

Fill in the blank spaces with the words listed below.

    samples   accurate
    waste   spit
    collecting   tests
    feces   sputum
    laboratory   specimens

1. As one of its natural living functions, the human body regularly gets rid
    of various _____ materials.

2. Most of the body's waste materials are discharged in the urine and
    _____.

3. The body also gets rid of wastes in the material coughed up and _____
    out of the mouth.

4. This expectorated material is called _____.

5. These body waste materials, when tested in the _____, often show
    changes in the sick person's body.

6. By examining the results of laboratory _____, the doctor gets
    information about the patient.

7. The doctor will sometimes need _____ of each of these waste
    products--urine, feces and sputum.

8. These samples are called _____.

9. Members of the nursing staff are responsible for _____ such
    specimens.

10. When collecting specimens you must be very _____.

WORKBOOK ASSIGNMENT #22, CHAPTER 13, SECTION 6
NEED FOR ACCURACY

Read the information titled "Accuracy" in your textbook.

Fill in the blanks in Column A with the letter of the correct explanation from
Column B.

           Column A   Column B

_____1. The right patient   A. how you approach and speak to
                                         the patient
_____2. The right specimen
                                    B. filled out properly from the
_____3. The right time   patient's identification bracelet

_____4. The right amount   C. from whom the specimen is to be
                                         collected
_____5. The right container

Column A	Column B

<table>
<tr><td></td><td>6.</td><td>The right label</td><td>D.</td><td>measured exactly for each specimen</td></tr>
<tr><td></td><td>7.</td><td>The right requisition or laboratory slip</td><td>E.</td><td>washing your hands before and after collecting the specimen</td></tr>
<tr><td></td><td>8.</td><td>The right method</td><td>F.</td><td>lists the kind of lab exam or test to be done</td></tr>
<tr><td></td><td>9.</td><td>The right asepsis</td><td>G.</td><td>as ordered by the doctor</td></tr>
<tr><td></td><td>10.</td><td>The right attitude</td><td>H.</td><td>procedure by which you collect the specimen</td></tr>
<tr><td></td><td></td><td></td><td>I.</td><td>when the specimen is to be collected</td></tr>
<tr><td></td><td></td><td></td><td>J.</td><td>the cup that is correct for each specimen</td></tr>
</table>

WORKBOOK ASSIGNMENT #23, CHAPTER 13, SECTION 6
COLLECTING A ROUTINE URINE SPECIMEN

Read the "Procedure: Collecting a Routine Urine Specimen" in your textbook.

Circle the letter of the correct response below.

1. You are collecting a routine specimen from Judy Barnet upon admission. You have just put the lid on the specimen container and placed the label on the container. Of the following three tasks, which should you do next?

    A. Pour the leftover urine into the toilet or hopper.
    B. Wash your hands.
    C. Identify the patient by checking the identification bracelet.

2. You are collecting a routine urine specimen from Mrs. Harris. You have just pulled the curtain around the bed for privacy. Of the following three tasks, which one should you do next?

    A. Clean and rinse out the graduate. Put it in its proper place.
    B. Ask the visitors to step out of the room.
    C. Have the patient urinate into the bedpan, urinal, or specimen.

3. You are collecting a routine urine specimen from Mr. John Baxter. You have just recorded the amount of urine on the output side of the I&O sheet. Of the following three tasks, which one should you do next?

    A. Put the lid on the specimen container. Place the correct label on the container for the correct patient.
    B. Pour urine from the graduate into a specimen container and fill it three-fourths full, if possible.
    C. Pour the leftover urine into the toilet or hopper.

WORKBOOK ASSIGNMENT #24, CHAPTER 13, SECTION 6
COLLECTING A 24-HOUR URINE SPECIMEN

Read the "Procedure: Collecting a 24-Hour Urine Specimen" in your textbook.

Write the word DO or DON'T next to each statement.

1. _____ wash your hands before beginning this procedure.

2. _____ tell the patient a 48-hour urine specimen is needed.

3. _____ post a sign saying NPO over the patient's bed.

4. _____ place tissue in the bedpan with the specimen.

5. _____ begin the test by having the patient void.

6. _____ be sure to measure the urine and enter the amounts on the I&O sheet
for all patients on I&O.

7. _____ use the first urine voided at the beginning of the test.

8. _____ be sure the bladder is empty when the test begins.

9. _____ end the test having the patient void exactly 24 hours after the
test started. If you started at 7 A.M. Monday, you would end at
7 A.M. Tuesday.

10. _____ collect more urine after the 24 hours is over.

WORKBOOK ASSIGNMENT #25, CHAPTER 13, SECTION 6
COLLECTING A STOOL SPECIMEN AND A SPUTUM SPECIMEN

Read the "Procedures: Collecting a Sputum Specimen and Collecting a Stool
Specimen" in your textbook.

In the blank space beside each of the following statements:

-- Write the word SPUTUM if the statement goes with the "Procedure: Collecting
a Sputum Specimen."
-- Write the word STOOL if the statement goes with the "Procedure: Collecting
a Stool Specimen."
-- Write the word NONE if the statement does not go with either of these two
procedures.
-- Write the word BOTH if the statement goes with both procedures.

1. _____ Tell the patient a sputum specimen is needed.

2. _____ Tell the patient a stool specimen is needed.

3. _____ Identify the patient by checking the ID bracelet.

4. _____ The patient may have to cough several times.

5. _____ Have the patient move his bowels into the bedpan.

164

6. _____ Take the covered bedpan to the patient's bathroom or to the dirty utility room.

7. _____ Wrap the tongue depressor in a paper towel and discard it.

8. _____ When the collection starts, have the patient void.

9. _____ Ask him to take three deep breaths in a row.

10. _____ One to two tablespoons is usually the required amount for this specimen.

WORKBOOK ASSIGNMENT #26, CHAPTER 13
WORDS TO REMEMBER/GLOSSARY

Read the definition carefully, then fill in the blanks with the vocabulary word to remember.

1. Coughing up matter from the lungs, trachea, or bronchial tubes and spitting it out is called _____.

2. Solid waste material is discharged from the body through the rectum and anus. Other names for _____ are stool, excreta, BM, bowel movement, and fecal matter.

3. Waste material coughed up from the lungs or trachea is referred to as _____.

4. A laboratory test of the patient's urine done for diagnostic purposes is called _____.

5. A condition in which the body has less than the normal amount of fluids is called _____.

6. To pass off as vapor, as to _____, or as water evaporating into the air.

7. Applies to both liquid and gaseous substances known as a _____.

8. When the same amount of fluid taken in by the body is given out by the body, it is called _____.

9. To discharge urine from the body. Other words used for this function are void, micturate, pass water, or _____.

10. A tube inserted into a body cavity, usually used to withdraw fluid, is called a _____.

11. A membranous sac that serves as a container within the body to hold urine is known as the _____.

12. The tube leading from the urinary bladder to the outside of the body is called the _____.

LEARNING BY DOING

As you study the procedures in this chapter, read every step carefully. Think
about the action words, the words that tell you what to do. Look at the pictures
closely and read the captions. You will be able to remember what to do more
easily if you try to do it after you have read about it. Learning by doing
involves your whole body in the learning process, not just your eyes or ears. It
is one of the most effective ways to learn.

Ask a fellow student or, if you are practicing at home, ask a friend or relative
to play the part of the patient. Actually do all of the steps of the procedure
several times, pretending you are a nursing assistant caring for several
patients. Work slowly at first. Look at the textbook whenever you are not sure
about what to do next. Practice in this way many times until you can work
quickly, and you no longer need to look at the textbook.

Switch roles with your partner, and you take several turns at being the patient.
Not only will this give your partner a chance to learn the procedure, but you
will benefit as well. By putting yourself in the patient's place, you will begin
to understand how it feels to be a patient, and you will be able to treat real
patients as you yourself would like to be treated.

CHAPTER 13 QUIZ

Circle the letter of the correct response.

1. When a patient's body loses more fluid than he is taking in or retains more than he is putting out, he has a:

    A. Fluid balance
    B. Fluid imbalance
    C. Measurable intake and output
    D. Tube feeding
    E. Cubic centimeter.

2. The amounts of intake and output are written on a special sheet of paper called:

    A. Institution identification
    B. A graduate
    C. Intake and output sheet
    D. Intravenous tube
    E. Parenteral intake records.

3. The term that includes everything the patient drinks -- water, milk, ice cream, fruit juices, soup, tea, coffee or anything liquid -- is:

    A. Fluid intake
    B. Fluid output
    C. Force fluid
    D. I&O
    E. Fluid imbalance.

4. When you measure liquids by ccs, rather than ounces, you are using the:

    A. British system
    B. Celsius system
    C. U.S. Customary System
    D. Metric system
    E. Centimeter system.

5. When a patient is to drink extra liquids, he is said to be on:

    A. Force fluids
    B. Restrict fluids
    C. Nothing by mouth
    D. Tube feedings
    E. Intake and output.

6. When a patient is to drink only a limited amount of liquids, he is said to be on:

    A. Force fluid
    B. Restrict fluids
    C. Nothing by mouth
    D. Tube feedings
    E. Intake and output.

7. When a patient cannot eat or drink anything at all, he is said to be on:

    A. FF
    B. RF
    C. N.P.O.
    D. cc
    E. I&O.

8. The term which includes urine, vomitus, drainage from a wound or from the stomach, and loss of blood is known as:

    A. Fluid intake
    B. Fluid output
    C. Force fluid
    D. I&O
    E. Fluid imbalance.

9. The catheter drains all the patient's urine into a:

    A. Graduate
    B. Bedpan
    C. Urinal
    D. Urine container
    E. Emesis basin.

10. If a patient is incontinent of urine, record this on the output side of the I&O sheet each time the patient:

    A. Gets out of bed
    B. Drinks anything
    C. Wets the bed
    D. Does something unusual
    E. Vomits.

11. _____ is a special method used to collect a patient's urine when the specimen must be free from contamination.

    A. 24-hour urine specimen
    B. Isolation technique
    C. Aseptic technique
    D. Midstream clean-catch urine specimen
    E. Straining the urine.

12. The urine is _____ to determine if a patient has passed stones or other matter from the kidney.

    A. Collected
    B. Strained
    C. Measured
    D. Cooled
    E. Tested.

13. _____ specimens should be thrown away.

    A. Cold
    B. Unlabeled
    C. Routine
    D. Measured
    E. Strained.

Here is a list of the procedures included in this chapter. Label each of the pictures on the following pages with the number of the procedure it is illustrating.

A. Routine urine specimen
B. Midstream clean-catch urine specimen
C. 24-hour urine specimen
D. Sputum specimen
E. Stool specimen
F. Straining the urine
G. Collecting a routine urine specimen from an infant

14. _____ .

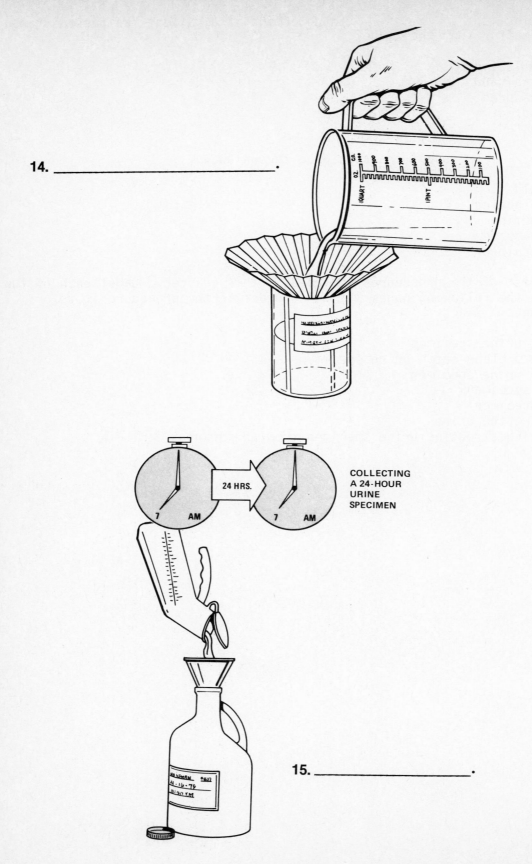

COLLECTING
A 24-HOUR
URINE
SPECIMEN

24 HRS.

7 AM   7 AM

15. _____ .

16._____.

17._____.

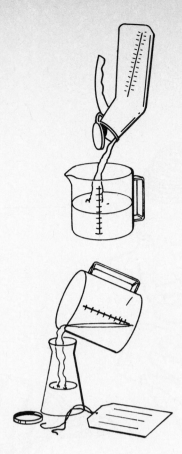

18. _____ .

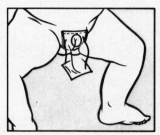

19. _____ .

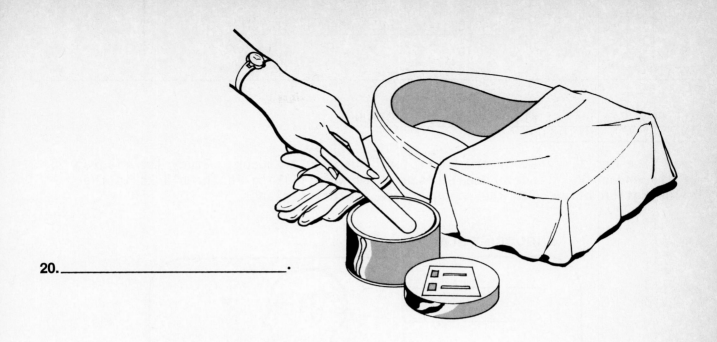

20. _____.

SECTION 1

WORKBOOK ASSIGNMENT #1, CHAPTER 14, SECTION 1
ANATOMY AND PHYSIOLOGY

Read "Section 1: Anatomy and Physiology" in your textbook. Study the diagram of the endocrine glands. Use it as a guide when filling in the blanks in the illustration below with the names of the endocrine glands.

ENDOCRINE GLANDS

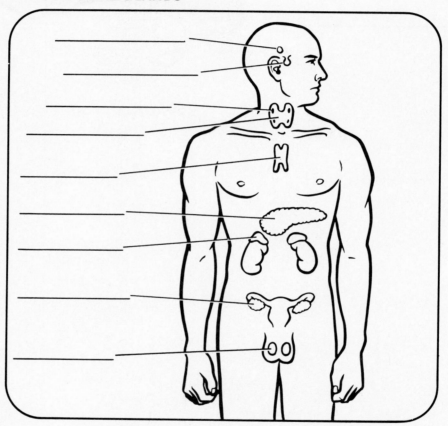

SECTION 2

WORKBOOK ASSIGNMENT #2, CHAPTER 14, SECTION 2
CARE OF THE DIABETIC PATIENT

Find the list of objectives for this section. Next to each objective, write the page numbers where you can find information to help you meet these objectives.

WORKBOOK ASSIGNMENT #3, CHAPTER 14, SECTION 2
DIABETES MELLITUS

Read "Key Ideas: Diabetes Mellitus" in your textbook.

There are three groups of signs and symptoms you need to know. Beside each sign and symptom listed, write the letter of the group to which it belongs.

A. Signs and symptoms of diabetes mellitus
B. Signs and symptoms of insulin shock
C. Signs and symptoms of diabetic coma

1. _____ Hunger

2. _____ Skin erosions

3. _____ Dulled senses

4. _____ Air hunger

5. _____ Excessive sweating

6. _____ Loss of appetite

7. _____ Abdominal pain

8. _____ Fainting, dizziness

9. _____ Headache

10. _____ Nausea, vomiting

11. _____ Weakness

12. _____ Polydipsia

13. _____ General aches

14. _____ Not able to awaken

15. _____ Large amounts of sugar
and ketones in the urine

16. _____ Loss of weight

17. _____ Blurred vision

18. _____ Increased thirst

19. _____ Fatigue, tiredness

20. _____ Tremors

21. _____ Low blood sugar

22. _____ Vaginitis

23. _____ Sweet breath odor

24. _____ Dry skin

25. _____ Polyuria

26. _____ Increased urination

27. _____ Irritability

28. _____ No sugar in urine

29. _____ High blood sugar

30. _____ Numbness of tongue and lips

WORKBOOK ASSIGNMENT #4, CHAPTER 14, SECTION 2
THE CLINITEST

Read "Key Ideas: The Clinitest and Clinistix Test" and the "Procedure: The Clinitest" in your textbook.

Circle the letter T if the statement is true, F if it is false:

T or F   1. The clinitest is a test that is done to determine the amount of glucose (sugar) in the patient's urine.

T or F   2.   With the dropper in the upright position, place 10 drops of urine in the center of the test tube.

T or F   3.   Place five drops of clean water in the center of the test tube.

T or F   4.   Using your thumb and index finger, take the tablet out of the bottle and drop it into the test tube.

T or F   5.   If your hands are wet and you touch the tablet, the moisture will start the reaction, and you will be burned.

WORKBOOK ASSIGNMENT #5, CHAPTER 14, SECTION 2
THE CLINISTIX TEST

Read the "Procedure: The Clinistix Test" in your textbook.

Write DO or DON'T in the space beside each statement.

1. _____ dip the reagent strip into the urine in the bedpan.

2. _____ remove it after it has been in the urine 10 seconds.

3. _____ tap the edge of the strip against the side of the urine container to remove excess urine.

4. _____ hold the strip in a vertical position.

5. _____ read the results immediately after removing the strip from the urine.

6. _____ read the results from the color chart.

WORKBOOK ASSIGNMENT #6, CHAPTER 14, SECTION 2
THE KETOSTIX REAGENT STRIP TEST

Read the "Procedure: The Ketostix Reagent Strip Test: in your textbook.

Circle the letter T if the statement below is true, F if it is false.

T or F   1.   Dip the Ketostix strip into the urine in a test tube.

T or F   2.   Remove the strip after 15 seconds.

T or F   3.   Tap the edge of the strip against the side of the urine container to remove excess urine.

T or F   4.   Hold the strip in a horizontal position.

T or F   5.   Read the results in 10 seconds after removing the strip from the urine.

T or F   6.   Read the results from the color chart on the bottle.

WORKBOOK ASSIGNMENT #7, CHAPTER 14
WORDS TO REMEMBER/GLOSSARY

Fill in the blanks with the vocabulary word to remember after reading the definition carefully.

1. A condition that develops when the body cannot change its sugar into energy. When this sugar collects in the blood, the patient needs a special diet and may have to be given insulin. This condition is called _____.

2. _____ is a hormone produced naturally by the pancreas. Insulin helps change sugar into energy. Insulin can be produced from animal pancreas, for use in the treatment of diabetes.

3. The _____ is a large gland, six to eight inches long, that secretes enzymes into the intestines for digestion of food. It also manufactures insulin, which is secreted into the bloodstream.

WORKBOOK ASSIGNMENT #8, CHAPTER 14
LEARNING BY DOING

As you study the procedure in this chapter, read every step carefully. Think about the action words, the words that tell you what to do. Look at the pictures closely and read the captions. You will be able to remember what to do more easily if you try to do it after you have read about it. Learning by doing involves your whole body in the learning process, not just your eyes or ears. It is one of the most effective ways to learn.

Ask a fellow student or, if you are practicing at home, ask a friend or relative to play the part of the patient. Actually do all of the steps of the procedure several times, pretending you are a nursing assistant caring for several patients. Work slowly at first. Look at the textbook whenever you are not sure about what to do next. Practice in this way many times until you can work quickly, and you no longer need to look at the textbook.

Switch roles with your partner, and you take several turns at being the patient. Not only will this give your partner a chance to learn the procedure, but you will benefit as well. By putting yourself in the patient's place, you will begin to understand how it feels to be a patient, and you will be able to treat real patients as you yourself would like to be treated.

CHAPTER 14 QUIZ

Here is a list of the procedures you learned in this chapter. Fill in the blanks with the letters of the correct procedures.

A.   Collecting a Fresh Fractional Urine Specimen
B.   The Clinitest
C.   The Clinistix Test
D.   The Acetest
E.   The Ketostix Reagent Strip Test

1.   In which procedure do you drop one drop of urine on a tablet? _____

2.   Which procedure requires the patient to void twice? _____

3.   Which tests are done to determine the amount of sugar in the patient's urine? _____ and _____

4.   Which procedures require you to dip a strip of chemically treated paper into the fresh fractional urine specimen? _____ and _____

5.   Which tests require you to use something that could burn you if you touch it with wet hands? _____ and _____

SECTION 1

WORKBOOK ASSIGNMENT #1, CHAPTER 15, SECTION 1
ANATOMY AND PHYSIOLOGY

Read "Section 1: Anatomy and Physiology" in your textbook. Study the diagrams of both the male and female reproductive systems. Use them as guides when filling in the blanks in the illustrations below with the names of the organs included in this system.

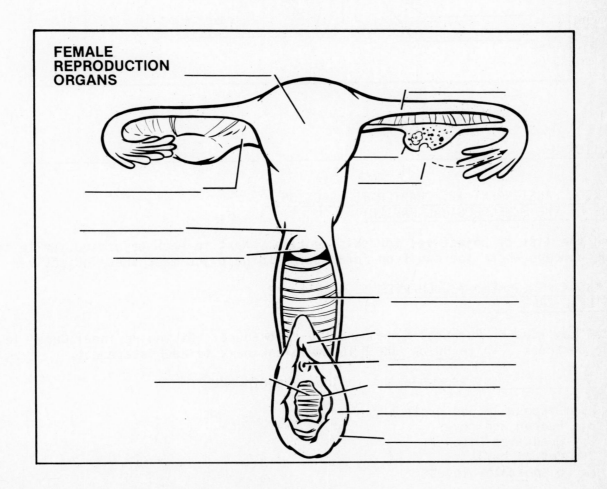

FEMALE
REPRODUCTION
ORGANS

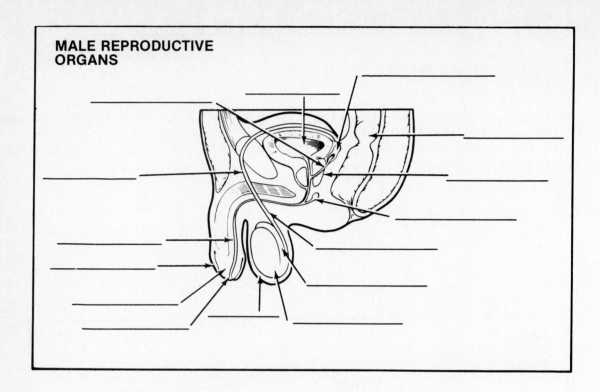

MALE REPRODUCTIVE ORGANS

SECTION 2
_____

WORKBOOK ASSIGNMENT #2, CHAPTER 15, SECTION 2
CARE OF THE GYNECOLOGICAL PATIENT

Find the list of objectives for this section. Next to each objective, write the page numbers where you can find information to help you meet these objectives.

WORKBOOK ASSIGNMENT #3, CHAPTER 15, SECTION 2
PERINEAL CARE

Read "Key Ideas: Perineal Care" and the "Procedure: Giving Perineal Care" in your textbook. Write <u>DO</u> or <u>DON'T</u> in the blank next to each statement.

1. _____ assemble the following equipment:

    A. Disposable bed protector
    B. Bedpan and cover
    C. Graduated pitcher
    D. Cotton balls
    E. Disposable gloves.

2. _____ darken the room.

3. _____ fill the graduated pitcher with cool water.
4. _____ place the disposable bed protector under the patient's buttocks.
5. _____ help the patient onto the bedpan.
6. _____ hold the pitcher 12 to 18 inches above the pubic area and pour the solution over the vulva (genital area).
7. _____ dry the patient gently with the cotton balls.
8. _____ remove the bedpan and disposable bed protector.
9. _____ place them on the floor.
10. _____ cover the patient with the top sheets. Remove the bath blanket.

WORKBOOK ASSIGNMENT #4, CHAPTER 15, SECTION 2
VAGINAL DOUCHE/NONSTERILE IRRIGATION

Read "Key Ideas: Vaginal Douche/Nonsterile Irrigation" and the "Procedure: Giving the Nonsterile Vaginal Douche" in your textbook.

Miss Brooks, nursing assistant, is giving a vaginal douche to her patient, Mrs. Van High. This is the first time since she finished her nursing assistant's training that she is performing this procedure. She didn't study well enough, and she has forgotten some of the steps in this procedure.

Keep your textbook open while you do this exercise, as you will have to look back at the procedure to answer the questions. We will go through this procedure with Miss Brooks. We will stop every so often so you can evaluate Miss Brooks' performance on that segment of the procedure. Circle GOOD is she has performed every step in that segment correctly and if she has not left out any steps. Circle POOR if she has performed any step incorrectly or if she has left out any steps. If you rate her POOR, you will then have to write down the step number (from the procedure as it is written in your textbook) that was wrong or left out.

SEGMENT 1. Miss Brooks began to assemble her equipment on the bedside table. She placed the disposable douche kit, graduated pitcher, disposable waterproof bed protector, solution, disposable gloves, and an emesis basin on the table. She washed her hands, checked Mrs. Van High's I.D. bracelet to identify her, and asked Mr. Van High to step out of the room for a few minutes. Then she explained to Mrs. Van High that she was going to give her a vaginal douche. Would you rate Miss Brooks' performance as GOOD or POOR? If you rated her POOR, which steps were wrong or left out?

SEGMENT 2. Miss Brooks pulled the curtains around the bed for privacy. Then she offered Mrs. Van High the bedpan and explained to her that her bladder must be empty to insure the desired results from the douche. When Mrs. Van High was finished, Miss Brooks removed the bedpan, measured and recorded output, emptied the bedpan, washed it, and placed it on a chair nearby. She helped Mrs. Van High to wash her hands and then Miss Brooks washed her own hands. Would you rate Miss Brooks' performance as GOOD or POOR because of steps _____?

SEGMENT 3. Miss Brooks covered Mrs. Van High with the bath blanket properly and placed the disposable bed protector under her hips. She raised the bed, opened the douche kit, and clamped the tubing. She filled the graduated pitcher with 500 cc of water. She measured the temperature of the water and found it to be 103°F. Then she poured the water into the container. Would you rate Miss Brooks' performance as GOOD or POOR because of steps _____?

181

SEGMENT 4. Miss Brooks poured cleansing solution over the cotton balls in a small disposable container to saturate them with solution. She placed Mrs. Van High in the dorsal recumbent position and draped her with a small sheet. She placed the bedpan under the patient's hips and put on the disposable gloves. Would you rate Miss Brooks' performance as GOOD or POOR because of steps _____?

SEGMENT 5. Miss Brooks began to clean the vulva using cotton balls saturated with cleansing solution. With the first cotton ball she wiped the labia majora from front to back on one side. She put the used cotton in the emesis basin. Next, she wiped from front to back over the other side of the labia majora and discarded the cotton in the emesis basin. She used a third cotton ball to wipe from front to back over the midline of the labia majora. She put the used cotton in the emesis basin. She separated the labia majora to expose the labia minora. She cleansed both sides of the labia minora and the midline always using a new cotton ball until the entire area was clean. Would you rate Miss Brooks' performance as GOOD or POOR because of steps _____?

SEGMENT 6. Miss Brooks opened the clamp to expel air and allowed the solution to flow over the vulva touching the vulva with the nozzle. With the solution flowing, she inserted the douche nozzle tip into the vagina two to three inches with a gentle upward and then downward and backward motion. She held the container 18 inches above the mattress and allowed the solution to flow. She rotated the nozzle until all the solution had been given. Would you rate Miss Brooks' performance as GOOD or POOR because of steps _____?

SEGMENT 7. Miss Brooks clamped the tubing and removed the douche nozzle. She wrapped it in paper and put the tubing into the container. She took off her gloves and threw them away. She dried the perineum with toilet tissue and discarded it into the bedpan. She removed the bedpan and placed it on the chair. Would you rate Miss Brooks' performance as GOOD or POOR because of steps _____?

SEGMENT 8. Miss Brooks helped Mrs. Van High to turn onto her side and dried her buttocks with toilet tissue. She removed the bed protector, raised the top sheets over the bath blanket, and then removed the bath blanket from under the top sheets. Would you rate Miss Brooks' performance as GOOD or POOR because of steps _____?

SEGMENT 9. After making Mrs. Van High comfortable, Miss Brooks cleaned the bedpan and emesis basin and put them away. She threw away all disposable supplies. She helped Mrs. Van High to wash her hands. Then she washed her own hands. Would you rate Miss Brooks' performance as GOOD or POOR because of steps _____?

SEGMENT 10. Miss Brooks reported to her team leader that she had given Mrs. Van High a vaginal douche. She told her the time the douche was given and that no specimen was collected. She related her observations concerning how the patient tolerated the procedure, the returned solution, the type of solution used, and her observations of anything unusual. Would you rate Miss Brooks' performance as GOOD or POOR because of steps _____?

WORKBOOK ASSIGNMENT #5, CHAPTER 15
WORDS TO REMEMBER/GLOSSARY

Fill in the blanks with the vocabulary word to remember, after reading the definition carefully.

1. The _____ is a pouch below the penis that contains the testicles.

2. The _____ is a small depression on the abdomen that marks the place where the umbilical cord was originally attached to the fetus.

3. Found in the female, the _____ is the birth canal leading from the vulva to the cervix of the uterus.

4. A procedure by which a stream of medicated or plain water is sent into the patient's vaginal opening. This is called a _____.

WORKBOOK ASSIGNMENT #6, CHAPTER 15
LEARNING BY DOING

As you study the procedures in this chapter, read every step carefully. Think about the action words, the words that tell you what to do. Look at the pictures closely and read the captions. You will be able to remember what to do more easily if you try to do it after you have read about it. Learning by doing involves your whole body in the learning process, not just your eyes or ears. It is one of the most effective ways to learn.

Ask a fellow student or, if you are practicing at home, ask a friend or relative to play the part of the patient. Actually do all of the steps of the procedure several times, pretending you are a nursing assistant caring for several patients. Work slowly at first. Look at the textbook whenever you are not sure about what to do next. Practice in this way many times until you can work quickly, and you no longer need to look at the textbook.

Switch roles with your partner, and you take several turns at being the patient. Not only will this give your partner a chance to learn the procedure, but you will benefit as well. By putting yourself in the patient's place, you will begin to understand how it feels to be a patient, and you will be able to treat real patients as you yourself would like to be treated.

CHAPTER 15 QUIZ

Fill in the blanks of questions 1 and 2 with the letters of the appropriate procedure below.

    A. Giving Perineal Care
    B. Giving the Nonsterile Vaginal Douche

1. The introduction of solution into the vaginal canal with an immediate return of the solution by gravity is called _____.

2. Which procedure is always given before indwelling catheter care and following childbirth? _____.

Fill in the blanks of questions 3, 4, and 5 with the words listed below:

    A. Malignant
    B. A.I.D.S.
    C. Comfort

3. Tumors of the breast can be benign or _____.

4. Acquired Immune Deficiency Syndrome is more commonly known as _____.

5. Perineal care provides cleanliness and _____ for the patient.

SECTION 1
_____

WORKBOOK ASSIGNMENT #1, CHAPTER 16, SECTION 1
ANATOMY AND PHYSIOLOGY

Read "Section 1: Anatomy and Physiology" in your textbook. Study the diagram
of both the motor neuron and sensory motor processes in operation. Use it as a
guide when filling in the blanks in the illustration below.

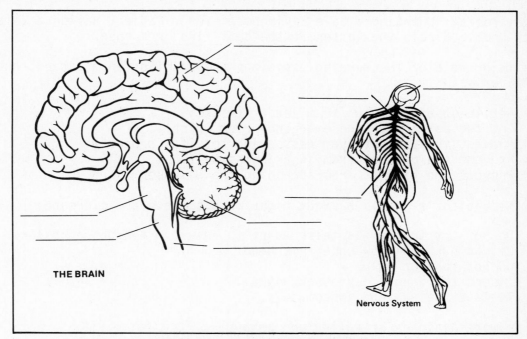

THE BRAIN

Nervous System

SENSORY AND MOTOR PROCESSES IN OPERATION

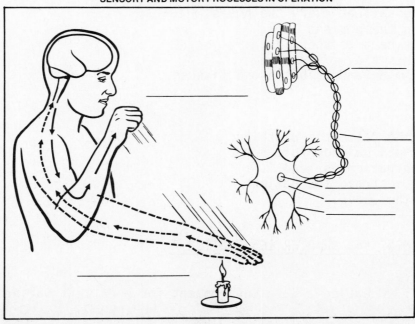

WORKBOOK ASSIGNMENT #2, CHAPTER 16, SECTION 2
CARE OF THE SEIZURE PATIENT

Find the list of objectives for this section. Next to each objective, write the page numbers where you can find information to help you meet these objectives.

WORKBOOK ASSIGNMENT #3, CHAPTER 16, SECTION 2
CARE OF THE SEIZURE PATIENT

Read "Key Ideas: Creating a Safe Environment for a Patient Having a Seizure" in your textbook. Circle the letter of the best first response.

1. The major role of the nursing assistant when caring for a patient having a seizure is to:

   A. Get the head nurse or team leader quickly.
   B. Get the patient to the emergency room quickly.
   C. Prevent the patient from destroying hospital property.
   D. Prevent the patient from injuring himself.
   E. Prevent the patient from spreading the disease.

2. If the patient's jaw is already tight or his teeth are clenched:

   A. Do not try to pry his teeth apart to insert a tongue depressor.
   B. Do not put a pillow under his head.
   C. Do not run for help.
   D. Insert the tongue depressor anyway.
   E. Isolate the patient immediately.

3. To promote drainage of saliva or vomitus:

   A. Turn the patient every two hours.
   B. Restrain the patient.
   C. Turn his head to the side.
   D. Loosen his tie.
   E. Offer him an emesis basin and tissues.

4. Never try to:

   A. Loosen the patient's clothing.
   B. Place a pillow under his head.
   C. Turn the patient's head.
   D. Move or restrain the patient.
   E. All of the above.

WORKBOOK ASSIGNMENT #4, CHAPTER 16, SECTION 2
SEIZURES

Read "Key Ideas: Creating a Safe Environment for a Patient Having a Seizure" in your textbook.

Circle the letter _T_ if the statement below is true, _F_ if it is false.

T or F 1. Seizures are an abnormality occurring from birth only.

T or F 2. A seizure can occur from a head injury, cancer, or disease.

T or F 3. A Grand Mal seizure is the same as a Petit Mal seizure.

T or F 4. In a Grand Mal seizure there may be stiffness of the total body, followed by jerking action of the muscles.

T or F 5. Only in a Petit Mal seizure will the patient bite his tongue.

T or F 6. A patient having a Petit Mal seizure may appear to be daydreaming.

T or F 7. Rolling of the eyes is common to Petit Mal seizures.

T or F 8. A Petit Mal seizure usually lasts more than 30 seconds.

T or F 9. While a patient is having a seizure, the nursing assistant should leave the room to go to her head nurse or team leader for help.

SECTION 3

WORKBOOK ASSIGNMENT #5, CHAPTER 16, SECTION 3
ARTIFICIAL EYE AND HEARING AID CARE

Find the list of objectives for this section. Next to each objective, write the page numbers where you can find information to help you meet these objectives.

WORKBOOK ASSIGNMENT #6, CHAPTER 16, SECTION 3
ARTIFICIAL EYE CARE

Read "Key Ideas: Care of the Patient's Artificial Eye" and the "Procedure: Caring for the Artificial Eye" in your textbook.

Fill in the blanks with the words listed below:

inner	gauge	solution
insert	drain	depress
nose	upper	hygiene
encrustation		

1. Cleaning the patient's artificial eye is part of daily personal _____.

2. _____ means formation of dried mucous material on the outside of the eye socket.

3. Clean any external secretions from the patient's _____ eyelid.

4. Clean from the _____ canthus to the outside of the eye area.

5. To remove the artificial eye, carefully _____ the lower eyelid with your thumb.

6. Place the eye in the cup on the 4x4 _____.

7. When cleaning the outside of the eye socket, move from the _____ to the outside of the eye.

8. When washing the artificial eye, be sure to close the _____ in the sink.

9. Use plain water unless the doctor has ordered a special _____.

10. If the patient is to _____ the eye, have him wash his hands.

SECTION 4 _____

WORKBOOK ASSIGNMENT #7, CHAPTER 16, SECTION 4
CARE OF THE CEREBRAL VASCULAR ACCIDENT PATIENT

Find the list of objectives for this section. Next to each objective, write the page numbers where you can find information to help you meet these objectives.

WORKBOOK ASSIGNMENT #8, CHAPTER 16, SECTION 4
THE CEREBRAL VASCULAR ACCIDENT PATIENT

Circle the letter T if the statement below is true, F if it is false.

T or F 1. A CVA (Cerebral Vascular Accident) occurs when the blood supply to a part of the brain is interrupted due to a blocked or ruptured blood vessel.

T or F 2. Frequently following a stroke, the patient remains paralyzed on one side of the body. This is called aphasia.

T or F 3. To prevent disability, position the patient in proper alignment.

T or F 4. When caring for a CVA patient, you should point out the positive aspects of his/her progress.

T or F 5. Provide good skin care and change the position of the patient frequently to prevent further paralysis.

T or F 6. Encourage the patient to permit you to do as much as possible for him/her.

T or F 7. In order to move the patient from the bed to the wheelchair, when one side of the body has been affected by the stroke, position the wheelchair on the side of the bed closest to the unaffected side of the patient's body.

T or F 8. When aphasia occurs, speech always returns completely.

9. When individuals experience a CVA, their lives change suddenly and drastically.

10. Anger, fear, frustration, depression, and withdrawal are common responses of the patient who has had a CVA.

WORKBOOK ASSIGNMENT #9, CHAPTER 16
WORDS TO REMEMBER/GLOSSARY

Read the definition carefully, then fill in the blanks with the vocabulary word to remember.

1. Convulsions (or paroxysms of involuntary muscular contractions and relaxations) can be localized or generalized, with spasms either violent or quiet. This is called a _____.

2. _____ pertains to the part of the brain called the cerebrum.

3. _____ is the loss of the ability to move a part or all of the body. Stroke/hemiplegia may be due to hemorrhage, cerebral thrombosis, emoblism, or a tumor of the cerebrum. Paralysis on only one half of the body is a result of this. The sudden apoplexy/hemiplegia is caused sometimes by hemorrhage, the result of rupture of a sclerosed or diseased blood vessel in the brain.

4. _____ refers to a loss of language/speech.

5. A _____ accident is also called a stroke or a CVA.

6. _____ is half of a sphere.

7. _____ means formation of dried mucous material.

8. _____ is fatty deposits within the blood vessels attached to the vessel walls.

9. _____ means breaking open.

10. _____ is a blood clot which remains at its site of formation.

11. Embolus is a clot that formed elsewhere in the body and traveled to the brain through the _____ system from its place of formation to another site, lodging in a small blood vessel and causing an obstruction.

WORKBOOK ASSIGNMENT #10, CHAPTER 16
LEARNING BY DOING

As you study the procedures in this chapter, read every step carefully. Think about the action words, the words that tell you what to do. Look at the pictures closely and read the captions. You will be able to remember what to do more easily if you try to do it after you have read about it. Learning by doing involves your whole body in the learning process, not just your eyes or ears. It is one of the most effective ways to learn.

Ask a fellow student or, if you are practicing at home, ask a friend or relative to play the part of the patient. Actually do all of the steps of the procedure several times, pretending you are a nursing assistant caring for several patients. Work slowly at first. Look at the textbook whenever you are not sure about what to do next. Practice in this way many times until you can work quickly, and you no longer need to look at the textbook.

Switch roles with your partner, and you take several turns at being the patient. Not only will this give your partner a chance to learn the procedure, but you will benefit as well. By putting yourself in the patient's place, you will begin to understand how it feels to be a patient, and you will be able to treat real patients as you yourself would like to be treated.

CHAPTER 16 QUIZ

Listed below are the four sections included in this chapter. Read each sentence.
Fill in the blank with the number of the section from which the sentence has been
taken.

Section 1: Anatomy and Physiology
Section 2: Care of the Seizure Patient
Section 3: Artificial Eye and Hearing Aid Care
Section 4: Care of the Cerebrovascular Accident/CVA/Stroke Patient

1. _____ Paralysis of the arm and leg interferes with the ability
   to perform all activities of daily living.

2. _____ The sense organs contain specialized endings of the sensory
   neurons.

3. _____ Cleaning the patient's artificial eye is part of daily
   personal hygiene.

4. _____ The major role of the nursing assistant in caring for a
   patient having a seizure is to prevent the patient from
   injuring himself.

5. _____ The cerebrovascular accident is actually a disease of the
   circulatory system, but the results affect the nervous
   system.

6. _____ Remember, even the best hearing aid cannot restore full
   normal hearing ability.

7. _____ A thrombus is a blood clot that remains at its site of
   formation.

8. _____ Never wash a hearing aid. You will ruin it.

9. _____ The most important aspect of caring for the aphasic patient
   is patience.

10. _____ The nervous system controls and organizes all body activity.

CHAPTER 17   WARM AND COLD APPLICATIONS

WORKBOOK ASSIGNMENT #1, CHAPTER 17
WARM AND COLD APPLICATIONS

Find the list of objectives for this section. Next to each objective, write the page numbers where you can find information to help you meet these objectives.

WORKBOOK ASSIGNMENT #2, CHAPTER 17
THE PRINCIPLES OF WARM AND COLD APPLICATIONS

Read "Key Ideas: Reasons for Warm and Cold Applications" in your textbook. Study the illustrations of the "Principles of Warm and Cold Applications."

Circle HEAT or COLD after each of the following statements:

1. Blood flow is reduced in the area of application. HEAT or COLD

2. Blood vessels are dilated by the application. HEAT or COLD

3. Blood flow to the body surface is increased. HEAT or COLD

4. Increased circulation can provide the body tissues with more food and oxygen. HEAT or COLD

5. This application causes the blood vessels to contract. HEAT or COLD

6. This prevents or reduces the pain that usually goes along with swelling. HEAT or COLD

WORKBOOK ASSIGNMENT #3, CHAPTER 17
LOCALIZED OR GENERALIZED

Read the "Key Ideas: Localized and Generalized Applications" in your textbook. Study the illustrations carefully. Write G for Generalized Applications or an L for Localized Applications beside each of the following statements.

1. _____ The application is applied to the patient's whole body.

2. _____ The application is applied to a specific part or area of the patient's body.

3. _____ The application is applied to the patient's arm.

4. _____ The application is applied to the patient's neck.

5. _____ The application involves sponging the patient's body with a solution of alcohol and water.

WORKBOOK ASSIGNMENT #4, CHAPTER 17
MOIST OR DRY

Read the information titled "Moist and Dry Applications" in your textbook. Write
M for Moist or D for Dry beside each of the following descriptions.

1. _____ Water touches the patient's skin

2. _____ Compresses and soaks

3. _____ No water touches the patient's skin

4. _____ Immerse the body or body part completely in water

5. _____ Warm water bottles

6. _____ The application has a dry surface

7. _____ Sitz bath

8. _____ Water is used only inside the equipment

9. _____ Heat lamp

10. _____ Ice caps.

WORKBOOK ASSIGNMENT #5, CHAPTER 17
KEEPING THE PATIENT SAFE

Read the information titled "Keeping the Patient Safe" in your textbook.

Circle the letter of the correct response in the multiple choice questions
below.

1. To prevent burning the patient's skin, check under warm applications for:

    A. Wrinkling
    B. Too much redness
    C. Darker discoloration
    D. Swelling
    E. Both B and C.

2. If you think a patient is being burned, you should:

    A. Remove the heat application immediately
    B. Report to your head nurse or team leader at once
    C. Apply a cold application
    D. Get the patient out of bed
    E. Both A and B.

193

3. Tell the head nurse or team leader at once if the area where cold is being applied looks:

   A. Blanched
   B. Very pale
   C. Bluish
   D. White
   E. All of the above.

4. If the patient's lips, fingernails, and eyelids look blue or turn a dark color, this is cyanosis and you should:

   A. Apply a warm application.
   B. Cover the patient with extra blankets and then report to your head nurse or team leader.
   C. Stop the treatment immediately and then report to your head nurse or team leader.
   D. Report to your head nurse or team leader and then stop the treatment.
   E. Either C or D.

5. When working with an unconscious patient, protect him from a burn by:

   A. Putting a blanket between his skin and the warm water bottle or ice cap
   B. Putting a blanket over the warm water bottle or ice cap
   C. Covering him with extra blankets during the application of a warm water bottle or ice cap
   D. Applying a warm water bottle and ice cap at the same time
   E. Lowering the temperature of the water in the warm water bottle or putting less ice in the ice cap.

WORKBOOK ASSIGNMENT #6, CHAPTER 17
KEEPING THE PATIENT COMFORTABLE

Read the information titled "Keeping the Patient Comfortable" in your textbook. Write DO or DON'T in the blanks before each of the following statements.

1. _____ make sure the patient is in a position that is comfortable for him and convenient for your work.

2. _____ stop the treatment if a patient shivers during a cold application.

3. _____ cover the patient with a blanket and report to your head nurse or team leader if the patient shivers.

4. _____ put the warm water bottle or ice bag on top of the painful area.

5. _____ fill a warm water bottle or ice bag more than half full.

6. _____ dry the bottle or bag.

7. _____ check the bottle or bag for leaks by turning it upside down.

8. _____ place the bottle or bag in a flannel cover.

9. _____ let the patient lie on the warm water bottle or ice bag.

10. _____ rub the patient's skin to dry it after an application.

WORKBOOK ASSIGNMENT #7, CHAPTER 17
THE WARM WATER BOTTLE

Read the "Procedure: Applying the Warm Water Bottle" in your textbook.

Here is a list of important actions or tasks from each step in a shortened form.
The order has been mixed up. Keep your book open while you do this exercise so
you can look at the procedure to determine the correct order for this list.
Number the list from 1 to 20 to show the correct order. Number 1 is done for
you, as an example:

A. _____ Ask visitors to step out.

B. _____ Fill it half full.

C. __1__ Assemble equipment.

D. _____ Place it in a cover.

E. _____ Check skin every hour.

F. _____ Apply it gently.

G. _____ Fasten the top.

H. _____ Wash hands before beginning.

I. _____ Fill pitcher and check temperature of water.

J. _____ Place it beside, not on, a painful area.

K. _____ Tell the patient what you will do.

L. _____ Make the patient comfortable.

M. _____ Dry and check for leaks.

N. _____ Report to head nurse or team leader.

O. _____ Squeeze air out by holding bag in horizontal position and neck upright.

P. _____ Pull the curtain.

Q. _____ Wash hands at end of procedure.

R. _____ Identify the patient.

S. _____ Clean or dispose of equipment.

T. _____ Squeeze air out by placing the bag on the edge of the counter and pressing out the air.

U. _____ Check temperature every hour. Change water as necessary.

WORKBOOK ASSIGNMENT #8, CHAPTER 17
HEAT LAMPS

Read the "Procedure: Applying a Heat Lamp" and "Key Ideas: The Perineal Heat Lamp" in your textbook.

Circle the letter of the correct response.

1. Expose only the body area that is to:

   A. Be covered with the bath blankets
   B. Be measured with the tape measure
   C. Receive the heat
   D. Be examined
   E. Both B and C.

2. The part of the patient's body that is being treated should be at least _____ away from the heat lamp.

   A. 18 inches
   B. 12 inches
   C.   9 inches
   D. 24 inches
   E. 36 inches.

3. Check the skin after:

   A.   2 hours
   B. 18 minutes
   C.   5 minutes
   D. 10 minutes
   E.   1 hour.

4. There is a danger of _____ when a heat lamp is being used.

   A. Wetting the bed
   B. Poisoning
   C. Diarrhea
   D. Fire
   E. Expectoration.

5. When you are using the heat lamp as a perineal lamp, help the patient into the _____ position.

   A. Fowler's
   B. Left Sims
   C. Trendelenburg
   D. Prone
   E. Lithotomy.

WORKBOOK ASSIGNMENT #9, CHAPTER 17
AQUAMATIC K-PAD

Read the "Procedure: Applying the Aquamatic K-Pad" in your textbook.

There are 16 steps in this procedure. Each step is an action -- something for you to do. Find the key word or words in each step that tell you what to do. These are the words that show <u>action</u>. They are the doing words called verbs. The first one is done for you as an example.

1. <u>Assemble</u> .   9. _____ .

2. _____ .   10. _____ , _____ .

3. _____ .   11. _____ .

4. _____ .   12. _____ .

5. _____ .   13. _____ .

6. _____ .   14. _____ .

7. _____ .   15. _____ .

8. _____ .   16. _____ .

WORKBOOK ASSIGNMENT #10, CHAPTER 17
DISPOSABLE SITZ BATH

Read the "Procedure: Using the Disposable Sitz Bath" in your textbook.

Circle the letter <u>T</u> if the statement below is true, <u>F</u> if it is false.

T or F   1. Measure the temperature of the water with a rectal thermometer.

T or F   2. Put the plastic bowl into the toilet bowl.

T or F   3. The opening for overflow must be towards the front of the toilet.

T or F   4. Fill the water bag with water only after closing the stopcock.

T or F   5. Hang the container 18 inches higher than the bowl.

WORKBOOK ASSIGNMENT #11, CHAPTER 17
WORDS TO REMEMBER/GLOSSARY

Fill in the blanks with the vocabulary word to remember after reading the definition carefully.

1. Because there is not enough oxygen in the blood, the skin looks blue or has a gray color. This condition is often seen in the patient's lips, eyelids, and in the skin under the fingernail. In a black patient, it may appear as a darkening of color. This is called _____.

2. An application of warm or cold in which no water touches the skin is called a _____ application.

3. One in which warm or cold is applied to the entire body is called a _____ application.

4. One in which warm or cold is applied to a specific area or small part of the body is called a _____.

5. An application of warm or cold in which water touches the skin is called a _____ application.

WORKBOOK ASSIGNMENT #12, CHAPTER 17
LEARNING BY DOING

As you study the procedures in this chapter, read every step carefully. Think about the action words, the words that tell you what to do. Look at the pictures closely and read the captions. You will be able to remember what to do more easily if you try to do it after you have read about it. Learning by doing involves your whole body in the learning process, not just your eyes or ears. It is one of the most effective ways to learn.

Ask a fellow student or, if you are practicing at home, ask a friend or relative to play the part of the patient. Actually do all of the steps of the procedure several times, pretending you are a nursing assistant caring for several patients. Work slowly at first. Look at the textbook whenever you are not sure about what to do next. Practice in this way many times until you can work quickly, and you no longer need to look at the textbook.

Switch roles with your partner, and take several turns at being the patient. Not only will this give your partner a chance to learn the procedure, but you will benefit as well. By putting yourself in the patient's place, you will begin to understand how it feels to be a patient, and you will be able to treat real patients as you yourself would like to be treated.

Here is a list of the procedures you learned in this chapter. Fill in the blanks with the letter of the correct response.

A. Applying the Warm Compress
B. Applying the Cold Compress
C. Applying the Cold Soak
D. Applying the Warm Soak
E. Applying the Warm Water Bottle
F. Applying the Ice Bag, Ice Cap, or Ice Collar
G. Applying the Commercial Unit Cold Pack
H. Applying the Commercial Unit Heat Pack
I. Applying a Heat Lamp
J. The Perineal Heat Lamp
K. Applying the Aquamatic K-pad
L. Using the Disposable Sitz Bath
M. Using the Portable Chair Type or Built-in Sitz Bath
N. The Alcohol Sponge Bath

1. Which of these are moist heat applications? _____, _____, _____, _____, _____.

2. Which of these are dry heat applications? _____, _____, _____, _____.

3. Which of these are moist cold applications? _____, _____, _____.

4. Which of these are dry cold applications? _____, _____.

Circle the letter of the correct response.

5. Heat or warm applications _____ blood vessels.

    A. Contract
    B. Discolor
    C. Expand.

6. Cold applications _____ blood vessels.

    A. Contract
    B. Discolor
    C. Expand.

Read the following list of actions. Decide which action is the best thing to do in the situation. Put the letter for that correct action in the blank. Choose the best response for each situation in the same way.

ACTIONS

A. Stop the treatment and report to your head nurse or team leader.
B. Use a bath thermometer to check the temperature.
C. Dry the patient's skin by patting gently.

7. After removing a patient's foot from a soak, _____.

8. If the patient says he feels weak or faint, _____.

9. If the patient's skin is red, _____.

10. After filling the pitcher with warm water, _____.

CHAPTER 18   ADMISSION, TRANSFER, AND DISCHARGE

SECTION 1

WORKBOOK ASSIGNMENT #1, CHAPTER 18, SECTION 1
ADMISSION

Find the list of objectives for this section. Next to each objective, write the page numbers where you can find information to help you meet these objectives.

WORKBOOK ASSIGNMENT #2, CHAPTER 18, SECTION 1
ADMITTING THE PATIENT

Read "Key Ideas" and "Procedure: Admitting the Patient" in your textbook.

Circle ALL the correct answers, as the questions below may have more than one response.

1. Which of the following is the single most important tool in providing quality patient care:

   A. The discharge plan
   B. The nursing care plan
   C. Admission check list
   D. Intake and output sheet
   E. Preoperative check list.

2. Which of the following items are necessary equipment for admitting the patient?

   A. Urine specimen container
   B. Thermometer
   C. Wheelchair
   D. Disposable enema bag, tubing, and clamp
   E. Portable scale.

3. Which of the following things should you try to observe when filling out the admission checklist?

   A. Color of stool
   B. How much the patient has eaten
   C. Unusual behavior
   D. Bruises, marks, rashes, or broken skin
   E. Patient's ability to speak and understand English.

4. Which of the following questions should you ask the patient (or a visitor if the patient is unable to answer) when filling out the admission check list?

   A. Are you allergic to any foods?
   B. Are you allergic to any drugs?
   C. Do you wear dentures?
   D. Do you wear glasses?
   E. Do you wear a hearing aid?

5. Which of the following things should you do to familiarize the patient with his surroundings?

    A. Show him where the signal cord is and how to work it.
    B. Show him how to operate the television.
    C. Explain how the bed works and show him how to adjust it.
    D. Ask visitors to leave the room while you finish admitting the patient.
    E. Raise the side rails of the bed.

WORKBOOK ASSIGNMENT #3, CHAPTER 18, SECTION 1
WEIGHING AND MEASURING THE PATIENT'S HEIGHT

Read the "Procedure: Weighing and Measuring the Height of a Patient Who is Able to Stand" in your textbook. Circle the letter T if the statement below is true, F if it is false.

T or F   1. Place a paper towel on the stand of the scale to protect the patient's feet.

T or F   2. The patient should be nude for an accurate weight.

T or F   3. The measuring rod should rest on the patient's shoulders.

T or F   4. Patients on complete bed rest cannot be weighed.

T or F   5. Note the patient's weight by adding the numbers on both the large balance and the small balance bar.

WORKBOOK ASSIGNMENT #4, CHAPTER 18, SECTION 1
THE PATIENT'S VALUABLES

Read "Key Ideas" and the "Procedure: Caring for the Patient's Valuables" in your textbook.

Circle the letter T if the statement below is true, F if it is false.

T or F   1. Make a list including every item of value.

T or F   2. A good description of a necklace might be, "a gold chain with a heart-shaped pendant containing three diamonds."

T or F   3. Count the patient's money and record the amount.

T or F   4. Be sure the patient sees you close the valuables envelope.

T or F   5. A good way to describe the patient's watch would be, "a silver-colored digital watch with a silver-colored metal band."

WORKBOOK ASSIGNMENT #5, CHAPTER 18, SECTION 2
TRANSFERRING THE PATIENT

Find the list of objectives for this section. Next to each objective, write the page numbers where you can find information to help you meet these objectives.

WORKBOOK ASSIGNMENT #6, CHAPTER 18, SECTION 2
TRANSFERRING THE PATIENT

Read "Key Ideas" and the "Procedure: Transferring the Patient" in your textbook. Fill in the blanks with the words listed below:

introduce   ready   after   number   transport

1. Check to be sure the new unit is _____ to receive the patient.

2. You may have to _____ the patient by stretcher or wheelchair to his new room.

3. If you are moving the patient's belongings and equipment on a cart, move them _____ the patient is settled and safe in his new unit.

4. Tell the patient that his family and friends will be given his new room _____.

5. _____ the patient to his new roommates and nursing staff.

SECTION 3

WORKBOOK ASSIGNMENT #7, CHAPTER 18
DISCHARGE PLANNING

Find the list of objectives for this section. Next to each objective, write the page numbers where you can find information to help you meet these objectives.

WORKBOOK ASSIGNMENT #8, CHAPTER 18
DISCHARGING THE PATIENT

Read "Key Ideas" and the "Procedure: Discharging the Patient" in your textbook.

Circle the word BEFORE or AFTER in each statement.

1. Help the patient into the wheelchair BEFORE or AFTER bringing it to the patient's bedside.

2. Get the discharge slip from the head nurse or team leader BEFORE or AFTER wheeling the patient off the floor.

3. Wipe the entire wheelchair with an antiseptic solution BEFORE or AFTER taking the release form and wheelchair back to the floor.

4. Strip the linen from the bed BEFORE or AFTER notifying environmental service that the discharge has taken place and the unit is ready to be cleaned.

5. Be sure the discharge plan has been explained to the patient BEFORE or AFTER wheeling him off the floor.

WORKBOOK ASSIGNMENT #9, CHAPTER 18, SECTION 2
WORDS TO REMEMBER/GLOSSARY

Fill in the blanks with the vocabulary word to remember after reading the definition carefully.

1. The administrative procedures followed when a person enters a health care institution and becomes an inpatient. _____ covers the period from the time the patient enters the door of the hospital until he is settled in his room.

2. When a patient is getting well or recovering after an illness or surgery, he is called a _____ patient.

3. This word has two meanings. 1) When a patient is ready to leave the hospital, the hospital's business office helps him with his arrangements and with the checking out procedure. This process is called _____. 2) The term used for unusual material coming out from some part of the body. For example, after a patient has had surgery, there may be a _____ of some kind of fluid coming out through the incision.

WORKBOOK ASSIGNMENT #10, CHAPTER 18, SECTION 2
LEARNING BY DOING

As you study the procedures in this chapter, read every step carefully. Think about the action words, the words that tell you what to do. Look at the picture closely and read the captions. You will be able to remember what to do more easily if you try to do it after you have read about it. Learning by doing involves your whole body in the learning process, not just your eyes or ears. It is one of the most effective ways to learn.

Ask a fellow student or, if you are practicing at home, ask a friend or relative to play the part of the patient. Actually do all of the steps of the procedure several times, pretending you are a nursing assistant caring for several patients. Work slowly at first. Look at the textbook whenever you are not sure about what to do next. Practice in this way many times until you can work quickly, and you no longer need to look at the textbook.

Switch roles with your partner, and take several turns at being the patient. Not only will this give your partner a chance to learn the procedure, but you will benefit as well. By putting yourself in the patient's place, you will begin to understand how it feels to be a patient, and you will be able to treat real patients as you yourself would like to be treated.

CHAPTER 18 QUIZ

Here is a list of procedures covered in this chapter:

A. Admitting the Patient
B. Weighing and Measuring the Height of a Patient Who is Able to Stand
C. Caring For the Patient's Valuables
D. Transferring the Patient
E. Discharging the Patient

Fill in the blanks with the letters of the correct procedures.

1. Which procedure involves welcoming a new patient to the health care institution? _____

2. Which procedure involves moving the patient and his belongings to a new unit? _____

3. Which procedure involves making a list of the patient's jewelry, money, and other valuable possessions? _____

4. Which procedure involves a patient who is ready to leave the health care institution? _____

5. In which procedure does the patient have to stand up very straight? _____

6. Which procedure might be done because the patient asked for a private room, but none were available when he was admitted? _____

7. Which two procedures involve stripping linen from a bed? _____ and _____

8. Which procedure involves filling out an admission check list? _____

9. Which procedure involves adding the numbers on both large and small balances to determine the number you will report? _____

10. In which procedure would the patient receive written instructions from the head nurse or team leader? _____

CHAPTER 19   PHYSICAL EXAMINATIONS

SECTION 1

WORKBOOK ASSIGNMENT #1, CHAPTER 19, SECTION 1
YOUR ROLE IN THE PHYSICAL EXAMINATION

Find the list of objectives for this section. Next to each objective, write the page numbers where you can find information to help you meet these objectives.

WORKBOOK ASSIGNMENT #2, CHAPTER 19, SECTION 1
THE EXAMINATION

Read "Rules to Follow: During the Physician's Examination" in your textbook.

Write <u>DO</u> or <u>DON'T</u> in the blank next to each statement below.

1. _____ touch the tongue depressor with your fingers.

2. _____ discard the tongue depressor after the examination.

3. _____ pull the covering completely off the tongue depressor as the doctor takes it.

4. _____ turn on the flashlight before handing it to the doctor.

5. _____ remove the patient's gown when the doctor is ready to examine the patient.

6. _____ place a towel across the patient's chest while the doctor examines the patient's abdomen.

7. _____ remove the drape when the doctor has finished examining the abdomen.

8. _____ expose one leg at a time when the doctor examines the patient's legs and feet.

9. _____ place the drape on the floor for the patient to stand on if the doctor asks the patient to stand.

10. _____ remake the entire bed when the examination is finished.

SECTION 2

WORKBOOK ASSIGNMENT #3, CHAPTER 19, SECTION 2
DRAPING AND POSITIONING THE PATIENT

Find the list of objectives for this section. Next to each objective, write the page numbers where you can find information to help you meet these objectives.

Read "Key Ideas: Draping and Positioning the Patient" in your textbook.

Study the pictures and the explanations under each one carefully. The best way
to study and remember these positions is to practice them yourself. Lie in the
first position while looking at its picture in your textbook. Say its name five
times. Repeat this for all 12 positions. Have a friend call out the names of
the positions and see if you can do them without looking in the book. Here is a
list of the positions. Write the letter of the position name beside its matching
picture.

A. Horizontal recumbent position
B. Side-lying position
C. Dorsal recumbent position
D. Trendelenburg position
E. Prone position
F. Reverse trendelenburg position

G. Dorsal lithotomy position
H. Fowler's position at 45°
I. Left Sims' position
J. Knee-chest position
K. Left lateral position

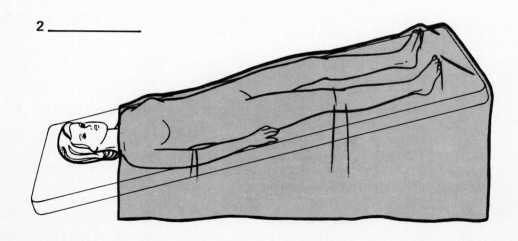

1 _____

2 _____

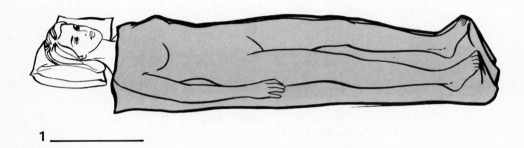

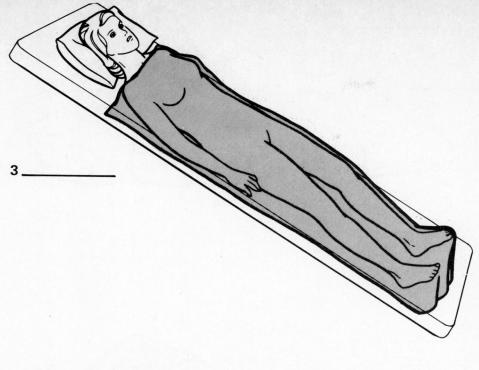

3 _____

4 _____

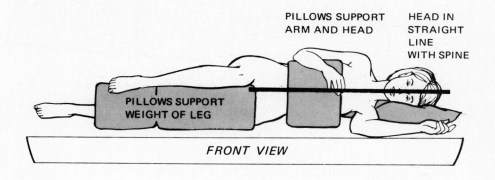

PILLOWS SUPPORT ARM AND HEAD

HEAD IN STRAIGHT LINE WITH SPINE

PILLOWS SUPPORT WEIGHT OF LEG

FRONT VIEW

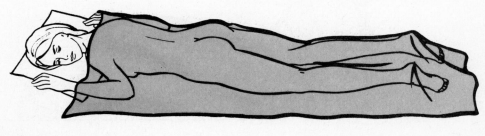

5 _____

6 _____

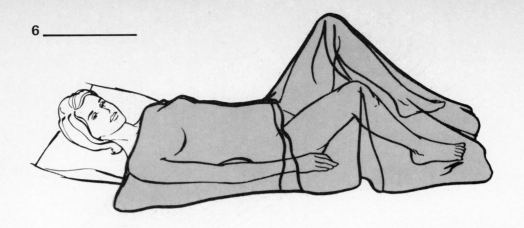

7 _____

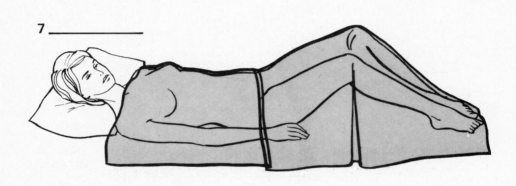

8 _____

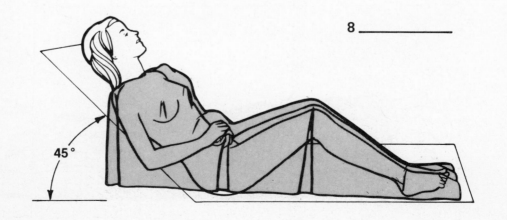

45°

9 _____

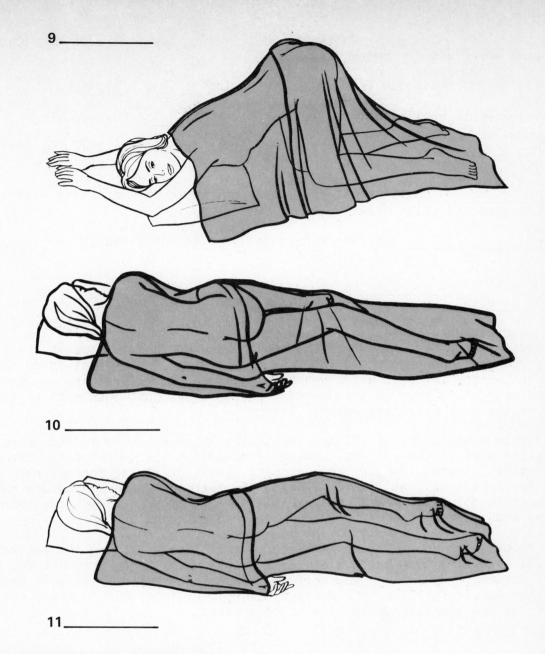

10 _____

11 _____

WORKBOOK ASSIGNMENT #5, CHAPTER 19
WORDS TO REMEMBER/GLOSSARY

Fill in the blanks with the vocabulary word to remember after reading the definition carefully.

1. Covering a patient or parts of the patient's body with a sheet, blanket, bath blanket, or other material is called _____ and is usually done during physical examination of the patient.

2. A covering used during an examination or an operation to cover the patient's body is called a _____.

3. The patient's position when the head of the bed is at a 45° angle is called _____ _____.

211

4. In _____ position the patient lies on her back with her legs spread apart and her knees bent.

5. Lying on one's stomach is referred to as the _____ position.

6. Lying down or reclining is called the _____ position.

7. The _____ lying position refers to the patient lying on his/her side.

8. _____ position refers to the patient on the left side with the right knee and thigh drawn up.

9. The _____ position refers to lying on one's back.

WORKBOOK ASSIGNMENT #6, CHAPTER 19
LEARNING BY DOING

As you study the procedures in this chapter, read every step carefully. Think about the action words, the words that tell you what to do. Look at the pictures closely and read the captions. You will be able to remember what to do more easily if you try to do it after you have read about it. Learning by doing involves your whole body in the learning process, not just your eyes or ears. It is one of the most effective ways to learn.

Ask a fellow student or, if you are practicing at home, ask a friend or relative to play the part of the patient. Actually do all of the steps of the procedure several times, pretending you are a nursing assistant caring for several patients. Work slowly at first. Look at the textbook whenever you are not sure about what to do next. Practice in this way many times until you can work quickly, and you no longer need to look at the textbook.

Switch roles with your partner, and take several turns at being the patient. Not only will this give your partner a chance to learn the procedure, but you will benefit as well. By putting yourself in the patient's place, you will begin to understand how it feels to be a patient, and you will be able to treat real patients as you yourself would like to be treated.

Fill in the blank with the word <u>PREPARE</u> if the task is done while preparing the patient for a physical examination. Write <u>DURING</u> in the blank if the task is done during the physician's examination.

1. _____ Tear the paper disposable covering on the tongue depressor halfway down.

2. _____ Remove the top sheet and bedspread from the bed without exposing the patient.

3. _____ Offer the bedpan or urinal to the patient.

4. _____ Place a towel or gown over the patient's chest and fold the bedding down to the patient's hips.

Circle the letter <u>T</u> if the statement below is true, <u>F</u> if it is false.

T or F   5.   Left Sims' position has the patient on her left side with the right knee bent against the abdomen. The left knee is also bent, but not as much.

T or F   6.   Trendelenburg position has the patient lying on her back. The bed is at an incline so the patient's head is lower than her feet.

WORKBOOK ASSIGNMENT #1, CHAPTER 20, SECTION 1
PREOPERATIVE NURSING CARE

Find the list of objectives for this section. Next to each objective, write the
page numbers where you can find information to help you meet these objectives.

WORKBOOK ASSIGNMENT #2, CHAPTER 20, SECTION 1
PREOPERATIVE CARE

Read "Key Ideas: Preoperative Care" in your textbook.

Match the terms in Column A with the definitions in Column B. Write the correct
letter in the space provided.

Column A		Column B	
_____	1. Post	A.	Operation or surgery
_____	2. Postoperative	B.	Before
_____	3. Operative	C.	After
_____	4. Preoperative	D.	Before surgery
_____	5. Pre	E.	After surgery

WORKBOOK ASSIGNMENT #3, CHAPTER 20, SECTION 1
THE PREOPERATIVE CHECK LIST

It is 7 a.m., and you have just arrived at work. Your head nurse gives you the
preoperative check list for Mr. Green. She tells you that he is scheduled to
have surgery in two hours, explains the care you are to give him, and that she
would like you to fill out the portion of the check list labeled "Morning of
Surgery."

After greeting Mr. Green and introducing yourself, you measure his vital signs,
height, and weight. His temperature is 100.2°F. His pulse is 68 beats per
minute. His respirations are 16 times per minute. His blood pressure is 120/80.
His weight is 186 pounds, and his weight is 5 feet 11 inches.

He is able to bathe himself and brush his own teeth. You obtain a urine sample
and send it to the lab. After his bath, he dresses in a clean hospital gown.
There is no urinary drainage bag. You ask him if he is allergic or sensitive to
any drugs and he answers, "none." He has no false teeth, prostheses, nail
polish, sanitary belts, makeup, hair pieces, or hair pins. He removes his
wedding ring and his contact lenses, which he gives to his wife to take home.

The head nurse comes in at 8 a.m. to give him his preoperative medications and
the siderails are up. At 8:30 a.m., the transportation attendant arrives and
takes him to the operating room by stretcher.

Use the information above to fill in the sample Preoperative Check List.

SAMPLE PREOPERATIVE CHECK LIST

COMPLETED BY NURSING ASSISTANT

EVENING BEFORE SURGERY

Patient's Name: _____

Identify the patient by checking his identification bracelet: Yes_____ No_____

Skin prep done by _____ at _____ P.M.

Skin prep checked by _____ at _____ P.M.

Food restrictions, if any, explained to the patient: Yes_____ No_____

"NPO AFTER MIDNIGHT" sign put on patient's bed and explained
   to the patient: Yes_____ No_____

Enema administered by _____ at _____ P.M.

MORNING OF SURGERY:

Bath?   Yes_____ No_____

Oral hygiene?   Yes_____ No_____

False teeth (dentures) and removable bridges removed?   Yes_____ No_____

Jewelry and pierced earrings removed?   Yes_____ No_____

Hairpiece, wig, hairpins removed?   Yes_____ No_____

Lipstick, makeup, and false eyelashes removed?   Yes_____ No_____

Sanitary belt removed?   Yes_____ No_____

Nail polish removed?   Yes_____ No_____

Eyeglasses and contact lenses removed?   Yes_____ No_____

Prostheses (artificial hearing aid, eye, leg, arm, and so
   forth) removed?   Yes_____ No_____

All clothing removed except clean hospital gown?   Yes_____ No_____

Patient allergic or sensitive to drugs?   Yes_____ No_____

Preop urine specimen obtained and sent to lab?   Yes_____ No_____

Urinary drainage bag emptied?   Yes_____ No_____

Side rails up in position?   Yes_____ No_____

Temperature _____   Pulse _____   Respiration _____

Blood pressure _____   Weight _____lbs.   Height _____ft. _____in.

Time patient leaves for the operating room: _____

Observations: _____

Signature: _____

WORKBOOK ASSIGNMENT #4, CHAPTER 20, SECTION 1
PREPARING THE PATIENT'S UNIT

Circle the letters of all the tasks you should do to prepare the patient's unit
to receive the patient after surgery.

A. Bring the I.V. pole to the bedside.
B. Attach a urine drainage bag to the bed frame.
C. Strip the linen from the bed.
D. Make the operating room bed.
E. Mop the floor.
F. Place tissues and emesis basin only on the bedside table.
G. Remove the drinking water.
H. Place a clean gown at the foot of the bed.

WORKBOOK ASSIGNMENT #5, CHAPTER 20, SECTION 1
PREOPERATIVE CARE

Decide which of the following actions is the best thing to do in the following
situations. Put the letter for that correct action in the space after the
situation:

ACTIONS

A. Listen and show interest in what the patient says.
B. Report this to your head nurse or team leader.
C. Check or record this information on the preoperative check list.

SITUATIONS

1. If you notice the patient is sneezing, sniffling, or coughing, _____
2. After you post the NPO sign and explain it to the patient, _____
3. After administering an enema the evening before surgery, _____
4. The patient wants to talk a lot. _____
5. The patient expresses concern for his family. _____
6. The patient's temperature rises the evening before surgery. _____
7. The patient begins to talk about the possibility of death or serious
    complications. _____
8. You prepared the patient's skin as instructed at 7:30 p.m. _____
9. On the morning of surgery, you helped the patient remove false
    teeth, jewelry, hairpins, and nail polish. _____

216

10. The patient complains of chest pains. _____
11. After weighing and measuring the patient, _____
12. After obtaining a urine specimen, _____.

WORKBOOK ASSIGNMENT #6, CHAPTER 20, SECTION 2
POSTOPERATIVE NURSING CARE

Find the list of objectives for this section. Next to each objective, write the page numbers where you can find information to help you meet these objectives.

WORKBOOK ASSIGNMENT #7, CHAPTER 20, SECTION 2
POSTOPERATIVE CARE

Read "Key Ideas: The Postoperative Patient" in your textbook. Decide which action is the best response for each situation. Fill in the blank next to each statement with the letter of the correct action.

ACTIONS

A. Signal for your head nurse or team leader immediately.
B. Turn the patient.
C. Change the patient's gown and bed linens.

SITUATIONS

1. You notice that I am a patient who is bleeding and the blood is bright red. What should you do? _____

2. I am a patient who has been in the same position for two hours. What should you do for me? _____

3. I am a postoperative patient. My gown and linens have become wet. What should you do for me? _____

4. I am a postoperative patient. You just noticed a rise in my blood pressure. What should you do? _____

5. My lips and fingernails are turning very pale or blue. What should you do?

   _____

6. You have just measured my vital signs, and my pulse is below 60. What should you do? _____

WORKBOOKS ASSIGNMENT #8, CHAPTER 20, SECTION 2
DEEP-BREATHING EXERCISES

Read "Key Ideas: Deep-Breathing Exercises" and the "Procedure: Helping the Patient With Deep-Breathing Exercises" in your textbook. Keep your book open to the procedure. Circle the letter of the correct response.

1. You are helping a patient with deep-breathing exercises. You have explained what you are going to do to the patient. You pulled the curtain around the bed and offered the bedpan. What should you do next?

    A. Place the pillow on the patient's abdomen for support.
    B. Dangle the patient's legs over the side of the bed, if allowed.
    C. Identify the patient by checking the identification bracelet.

2. If the patient is not permitted to dangle his legs, what should you do?

    A. Place the patient in as much of a sitting position as possible.
    B. Do the exercises with the patient lying down.
    C. Prop the patient up with the pillows.

3. You placed a pillow on the patient's abdomen and asked him to breathe deeply 10 times. What should you do while he breathes?

    A. Take care of another patient.
    B. Count his pulse.
    C. Count the respirations out loud to the patient.

SECTION 3

WORKBOOK ASSIGNMENT #9, CHAPTER 20, SECTION 3
INTRAVENOUS INFUSION EQUIPMENT

Find the list of objectives for this section. Next to each objective, write the page numbers where you can find information to help you meet these objectives.

WORKBOOK ASSIGNMENT #10, CHAPTER 20, SECTION 3
INTRAVENOUS INFUSION EQUIPMENT

Read "Key Ideas: Intravenous Infusion Equipment" and the "Procedure: Changing the Patient's Gown with Intravenous Tubing" in your textbook. Keep your book open to the procedure.

1. You are changing Miss Farrari's gown. You have just pulled the curtain around the bed for privacy and untied the gown. Which of the following three tasks should you do next?

    A. Place the soiled gown on a chair.
    B. Remove the arm without the intravenous tubing from the sleeve.
    C. Move the sleeve down the arm, over the tubing, and up to the bottle or container.

2. You have just removed Miss Farrari's arm without the intravenous tubing from the sleeve. Which of the following three tasks should you do next?

    A. Slip the gown over the bottle and return the bottle or container to its hook.
    B. Remove the container or bottle from the hook.
    C. Carefully remove the gown from the arm with the intravenous tubing, considering the tube and container of fluid as part of the arm.

3. To remove the gown from the arm with the intravenous tubing, you are supposed to think of the tube and the container of fluid as part of the arm. To do this you should:

   A. Move the sleeve down the arm, over the tubing, and up to the bottle or container.
   B. Remove the container or bottle from the hook.
   C. Be careful not to lower the bottle below the area on the patient's arm where the needle is inserted.

4. You have just removed the container or bottle from the hook. You did not lower the bottle below the area on the patient's arm where the needle is inserted. Which of the following three tasks should you do next?

   A. Place the soiled gown on chair.
   B. Untie the gown.
   C. Slip the gown over the bottle and return the bottle or container to its hook.

5. To put the clean gown on the patient, you will also think of the bottle or container and the tube as part of the patient's arm. Which of the following three tasks should you do first?

   A. Slip the sleeve of the gown over the bottle or container quickly.
   B. Carefully lift the bottle from the hook without moving it below the area on the patient's arm where the needle has been inserted.
   C. Make the patient comfortable.

6. While putting the clean gown on your patient, you have just lifted the bottle from the hook and you are holding it in your hand above the patient's arm. Which of the following three tasks should you do next?

   A. Slip the sleeve of the gown over the bottle or container quickly.
   B. Tie the back straps for the patient's comfort.
   C. Replace the bottle on the hook.

7. You have just slipped the sleeve of the gown over the bottle and replaced the bottle on the hook. Which of the following three tasks should you do next?

   A. Make sure the patient is not lying on top of the intravenous tubing.
   B. Slip the gown over the other arm.
   C. Slip the gown down the tube and then over the patient's arm.

SECTION 4
_____

WORKBOOK ASSIGNMENT #11, CHAPTER 20, SECTION 4
CARE OF THE OSTOMY PATIENT

Find the list of objectives for this section. Next to each objective, write the page numbers where you can find information to help you meet these objectives.

WORKBOOK ASSIGNMENT #12, CHAPTER 20, SECTION 4
CARING FOR AN OSTOMY

Read the "Procedure: Caring for an Ostomy" in your textbook. Keep your book open to the procedure. In each of the following situations, a nursing assistant is caring for a patient with an ostomy, but there will be one step missing or forgotten. Write the number, from the procedure in your textbook, of the missing step in the blank.

1. Mr. Kinley covered his patient with a bath blanket and without exposing him, fan-folded the top sheet and bedspread to the foot of the bed under the blanket. He placed the emesis basin within easy reach and filled the wash basin half full with water at 115°F (46.1°C). Between steps 7 and 10, one step has been forgotten. Which one is missing? _____

2. Miss Green removed the soiled plastic stoma bag from the belt. After opening the belt, she wet and soaped the washcloth. She washed the entire ostomy area with a gentle circular motion. Between steps 11 and 14, one step has been forgotten. Which one is missing? _____

3. Mrs. Taylor rinsed the entire area very well. She applied a small amount of lubricant around the ostomy. After wiping off any excess, she put a clean belt and stoma bag on the patient. Between steps 15 and 18, one step has been forgotten. Which one is missing? _____

4. After making the patient comfortable, Mr. Kinley removed all used equipment and disposed of waste material. He discarded all disposable equipment, cleaned the bedpan, and put it away. He washed his hands and reported to his head nurse. Between steps 21 and 27, one step has been forgotten. Which one is missing? _____

WORKBOOK ASSIGNMENT #13, CHAPTER 20, SECTION 4
THE OSTOMY

Read "Key Ideas: The Ostomy" in your textbook.

Fill in the blanks with the words listed below.

abdomen   belt   ostomy appliance   rectum
bag   feces   surgical procedure   stoma

1. The creation of an ostomy is an _____.

2. The new opening is created on the _____.

3. The opening is for the release of _____ from the body.

4. The opening is called a _____.

5. The stoma is created surgically to change the path of the patient's feces from the _____.

6. A person with a stoma must wear an _____.

7. The ostomy appliance is a collecting _____.

8. The appliance is held over the opening by special types of adhesive material and/or a _____ .

SECTION 5

WORKBOOK ASSIGNMENT #14, CHAPTER 20, SECTION 5
BINDERS AND ELASTIC BANDAGES

Find the list of objectives for this section. Next to each objective, write the page numbers where you can find information to help you meet these objectives.

WORKBOOK ASSIGNMENT #15, CHAPTER 20, SECTION 5
BINDERS

Read "Key Ideas: Binders" and "Rules to Follow" in your textbook.

Fill in the blanks with the words listed below.

bandages	reddened	support
smooth	bedsores	pressure

1. Binders give _____ to a weakened body part.

2. Binders hold dressings and _____ in place.

3. Binders put _____ on parts of the body.

4. Keep the binder _____ and clean.

5. _____ can be caused by wrinkled or wet binders.

6. Watch for _____ areas on the patient's skin.

WORKBOOK ASSIGNMENT #16, CHAPTER 20, SECTION 5
ELASTIC STOCKINGS AND BANDAGES

Read the information titled "Using Elastic Stockings and Elastic Bandages, Applying Anti-Embolism Elastic Stockings, Elastic Bandages" and the "Procedure: Applying Elastic Bandages" in your textbook.

Circle the letter T if the statement below is true, F if it is false.

T or F 1. Anti-embolism elastic stockings should be applied while the patient is sitting in a chair.

T or F 2. Smooth out all wrinkles and be sure the stocking is pulled up firmly.

T or F 3. Check for paleness, coldness, blueness, pain, swelling, or numbness once per shift.

T or F 4. Anchor the bandage by two circular turns around the body part at its smallest point.

WORKBOOK ASSIGNMENT #17, CHAPTER 20
WORDS TO REMEMBER/GLOSSARY

Read the definition carefully, then fill in the blanks with the vocabulary word to remember.

1. The preparation for making the patient's abdomen ready for surgery includes thorough cleansing of the skin and careful shaving of the body hair in the abdominal area. This procedure is called Abdominal _____.

2. Refers to the injection of fluids into a vein. Foods in liquid form and medications can be put into the patient's body in this way, which is known as _____ _____.

3. Loss of feeling or sensation in part or all of the body. Local _____ is the loss of sensation in a part of the body. General anesthesia is complete loss of sensation in the entire body.

4. Throwing up, when the contents of the stomach are cast up and out of the mouth, is called _____.

WORKBOOK ASSIGNMENT #18, CHAPTER 20
LEARNING BY DOING

As you study the procedure in this chapter, read every step carefully. Think about the action words, the words that tell you what to do. Look at the pictures closely and read the captions. You will be able to remember what to do more easily if you try to do it after you have read about it. Learning by doing involves your whole body in the learning process, not just your eyes or ears. It is one of the most effective ways to learn.

Ask a fellow student or, if you are practicing at home, ask a friend or relative to play the part of the patient. Actually do all of the steps of the procedure several times, pretending you are a nursing assistant caring for several patients. Work slowly at first. Look at the textbook whenever you are not sure about what to do next. Practice in this way many times until you can work quickly, and you no longer need to look at the textbook.

Switch roles with your partners, and take several turns at being the patient. Not only will this give your partner a chance to learn the procedure, but you will benefit as well. By putting yourself in the patient's place, you will begin to understand how it feels to be a patient, and you will be able to treat real patients as you yourself would like to be treated.

Circle the letter of the correct response. There may be more than one answer for each question:

1. Circle all the items you would remove from the patient on the morning of surgery.

   A. Nail polish
   B. Dentures
   C. Jewelry
   D. Blankets
   E. Hospital gown.

2. On the morning of surgery, patients usually _____.

   A. Aren't hungry or thirsty
   B. Eat a hearty breakfast
   C. Are not permitted to eat or drink anything
   D. Can have liquids only
   E. Can eat whatever they want.

3. It is important to make the patient's body as clean as possible:

   A. To prevent chest complications
   B. To prevent infections
   C. To make the patient more comfortable
   D. To regulate the vital signs
   E. Both B and C.

4. Preoperative care is given:

   A. Before the operation
   B. After the operation
   C. During the operation
   D. While shaving the patient
   E. Both A and D.

5. In caring for the postoperative patient, you will be watching for certain signs. When you observe these, you should signal the head nurse or team leader immediately. Which one of the following does <u>not</u> belong in the list?

   A. The patient is breathing in an irregular way.
   B. There is sudden, bright red bleeding where the patient had his operation.
   C. The patient says he is hungry.
   D. The patient is unusually restless.
   E. The patient says he is very thirsty.

6. When a patient is under the influence of special medications that cause a loss of feeling, he is in a state of:

   A. Anesthetic
   B. General anesthetic

C. Unconsciousness
D. Anesthesia
E. Anesthesiologist.

7. Postoperative care means taking care of the patient:

    A. Before an operation
    B. After an operation
    C. During anesthesia
    D. During surgery
    E. Until the anesthetic wears off.

8. A postoperative patient should be turned to a new position every:

    A. Hour
    B. 30 minutes
    C. Four hours
    D. Time he appears restless
    E. Two hours.

9. To expand the lungs, assist in bringing up lung secretions, and to help in preventing postoperative pneumonia, you should:

    A. Help the patient with deep-breathing exercises
    B. Encourage the first voiding after surgery
    C. Apply anti-embolism stockings
    D. Change the patient's position every two hours
    E. Call the patient by his first name when he awakens.

10. To prep--where you shave from the nipple line on male patient, and from below the breasts on female patients, down to and including the pubic area--is known as:

    A. Th thoracic prep
    B. The vaginal prep
    C. The abdominal prep
    D. The scrotal prep
    E. None of the above.

Circle the letter T if the statement below is true, F if it is false.

T or F   11. A nursing assistant never touches the clamp on intravenous tubing.

T or F   12. After changing the gown of a patient with an intravenous tubing, the nursing assistant should not report that all the solution has run out of the container.

T or F   13. Intravenous tubing should have some blood in it.

T or F   14. An ostomy is a surgically created opening in the abdomen.

CHAPTER 21   GERIATRIC CARE

WORKBOOK ASSIGNMENT #1, CHAPTER 21
GERIATRIC CARE

Find the list of objectives for this section. Next to each objective, write the page numbers where you can find information to help you meet these objectives.

WORKBOOK ASSIGNMENT #2, CHAPTER 21
GERIATRIC PATIENT CARE

Read "Key Ideas: The Geriatric Patient" in your textbook. Complete each statement with the letter of the correct nursing task listed below.

A.   Getting in and out of bed or walking from room to room
B.   The use of a cane or walker
C.   Give frequent and thorough skin care
D.   Urge the patient to move about as often as he is able
E.   Turn the patient many times each day
F.   Treating him with kindness and respect.

1.   If your patient has poor circulation and dry, flaky, wrinkled skin, then it is your responsibility to _____.

2.   If your patient is unsteady on his feet, he may benefit from _____.

3.   If your patient's problems are related to lack of physical activity, then it is your responsibility to _____.

4.   You can show sensitivity to the emotional needs of your patient by _____.

5.   If the patient is helpless or nonambulatory, then it is your responsibility to _____.

6.   Some patients may need extra assistance when _____.

WORKBOOK ASSIGNMENT #3, CHAPTER 21
THE GERIATRIC PATIENT

Read "Key Ideas: The Geriatric Patient" in your textbook.

Match the items listed in Column A with the correct description in Column B.
Write the correct letter in the blank provided.

Column A	Column B
_____1. Skin	A. Brittle, fracture easily
_____2. Joints	B. May wear dentures
_____3. Muscle tone	C. Dry, flaky, wrinkled
_____4. Appetite	D. Frequent urination
_____5. Bones	E. Stiffness
_____6. Hair	F. Detecting heat, pain, cold
_____7. Teeth	G. Neglectful of personal care
_____8. Hearing	H. May decrease
_____9. Central nervous system	I. Change of color
_____10. Behavior	J. Louder talking

WORKBOOK ASSIGNMENT #4
GERIATRIC CARE

Read Chapter 21 "Geriatric Care" in your textbook.

Circle the letter of the correct respose in the multiple choice questions below.
There may be more than one correct answer.

1. If a patient does not seem to know where he is or seems to be speaking to
    people who are not in the room, you should:

    A. Call your supervisor immediately.
    B. Tell the patient the time and day and where he/she is.
    C. Call an ambulance.
    D. Tell the patient who you are and why you are there.
    E. Give the patient a back rub to stimulate circulation.

2. Assisting with _____ will be part of your job when caring for the bed-
    bound geriatric patient.

    A. Food service
    B. Range of motion exercises
    C. Activities of daily living
    D. Recording of intake and output
    E. All of the above.

3. Your responsibilities for meeting the psychosocial needs of the geriatric patient include:

    A. Maintaining a safe environment
    B. Being a good listener
    C. Watching television
    D. Providing for the patient's privacy
    E. A, B, and D.

4. Along with the normal body changes that occur as a person grows older, there are many chronic disease/conditions that may result including:

    A. Cerebral vascular accident
    B. Appendicitis
    C. Arteriosclerosis
    D. Whooping cough
    E. A and C.

5. When geriatric patient appears to be confused, you should:

    A. Give him/her a drink of cold water
    B. Stay away from him
    C. Give him/her something to read
    D. Talk to him/her gently. Repeat frequently where he/she is (hospital, long-term care facility, or at home), the date, the time, and what you are trying to do for him/her.

WORKBOOK ASSIGNMENT #5, CHAPTER 21
COMMON CHRONIC CONDITIONS

Read the information titled "Common Chronic Diseases/Conditions" in your textbook. Study the chart carefully. Match the description with its name by writing the letter of the condition or disease in the blank below.

A. Arthritis   E. Cancer
B. Cataracts   F. Cerebral vascular accident
C. Parkinson's disease   G. Diabetes
D. Heart disease

1. _____ A change in cell growth causing pain and loss of weight.

2. _____ Clouding of the lens of the eye causing decreased vision.

3. _____ A disturbance of the carbohydrate metabolism because of an imbalance of hormones (insulin).

4. _____ Inflammation of the body joints causing pain and loss of movement.

5. _____ A disease of the central nervous system causing tremors in the body. This patient may shuffle his feet instead of taking steps.

6. _____ A number of different problems in the circulatory system sometimes causing pain, fatigue, and anxiety.

7. _____ Arterial changes in the brain possibly leading to stroke and paralysis.

Fill in the blanks with the vocabulary word to remember after reading the definition carefully.

1. _____ patients are those over 65 years of age.

2. Psycho refers to mental or _____ processes.

3. Social refers to interactions and _____ between people.

4. Walking is another word for being _____.

5. Bed-bound means unable to get out of _____.

6. Aging process refers to changes in the body caused by growing _____.

CHAPTER 21 QUIZ

Write <u>SOMETIMES</u>, <u>ALWAYS</u>, or <u>NEVER</u> in the spaces provided to complete each sentence.

1. When greeting a geriatric patient in the morning, _____ refer to the day, date and time.

2. The geriatric patient wants her side rails lowered. The nursing assistant should _____ lower the side rails without asking the head nurse, team leader, or supervisor.

3. _____ provide an ashtray for patients who smoke.

4. _____ encourage the patient to do as much as he or she is able to do.

5. _____ the geriatric patient may feel unsteady on his feet and may benefit from the use of a walker.

6. _____ provide care with a gentle touch and in a kind and considerate manner.

7. _____ call the geriatric patient mom or pop.

8. _____ ignore what the patient tells you.

9. _____ be alert for any condition which might cause an accident or injury to the patient.

10. _____ geriatric patients have difficulty hearing.

CHAPTER 22   REHABILITATION

WORKBOOK ASSIGNMENT #1, CHAPTER 22, SECTION 1
HOLISTIC APPROACH TO REHABILITATION

Find the list of objectives for this section. Next to each objective, write the page numbers where you can find information to help you meet these objectives.

WORKBOOK ASSIGNMENT #2, CHAPTER 22, SECTION 1
REHABILITATION

Read "Key Ideas: Rehabilitation" in your textbook. Using the following list of terms, fill in the spaces provided in each sentence. Each term will be used only once.

A. poor positioning   F. patient
B. small   G. alignment
C. emotional   H. therapy
D. occupational   I. recreational
E. depression   J. relationship

1. Rehabilitation programs are designed to offset the consequences of
    _____ for long periods of time.

2. To rehabilitate requires meeting the total needs of the patient, including
    physical needs, _____ needs, social/economic needs, and spiritual
    needs.

3. Rehabilitation includes learning to accept the accomplishment of _____
    goals.

4. The rehabilitation team includes the physical therapist and the _____
    therapist.

5. The nursing assistant helps the physical therapist to maintain the patient
    in good body _____.

6. Constant fatigue is one of the signs of _____ which the nursing
    assistant must report.

7. Involve the patient in programs where the decisions are made by the
    _____.

8. Listening, understanding, and respecting the patient's individuality
    establishes a genuine _____ with the patient.

9. Speech _____ is part of rehabilitation services.

10. Involve the patient in _____ activities to provide a creative change
    of pace.

WORKBOOK ASSIGNMENT #3, CHAPTER 22, SECTION 2
RANGE OF MOTION

Find the list of objectives for this section. Next to each objective, write the page numbers where you can find information to help you meet these objectives.

WORKBOOK ASSIGNMENT #4, CHAPTER 22, SECTION 2
RANGE OF MOTION

Read "Section 3: Range of Motion" in your textbook.

Circle the letter T if the statement below is true, F if it is false.

T or F   1.   A patient who is confined to bed or is unable to get out of bed does not need his muscles and joints exercised.

T or F   2.   ROM is the abbreviation for range of motion exercises.

T or F   3.   The nursing assistant may need to help a bedridden patient get the necessary exercise by performing ROM.

T or F   4.   Each ROM exercise should be done one time.

T or F   5.   The nursing assistant should encourage the patient to do as little as possible.

T or F   6.   Start at the patient's head and work your way down to the patient's feet.

T or F   7.   When performing ROM with a patient, the nursing assistant should be gentle. Never bend or extend a body part further than it can go.

T or F   8.   During ROM exercises, a patient complains to the nursing assistant that when he extends his arms he gets a sharp pain across his chest. The correct action for the nursing assistant to take would be to report this to her head nurse or team leader.

T or F   9.   A large amount of equipment is needed to perform ROM exercises.

T or F 10.   ROM exercises are always performed with the patient in a wheelchair.

WORKBOOK ASSIGNMENT #5, CHAPTER 22, SECTION 2
RANGE OF MOTION

Read "Section 3: Range of Motion" in your textbook.

Circle the letter of the correct answer for each question below.

1. Miss Burns, nursing assistant, is performing ROM exercises with one of her patients, Mr. Blake, who is confined to his bed due to a nerve disorder. As Miss Burns flexes Mr. Blake's leg, he complains of a sharp pain in his leg. What would be the proper action for Miss Burns to take?

   A. Tell Mr. Blake not to worry; this is normal when exercising.
   B. Stop the exercises, and report Mr. Blake's complaint to the head nurse or team leader.
   C. Ignore Mr. Blake's complaint and continue the ROM exercises.
   D. Let Mr. Blake rest for 15 minutes and then resume the exercises.
   E. None of the above.

2. A logical way to perform ROM so that each joint and muscle is exercised would be:

   A. To exercise the arms and feet first, then exercise the rest of the body
   B. To flex the neck, wrists, and ankles and then exercise the rest of the body
   C. Start at the waist and work your way down, then exercise the upper portion of the body
   D. Start at the head and work your way down to the feet
   E. Any way you do it would be logical.

SECTION 3

WORKBOOK ASSIGNMENT #6, CHAPTER 22, SECTION 3
RETURN TO SELF-CARE/ACTIVITIES OF DAILY LIVING

Find the list of objectives for this section. Next to each objective, write the page numbers where you can find information to help you meet these objectives.

WORKBOOK ASSIGNMENT #7, CHAPTER 22, SECTION 3
BATHING, DRESSING, AND GROOMING THE HANDICAPPED PATIENT

Read "Rules to Follow: Bathing the Handicapped Patient" and "Rules to Follow: Dressing and Grooming the Handicapped Patient" in your textbook.

Write DO or DON'T in the space beside each statement.

1. _____ place all equipment where the patient can reach it.

2. _____ encourage the patient to remain in pajamas all day.

3. _____ wash the involved arm first.

4. _____ place the soap on a dampened sponge or washcloth.

5. _____ be sure the patient turns on the hot water first.

6. _____ let the patient select his own clothing.

7. _____ undress the weak or involved extremity first.

8. _____ remind the patient to rinse off the soap and dry each part of the body.

9. _____ wash the areas the patient cannot reach.

10. _____ attempt any technique which has not been taught or outlined to you or to the patient by the occupational therapist, head nurse, team leader, or rehabilitation nurse.

WORKBOOK ASSIGNMENT #8, CHAPTER 22, SECTION 3
BOWEL AND BLADDER REHABILITATION FOR THE INCONTINENT PATIENT

Read "Key Ideas: Bowel and Bladder Rehabilitation for the Incontinent Patient" and the procedure that follows in your textbook.

Circle the correct response below.

1. To stimulate evacuation of the bowel and bladder, place the patient on a bedpan or on the bedside commode or walk him to the bathroom:

   A. Every four hours
   B. After meals and at bedtime
   C. First thing in the morning and at bedtime
   D. Every two hours
   E. Four times a day.

2. Pour _____ over the genital area into the bedpan to stimulate elimination.

   A. A soapsuds solution
   B. A saline solution
   C. Water at 105°F (40.5°C)
   D. Water at 115°F (46.1°C)
   E. Any of the above.

3. Which of the following should you do first?

   A. Remove the bedpan.
   B. Help the patient back into bed.
   C. Dry the patient with toilet tissue.
   D. Make the patient comfortable.
   E. Wash the patient's hands.

WORKBOOK ASSIGNMENT #9, CHAPTER 22, SECTION 3
RECTAL SUPPOSITORIES

Read "Key Ideas: Rectal Suppositories" and the "Procedure: Inserting a Rectal Suppository" in your textbook.

Fill in the blanks with the words listed below:

finger   signal   position
bedpan   gloves   training
sheets   thumb   press
                                        rectum

1. When inserting a suppository hold it between your _____ and index
    finger.

2. Gently insert it through the anus and along the wall of the _____.

3. Push it in as far as your index _____ will reach (two inches).

4. _____ folded toilet tissue against the anus briefly.

5. Remove the _____ turning them inside out as you remove them.

6. Replace the top _____.

7. Turn the patient into a _____ of comfort.

8. Give the patient the _____ cord.

9. Instruct the patient to signal you when he needs the _____.

10. If you are re-toilet _____ the patient, place him on a bedpan.

WORKBOOK ASSIGNMENT #10, CHAPTER 22
WORDS TO REMEMBER/GLOSSARY

Fill in the blanks with the vocabulary word to remember, after reading the
definition carefully.

1. _____ refers to all aspects of the mind such as feelings, thoughts,
    etc.

2. _____ refers to all aspects of living together in a group with
    other human beings.

3. _____ refers to low spirits that may or may not cause a change of
    activity.

4. _____ is a semi-solid preparation that is inserted into the rectum.

5. _____ is a person trained to assist the patient with
    activites related to motion.

6. _____ _____ is a trained person who assists the patient with
    performing their daily living tasks.

7. _____ means to bend.

8. These exercises move each muscle and joint through its full range of motion. Therefore, they assist confined patients to exercise their muscles and joints. These exercises are called _____ _____ _____.

9. The inability to control one's bladder or bowels. Incontinent patients cannot stop themselves from urinating or defecating. This is called _____.

10. The processes by which people who have been disabled by injury or sickness are helped to recover as much as possible of their original abilities to perform activities of daily living is called _____.

WORKBOOK ASSIGNMENT #11, CHAPTER 22, SECTION 3
LEARNING BY DOING

As you study the procedures in this chapter, read every step carefully. Think about the action words, the words that tell you what to do. Look at the pictures closely and read the captions. You will be able to remember what to do more easily if you try to do it after you have read about it. Learning by doing involves your whole body in the learning process, not just your eyes or ears. It is one of the most effective ways to learn.

Ask a fellow student or, if you are practicing at home, ask a friend or relative to play the part of the patient. Actually do all of the steps of the procedure several times, pretending you are a nursing assistant caring for several patients. Work slowly at first. Look at the textbook whenever you are not sure what to do next. Practice in this way many times until you can work quickly, and you no longer need to look at the textbook.

Switch roles with your partner, and you take several turns at being the patient. Not only will this give your partner a chance to learn the procedure, but you will benefit as well. By putting yourself in the patient's place, you will begin to understand how it feels to be a patient, and you will be able to treat real patients as you yourself would like to be treated.

Circle the letter of the correct answer.

1. Range of motion exercises:

    A. Move each muscle and joint through the full range of motion
    B. Exercise the patient's muscles and joints while he is in bed
    C. Are done in the hospital gym
    D. All of the above
    E. A and B only.

2. Which procedure is used to help the patient regain some or all of his lost bladder or bowel control?

    A. Making the Occupied Bed
    B. Straining the Urine
    C. Bowel and Bladder Rehabilitation/Training of the Incontinent Patient
    D. Applying a Warm Moist Compress
    E. A and D.

3. In the holistic approach, the health care team is concerned with:

    A. Only the disease or ailment for which the patient was admitted to the health care institution
    B. Only the psychological needs of the patient
    C. Only restoring the patient to a physical state of wellness
    D. Every aspect of the patient
    E. Only the patient's social and cultural environment.

4. The nursing assistant will assist the rehabilitation team by:

    A. Repeating exercises with the patient
    B. Observing the patient
    C. Listening to the patient
    D. Maintaining the patient in good body alignment
    E. All of the above.

5. The nursing assistant must report signs of depression which include:

    A. Low self-esteem
    B. Constant fatigue
    C. Constant talking and complaining
    D. A and B only
    E. All of the above.

SECTION 1

WORKBOOK ASSIGNMENT #1, CHAPTER 23, SECTION 1
THE TERMINALLY ILL PATIENT

Find the list of objectives for this section. Next to each objective, write the page numbers where you can find information to help you meet these objectives.

WORKBOOK ASSIGNMENT #2, CHAPTER 23, SECTION 1
THE TERMINALLY ILL PATIENT

Read "Key Ideas: The Psychological Aspects of Caring for a Terminally Ill Patient" in your textbook.

Circle the letter <u>T</u> if the statement below is true, <u>F</u> if it is false.

T or F   1.   The most important fact to remember when you are caring for a dying patient is that he is just as important as the patient who is going to recover.

T or F   2.   When a patient suspects he is going to die, he may be afraid to die alone.

T or F   3.   Your first responsibility is to help make the patient as comfortable as possible.

T or F   4.   Show respect for beliefs that are different from your own.

T or F   5.   Your second responsibility is to assist in meeting the emotional needs of the patient and his family.

WORKBOOK ASSIGNMENT #3, CHAPTER 23, SECTION 1
SIGNS OF APPROACHING DEATH

Read the list titled "Signs of Approaching Death" in your textbook. Write YES beside each statement that is a sign of approaching death. Write NO beside each statement that is not.

1. _____ The patient is incontinent of urine.

2. _____ The patient may perspire heavily even though his body is cold.

3. _____ The patient's feces look like black tar or coffee grounds.

4. _____ Mucous collecting in the patient's throat and bronchial tubes may cause a sound that is sometimes called "death rattle."

5. _____ The pulse often is rapid, but it becomes weak and irregular.

6. _____ The patient's lips and fingernails turn blue.

WORKBOOK ASSIGNMENT #4, CHAPTER 23, SECTION 2
POSTMORTEM CARE

Find the list of objectives for this section. Next to each objective, write the page numbers where you can find information to help you meet these objectives.

WORKBOOK ASSIGNMENT #5, CHAPTER 23, SECTION 2
POSTMORTEM CARE (PMC)

Read the "Procedure: Postmortem Care" in your textbook. Circle the letter of the correct response.

1. You are giving postmortem care, and you have removed all pillows except one. You placed the body in the supine or dorsal recumbent position and straightened the arms and legs. Which one of the following three tasks should you do next?

    A. Bathe the body, if necessary.
    B. Lower the backrest.
    C. Close the patient's eyes.

2. You closed the eyes and bathed the patient's body. Which one of the following three tasks should you do next?

    A. Comb the hair.
    B. Replace dentures in the mouth.
    C. Get postmortem care kit from CSR.

3. You closed the patient's mouth, fastened a chin strap in place, and combed the patient's hair. Which one of the following three tasks should you do next?

    A. Remove all jewelry and give it to the head nurse or team leader.
    B. Remove all soiled dressings, bandages, and tubes as per your head nurse's or team leader's instructions.
    C. Remove old marks from adhesive tape with adhesive remover.

4. You covered all wounds or open incisions with fresh, small, clean dressings, using adhesive tape to hold them in place. Which one of the following tasks should you do next?

    A. Remove all jewelry and give it to the head nurse or team leader.
    B. Attach identification tags to the bandage on the right big toe.
    C. Fold the arms over the abdomen.

5. The patient's ring cannot be removed because of swelling. Which one of the following three tasks should you do next?

    A. Leave it alone.
    B. Secure it in place with a one-inch bandage tied around it or a piece of tape, and report this to your head nurse or team leader.
    C. Report to your head nurse or team leader that you could not remove the ring.

WORKBOOK ASSIGNMENT #6, CHAPTER 23
WORDS TO REMEMBER/GLOSSARY

Fill in the blanks with the vocabulary word to remember after reading the definition carefully.

1. After death is also called _____.

2. Stiffening of a person's body and limbs shortly after death is called _____ _____.

3. A program of care that allows a dying patient to remain at home and die at home while receiving professionally supervised care is called _____.

4. Another word for dead is _____.

WORKBOOK ASSIGNMENT #7, CHAPTER 23
LEARNING BY DOING

As you study the procedures in this chapter, read every step carefully. Think about the action words, the words that tell you what to do. Look at the pictures closely and read the captions. You will be able to remember what to do more easily if you try to do it after you have read about it. Learning by doing involves your whole body in the learning process, not just your eyes and ears. It is one of the most effective ways to learn.

Ask a fellow student or, if you are practicing at home, ask a friend or relative to play the part of the terminally ill patient. Actually do all of the steps of the procedure several times, pretending you are a nursing assistant caring for several patients. Work slowly at first. Look at the textbook whenever you are not sure about what to do next. Practice in this way many times until you can work quickly, and you no longer need to look at the textbook.

Switch roles with your partner, and you take several turns at being the patient. Not only will this give your partner a chance to learn the procedure, but you will benefit as well. By putting yourself in the patient's place, you will begin to understand how it feels to be a patient, and you will be able to treat real patients as you yourself would like to be treated.

CHAPTER 23 QUIZ

Read the situations listed below. Then read the list of actions. Decide which action is the best thing to do in that situation. Put the letter of that correct action in the blank. Choose the correct response for each situation in the same way.

ACTIONS

A. Report this to your head nurse or team leader.
B. Be as helpful to them as you can.
C. Listen to the patient.
D. Change the position of the patient's body.

SITUATIONS

_____1. When a member of the family spends a lot of time with the patient

_____2. When a patient has been in the same position for several hours

_____3. When a dying patient talks a lot

_____4. When a dying patient says he needs spiritual help

_____5. When you think a dying patient has stopped breathing

_____6. When the patient seems to complain constantly.

Circle the letter T if the statement below is true, F if it is false.

T or F   7. If you notice any signs of approaching death, call a Code Blue.

T or F   8. Until you receive direct instructions from your head nurse or team leader, no postmortem care may be given to the patient.

T or F   9. After a patient has died, his body still must be treated with respect and given gentle care.

T or F 10. The patient's belongings are sent to the morgue with the body.

SECTION 1

WORKBOOK ASSIGNMENT #1, CHAPTER 24, SECTION 1
INTRODUCTION TO HOME HEALTH CARE

Find the list of objectives for this section. Next to each objective, write the page numbers where you can find information to help you meet these objectives.

WORKBOOK ASSIGNMENT #2, CHAPTER 24, SECTION 1
THE HOME HEALTH ASSISTANT

Read "Key Ideas: The Home Health Assistant" in your textbook. In the following list, circle the letters of all the items that are duties of the home health assistant.

A. Collecting specimens
B. Cleaning any equipment used in the care of the patient
C. Preparing and serving the patient's food
D. Applying heat applications
E. Housecleaning to maintain a clean environment for the patient
F. Making the patient's bed and changing linens
G. Administering medications
H. Preventing decubitus ulcers through proper skin care and frequent back rubs
I. Performing basic urine tests for sugar and/or acetone
J. Observing, measuring, and recording vital signs
K. Administering enemas
L. Assisting with personal care
M. Washing the patient's clothing, bed linens, and towels
N. Gastric lavage or gavage
O. Assisting the patient during the use of special equipment such as wheelchair, walker, or a commode.

WORKBOOK ASSIGNMENT #3, CHAPTER 24, SECTION 1
SAFETY IN THE HOME

Read the information titled "Safety in the Home and Safety Hazards" in your textbook.

Read Situation 1, then read the list of actions. Put the letter for the correct action in the space provided. Choose the correct response for each situation in the same way.

ACTIONS

A. Report this to the responsible family member and your supervisor.
B. Correct and unsafe condition immediately.
C. Remove the unsafe object from the patient's environment.

SITUATIONS

_____1. The patient spilled orange juice on the kitchen floor.

_____2. You notice that the electric cord from the washing machine is frayed.

_____3. You see a razor in the baby's room.

_____4. You notice the rug in the hallway is loose.

_____5. You notice an open bottle of pills on the coffee table.

_____6. The patient left a burning cigarette in the ashtray, and he is sleeping.

SECTION 2
_____

WORKBOOK ASSIGNMENT #4, CHAPTER 24, SECTION 2
NEWBORN AND INFANT CARE

Find the list of objectives for this section. Next to each objective, write the page numbers where you can find information to help you meet these objectives.

WORKBOOK ASSIGNMENT #5, CHAPTER 24, SECTION 2
INFANT FORMULA

Read "Key Ideas: Care of the Infant in the Home" in your textbook.

Circle the letter T if the statement below is true, F if it is false.

T or F   1. Formula will begin to spoil within two hours when it is left at room temperature.

T or F   2. Formula can be kept refrigerated for three to four days without spoiling.

T or F   3. Wash all cans and bottles before opening.

T or F   4. Powdered formula must be mixed with plain tap water.

T or F   5. Concentrated liquid formula must be mixed in equal parts with sterile water.

T or F   6. Formula must be kept refrigerated once the can has been opened or the formula has been mixed with water.

T or F   7. A bottle of formula should be kept refrigerated until 30 minutes before the feeding.

WORKBOOK ASSIGNMENT #6, CHAPTER 24, SECTION 2
STERILIZING BOTTLES

Read the "Procedure: Sterilizing Bottles" in your textbook.

Circle the letter of the correct answer below.

1. Why should you squirt hot, soapy water through the holes in the nipples before sterilizing them?

    A. To soften the rubber for more effective sterilizing
    B. To avoid having to sterilize the nipples
    C. To make sure there is a big enough hole in each nipple
    D. To clean out any dried-on formula
    E. None of the above.

2. In order to sterilize bottles, water must remain at a full boil for:

    A. 15 minutes
    B. 20 minutes
    C. 25 minutes
    D. 30 minutes
    E. None of the above.

WORKBOOK ASSIGNMENT #7, CHAPTER 24, SECTION 2
FEEDING AND BURPING THE INFANT

Read "Key Ideas: Burping the Infant" and "When Feeding the Baby from a Bottle" in your textbook. Complete the following sentences by filling in the blanks with the correct word from the list below. Each of the following words is used only once.

slowly   air
full   rub
vomiting   abdominal
two   held
temperature   pat

1. Most infants, especially those who are bottle-fed, swallow some _____ while drinking.

2. Air in the gastrointestinal tract can cause _____ and _____ pain.

3. You can prevent a buildup of air in the gastrointestinal tract by feeding the infant _____.

4. Burping the infant after every _____ ounces will also help to minimize the buildup of air in the gastrointestinal tract.

5. Gently _____ and/or _____ the infant's back until you hear the burp.

6. When feeding an infant, always tilt the bottle so the nipple is always _____ of formula.

243

7. An infant should always be _____ during the feeding.

8. You can check the _____ of the formula by shaking a few drops on the inside of your wrist.

WORKBOOK ASSIGNMENT #8, CHAPTER 24, SECTION 2
OBSERVING THE INFANT'S STOOL

Circle the letter of the correct answer for each question.

1. The normal bottle-fed infant may have stools that are:

   A. Dry and formed, brown
   B. Loose and seedy, yellow
   C. Green and watery
   D. Mustard color or yellow, lumpy and soft
   E. None of the above.

2. The normal breast-fed infant may have stools that are:

   A. Dry and formed, brown or black
   B. Mustard color or yellow, lumpy but soft
   C. Mustard color sometimes with a greenish tint, loose, seedy
   D. Green and watery
   E. None of the above.

3. A constipated infant's stool will appear:

   A. Dry and formed
   B. Mustard color or yellow, lumpy but soft
   C. Green and watery
   D. Loose and seedy, yellow
   E. None of the above.

4. "Infants can lose all of their body fluids and chemicals very quickly."
   The word that BEST describes this condition is:

   A. Constipation
   B. Fluid balance
   C. Diarrhea
   D. Dehydration
   E. None of the above.

5. Miss Perkins, nursing assistant, is helping to care for an infant in the home. One day while changing the infant's diaper Miss Perkins noticed a change in the infant's elimination pattern. The infant's stool appeared green and watery, and there was a distinct odor. Which would be the appropriate action for Miss Perkins to take in this situation?

   A. Miss Perkins should do nothing special because this type of infant stool is normal.
   B. Miss Perkins should report this to the infant's mother and let her take care of it.

C. Miss Perkins should ask the infant's mother to contact the physician for specific instructions, and she should also report this situation to her supervisor.

D. Miss Perkins should give the infant extra plain sterile water to correct the situation.

E. None of the above.

6. What important role can proper and frequent handwashing play in the care of an infant in the home?

A. Prevent and limit unnecessary diarrhea
B. To prevent and limit passing bacteria to the infant from the hands of those who handle him
C. To prevent having to bathe the infant
D. Both A and B
E. None of the above.

WORKBOOK ASSIGNMENT #9, CHAPTER 24, SECTION 2
CARING FOR THE UMBILICAL CORD

Read the information titled "Care of the Umbilical Cord" in your textbook.

Circle the letter T if the statement below is true, F if it is false.

T or F   1. Within two to three days the cord will dry, turn black, and fall off.

T or F   2. A wet diaper on top of a cord could cause an infection and slow the healing process.

T or F   3. The diaper should always be folded down away from the cord.

T or F   4. Laying an infant on his abdomen can hurt the cord.

T or F   5. Never pull on an umbilical cord.

WORKBOOK ASSIGNMENT #10, CHAPTER 24, SECTION 2
SPONGE BATHING THE INFANT

Read the information titled "Sponge Bathing the Infant" in your textbook.

Complete the following sentences by filling in the blanks with the correct word from the list below.

safety   dry   cover
once   sponge
water   mild

1. While the cord is still attached to the infant, only a _____ bath may be given.

2. An infant should be bathed at least _____ daily, usually in the morning.

3. Sponge bathing means gently washing each part of the baby's body with _____ soap and warm _____.

4. _____ of the infant during the sponge bath is very important.

5. Wash, rinse, and _____ each part of the baby's body very well.

6. Then _____ the body parts right away with the bath blanket.

WORKBOOK ASSIGNMENT #11, CHAPTER 24, SECTION 2
TUB BATHING THE INFANT

Read the information titled "Tub Bathing the Infant" in your textbook.

Circle the letter of the correct answer for each question.

1. You should fill the tub or sink with _____ of water.

   A. 1/2 full
   B. 1 to 2 inches
   C. 5 inches
   D. A or C
   E. None of the above.

2. To clean the infant's eyes you should:

   A. Gently wipe with a cotton ball moistened with warm water from the nose towards the ears.
   B. Splash the infant's face with warm water.
   C. Rub briskly back and forth over the infant's eyes with a soft cloth moistened with warm water.
   D. Any of the above.
   E. None of the above.

3. If the infant is female, always wash the perineal area:

   A. With alcohol
   B. From front to back
   C. From back to front
   D. With warm water and mild soap
   E. B and D.

4. To avoid having to leave the infant unattended in the tub or on the counter, you should:

   A. Lock the front door so no one can come in and distract you or the infant's mother.
   B. Take the telephone off the hook to prevent it from ringing during the bath, if the mother agrees.
   C. Keep your hands and eyes on the infant throughout the bath.
   D. Assemble your equipment before you begin.
   E. All of the above.

WORKBOOK ASSIGNMENT #12, CHAPTER 24, SECTION 2
INFANT SAFETY

Read the information titled "Infant Safety" in your textbook.

Circle the letter T if the statement below is true, F if it is false.

T or F 1. Even if an infant has not yet learned to roll over, he can still wiggle and kick until he falls.

T or F 2. Never leave an infant unattended in a crib.

T or F 3. Always wash your hands before handling the infant or his supplies.

T or F 4. After a feeding, always place the infant on his belly or on his side to prevent aspiration.

T or F 5. Never keep the side rails of the crib in the up position when the baby is sleeping.

T or F 6. Always check the temperature of the bath water before placing the infant in the tub or sink.

SECTION 3

WORKBOOK ASSIGNMENT #13, CHAPTER 24, SECTION 3
HOUSEHOLD MANAGEMENT

Find the list of objectives for this section. Next to each objective, write the page numbers where you can find information to help you meet these objectives.

WORKBOOK ASSIGNMENT #14, CHAPTER 24, SECTION 3
HOUSEKEEPING

Read "Key Ideas: Household Management" in your textbook.

Circle the letter of the correct response.

1. Cleaning the bathroom frequently with a disinfectant detergent will help to eliminate odors and:

    A. Make the bathroom look more appealing
    B. Cut down on the growth of bacteria.
    C. Cut down on the growth of plants.
    D. Make the patient get well more quickly.
    E. All of the above.

2. Wash dishes with _____ to control the spread of microorganisms.

    A. Cold water and soap powder
    B. Cold water and detergent
    C. Hot water and soap powder
    D. How water and bleach
    E. Hot water and detergent.

3. Even if the patient's meals are small, they must be:

   A. Soft and bland
   B. Therapeutically prescribed
   C. Hot and hearty
   D. Well-balanced
   E. The patient's favorites.

WORKBOOK ASSIGNMENT #15, CHAPTER 24, SECTION 3
REPORTING AND RECORDING

Read the information titled "Reporting and Recording" and "Activities of Daily Living -- A Sample Daily Report" in your textbook.

Here is a small portion of a daily report written by Miss White. Write <u>YES</u> or <u>NO</u> in the blanks to answer the questions that follow.

Home Health Assistant: Miss White 9-13-85

Patient's Name: Howard Bloom

8:00 A.M. Greeted the patient. Made coffee and chatted with Mr. Bloom while we both had a cup of coffee.

8:30 Mr. Bloom washed his hands and face, and I assisted him with oral hygiene. He listened to the radio while I made his breakfast.

9:00 Mr. Bloom read the paper while I did the dishes.

9:15 I assisted Mr. Bloom with a shower. I shaved his beard, and he got into bed to finish reading the newspaper.

10:00 His daughter arrived. While they visited, I did the laundry and mopped the kitchen floor.

11:00 His daughter offered to make lunch so while she cooked, I took Mr. Bloom for a walk in front of the house.

11:30 We all had lunch together. Mr. Bloom's daughter left. Mr. Bloom took a nap, and I cleaned up the lunch dishes.

_____1. Does this report tell what time Mr. Bloom had breakfast?

_____2. Does this report tell what Mr. Bloom actually ate for breakfast?

_____3. Does this report tell what type of bath Mr. Bloom had?

_____4. Does this report tell how long Mr. Bloom walked?

_____5. Does this report tell how he tolerated this activity?

_____6. Does this report tell what Miss White did while the patient napped?

WORKBOOK ASSIGNMENT #16, CHAPTER 24
WORDS TO REMEMBER/GLOSSARY

Fill in the blanks with the vocabulary word to remember after reading the definition carefully.

1. An abnormally frequent discharge of fluid fecal matter from the bowel is called _____.

2. Solid waste material discharged from the body through the rectum and anus is called _____.

3. A rather long, flexible, round organ that carries nourishment from the mother to the baby. It connects the umbilicus of the unborn baby in the mother's uterus to the placenta. This is called the _____ cord.

4. A diet containing a variety of foods from each of the basic food groups is called a _____ _____ diet.

WORKBOOK ASSIGNMENT #17, CHAPTER 24
LEARNING BY DOING

As you study the procedures in this chapter, read every step carefully. Think about the action words, the words that tell you what to do. Look at the pictures closely and read the captions. You will be able to remember what to do more easily if you try to do it after you have read about it. Learning by doing involves your whole body in the learning process, not just your eyes and ears. It is one of the most effective ways to learn.

Ask a fellow student or, if you are practicing at home, ask a friend or relative to play the part of the patient. Actually do all of the steps of the procedure several times, pretending you are a nursing assistant caring for several patients. Work slowly at first. Look at the textbook whenever you are not sure about what to do next. Practice in this way many times until you can work quickly, and you no longer need to look at the textbook.

Switch roles with your partner, and take several turns at being the patient. Not only will this give your partner a chance to learn the procedure, but you will benefit as well. By putting yourself in the patient's place, you will be able to treat real patients as you yourself would like to be treated.

Circle all the correct responses. There may be more than one answer to each question.

1. The home health assistant always works under the direct supervision of a:

    A. Physician
    B. Employer
    C. Registered nurse
    D. Home health agency
    E. Licensed practical nurse.

2. Safety in the home includes:

    A. Proper infection control
    B. Electrical and fire safety
    C. Accident prevention
    D. Proper nutrition
    E. Activities of daily living.

3. Infant formula must be mixed with _____.

    A. Sterile water
    B. Tap water
    C. A wooden spoon
    D. Concentrated liquids
    E. Fresh milk.

4. You will need to observe the infant's stool at each _____ in order to detect constipation or diarrhea.

    A. Feeding
    B. Burping
    C. Nap
    D. Diaper change
    E. Bath.

5. The cord will dry, turn black, and eventually fall off within:

    A. 5 to 21 days
    B. 5 to 10 days
    C. 10 to 20 days
    D. 3 to 10 days
    E. 2 to 6 days.

6. The infant can be given a tub bath after:

    A. Returning home from the hospital
    B. The cord has fallen off
    C. He has gained two pounds
    D. Your supervisor gives permission
    E. He is eight days old.

7. <u>NEVER</u> leave an infant unattended in the following places:

   A. Counters
   B. Chairs
   C. Cribs
   D. Beds
   E. Carriages.

8. The following are convenient times for you to perform housekeeping tasks:

   A. While the patient is sleeping
   B. While the patient is reading
   C. When the patient needs a back rub
   D. While feeding the patient
   E. While the patient is bathing.

FINAL TEST FOR BEING A NURSING ASSISTANT

1. For which of the following incidents must you make out an incident report?

   A. A patient falling out of bed
   B. Theft of a patient's purse
   C. A visitor slipping in the hallway
   D. Sticking your finger with a pin
   E. All of the above.

2. A nursing assistant serves a regular diet to a diabetic patient. She is guilty of:

   A. Nothing, it is the team leader's fault
   B. Professional abandonment
   C. Negligence
   D. Nothing, it is the dietician's fault
   E. Nothing, it is the fault of the doctor.

3. The urinary drainage bag should be emptied, measured in a graduate, and recorded on the intake and output sheet.

   A. At the beginning of each shift
   B. At the end of each shift
   C. Every two hours
   D. When the doctor asks you
   E. When the head nurse asks you.

4. The patient's first voiding after surgery should always be:

   A. Sent to the lab
   B. Measured and recorded on the I&O sheet
   C. Discarded
   D. Placed in a 24-hour collection container
   E. Saved in the patient's bathroom.

5. Normal body temperature taken by axilla is:

   A. 98.6°F
   B. 97.6°F
   C. 97.6°C
   D. 99.6°C
   E. 100.2°F.

6. After completing your work with an isolated patient, you should remove your dirty isolation gown:

   A. Before leaving the patient's room
   B. In the hall outside of the isolation unit
   C. Upon arriving at the central supply room
   D. Upon completion of all your isolation area duties for several patients
   E. After your day's work is finished.

252

7. B.P. means:

A. Bathroom privileges
B. Blood pressure
C. Bath privileges
D. Bed bath
E. Bottle for blood.

8. The temperature of enema solution should be:

A. 100°F
B. 105°F
C. 105°C
D. 115°C
E. 115°F.

9. When you have to feed a patient:

A. Serve the tray along with all the other trays, then come back to feed the patient
B. Bring the tray to the patient first and feed him after you have served all the other patients
C. Do not bring the tray into the room until you are ready to feed the patient
D. Have the kitchen hold the tray for one hour
E. Tell the visitors to feed the patient whenever they arrive

10. The brachial pulse is found:

A. At the wrist
B. Over the fold of the elbow, on the side closest to the patient's body
C. At the temple
D. In the groin
E. In the neck.

11. To prevent chest complications after surgery, watch for:

A. Signs of respiratory infection
B. Sneezing, sniffling, or coughing
C. Complaints or signs of chest pains
D. Elevated temperature
E. All of the above.

12. Generalized heat application means:

A. Heat put on one small area of the body
B. Heat applied to the entire body
C. Heat applied only to the feet
D. Heat applied only to the hands
E. Heat applied only to the head.

13. T.L.C. means:

    A. Temperature, pulse, and respiration
    B. Tender loving care
    C. Three times a day
    D. Physical therapy
    E. Weight.

14. When doing a clinitest, the amount of urine that you put into the test tube is:

    A. Two drops
    B. Four drops
    C. Five drops
    D. Ten drops
    E. Fifteen drops.

15. Rectal temperatures are taken when the patient:

    A. Is in a coma
    B. Has a nasogastric tube in place
    C. Has had oral surgery
    D. Is under 12 years of age
    E. All of the above.

16. When water spills on the floor, you wipe it up immediately:

    A. To help the maid
    B. To have something to do
    C. To prevent an accident
    D. So the hospital or home looks nice
    E. So the head nurse or team leader thinks you are being very cooperative.

17. A bed cradle is a:

    A. Box
    B. Place for a baby
    C. Frame to keep the top sheets from touching the patient
    D. Treatment
    E. Procedure.

18. When feeding a patient you should:

    A. Feed him/her all of the meat first
    B. Feed him/her all of the vegetables first
    C. Feed him/her all of the foods in variety
    D. Feed him/her all of the liquids first
    E. Feed him/her all of the salad first then all of the meat.

19. When filling an ice bag you fill it:

   A. One-half full
   B. Completely full
   C. One-third full
   D. Two-thirds full
   E. One-fourth full.

20. When giving daily indwelling catheter care, the nursing assistant should:

   A. Remove the catheter tip and apply antiseptic solution
   B. Remove the collection bag and replace with a new one
   C. Apply an antiseptic solution to the area of insertion and to the four inches of tubing closest to the patient
   D. Remove and change the entire system
   E. Wash the bag and the tubing.

21. The head nurse tells you to take vital signs. This means you should measure and record the patient's:

   A. Temperature, pulse, respiration, and blood pressure
   B. Temporal pulse
   C. Blood pressure
   D. Apical pulse
   E. Apical pulse deficit.

22. 1000 cc is the same as one:

   A. Pint
   B. Quart
   C. Milliliter
   D. Gallon
   E. Ounce.

23. The water temperature for a tub bath is:

   A. 98°F
   B. 212°F
   C. 105°F
   D. 115°F
   E. 115°C.

24. The normal diet is sometimes changed to meet a patient's special needs. These diets are known as:

   A. Special
   B. Restricted
   C. Modified
   D. Therapeutic
   E. All of the above.

25. A shampoo is given:

    A. When the patient's hair is dirty
    B. When the doctor orders the shampoo
    C. As part of morning care
    D. During evening care
    E. As part of activities of daily living.

26. The patient's liquid intake is measured when he consumes:

    A. Water
    B. Milk
    C. Soda
    D. Ice cream
    E. All of the above.

27. The correct positioning of a patient is:

    A. Therapeutic positioning
    B. Body alignment
    C. Diagnostic positioning
    D. Transporting a patient
    E. Restricted positioning.

28. When giving a complete bed bath, the water temperature should be:

    A. Room temperature
    B. 115°F
    C. 150°F
    D. 32°F
    E. 120°F.

29. A decubitus ulcer is a:

    A. Stomach ulcer
    B. Bedsore
    C. Duodenal ulcer
    D. Oral ulcer
    E. Rectal ulcer.

30. Your patient has just been placed on "nothing by mouth." You should:

    A. Partly fill the water container as directed
    B. Keep encouraging the patient to eat and drink
    C. Remove the water pitcher and all items of food and drink from the
        patient's reach
    D. Constantly keep the patient's water pitcher filled
    E. Offer the patient a soda.

31. When the patient is on intake and output, you should measure output each time the patient uses the:

    A. Commode
    B. Bedpan
    C. Urinal
    D. Specipan
    E. All of the above.

32. The patient with an indwelling urinary catheter constantly complains of pain in the lower abdomen. You should:

    A. Report to the head nurse or team leader
    B. Report to a doctor
    C. Question the patient about how much liquid he has taken
    D. Unless the bag is near full, continue your assignment
    E. Empty the bag, measure the graduate, and record on the intake and output sheet.

33. A specimen collected by having the patient cough up a substance from the lungs and bronchial tubes is called:

    A. Saliva
    B. Mucus
    C. Sputum
    D. Spit
    E. Excreta.

34. When giving a patient an enema, the normal adult patient should be placed in the:

    A. Fowler's position
    B. Trendelenburg position
    C. Sims' position
    D. Harris position
    E. Dorsal recumbent position.

35. Diastolic blood pressure is:

    A. The top number
    B. The bottom number
    C. The number you hear at the first clear sound
    D. The number after the sound starts
    E. The top number multiplied by two.

36. When a postoperative patient vomits, your first step is to:

    A. Wipe off the vomitus
    B. Immediately begin mechanical suctioning
    C. Turn the patient's head to one side
    D. Immediately begin manual suctioning
    E. Turn the patient to the prone position.

37. B.I.D. means:

    A. Twice a day
    B. Three times a day
    C. Four times a day
    D. Every six hours
    E. Every two hours.

38. When answering the patient's call signal:

    A. Go to the patient at once
    B. Go and ask the head nurse to respond
    C. Consider the condition of the patient and call the doctor
    D. Yell to the patient that you are coming
    E. All of the above.

39. Axillary temperature is taken at the:

    A. Groin
    B. Abdomen
    C. Armpit
    D. Neck
    E. Temple.

40. Which of the following is the routine site for taking the pulse?

    A. Carotid
    B. Radial
    C. Femoral
    D. Brachial
    E. Temporal.

41. When counting respirations, you should:

    A. Tell the patient what you are going to do
    B. Not tell the patient what you are going to do
    C. Count five respirations and then check your watch
    D. Have the patient count respirations while you take his pulse
    E. Take respirations before you count the pulse.

42. Normal body temperature taken orally is:

    A. 99.8°F
    B. 98.6°C
    C. 98.6°F
    D. 94.6°F
    E. 68.8°F.

43. Normal average range of pulse for adults is:

    A. 72 to 80 beats per minute
    B. 80 to 100 beats per minute
    C. 60 to 100 beats per minute
    D. 62 to 104 beats per minute
    E. 88 to 98 beats per minute.

44. The nursing assistant must report respirations when they are:

    A. Below 14 or over 28 per minute
    B. Below 10 or over 38 per minute
    C. Below 4 or over 22 per minute
    D. Below 16 or over 34 per minute
    E. Below 22 or over 88 per minute.

45. To prevent bedsores (decubitus ulcers) on the nonambulatory patient, the nursing assistant should:

    A. Turn the patient every two hours
    B. Keep the patient's body as clean and dry as possible
    C. Keep linen wrinkle-free and dry at all times
    D. Remove crumbs and any hard objects from the bed promptly
    E. All of the above.

46. Rules to follow for good body mechanics are:

    A. When an action requires physical effort, use as many muscles or groups of muscles as possible
    B. Keep your body aligned properly
    C. Keep your back straight
    D. Have your knees bent
    E. All of the above.

47. Examples of objective reporting are:

    A. Mrs. Smith in 404-B bed is breathing rapidly and the breaths appear to be shallow
    B. Mr. Williams in 204-B bed has voided urine that looks as if there is blood in it
    C. Mrs. Adams in 119-C bed cannot hold a glass without dropping it; she was able to do this at lunch time
    D. Mr. Cass in 103-D bed said he did not want to get out of bed today
    E. All of the above.

48. When collecting specimens you must be very accurate by:

    A. Collecting the specimen from the right patient
    B. Collecting the right specimen
    C. Collecting the specimen at the right time
    D. Using the right label
    E. All of the above.

49. When reporting that an enema was given you report:

    A. The time and type of enema given
    B. The results of the enema and the patient's reaction to the procedure
    C. Whether or not a specimen was obtained
    D. Your observations of anything unusual
    E. All of the above.

50. Intravenous poles should be wiped with an antiseptic solution:

    A. Once a shift
    B. Once a week
    C. Once in 24 hours
    D. After each use
    E. Before each use.

CHAPTER 1

CHAPTER 1, SECTION 1
Assignment #2--1. Ill   2. Prevent   3. Community   4. Education   5. Sciences

Assignment #3--1. B   2. A   3. E   4. C   5. E

Assignment #4--A. Teams   B. Leader   C. Group   D. Assignments   E. Team
        F. Registered Nurses (R.N.)   G. Licensed Practical Nurses
        (L.P.N.)   H. Nursing Assistants (N.A.)   I. Advisor   J. Members
        K. Task   L. Done

Assignment #5--A. Delivery   B. Professional   C. Accountable   D. Nursing
        E. Needs   F. Evaluating   G. Care   H. Works
        I. Patient   J. Responsibilities K. Patient   L. Individual

CHAPTER 1, SECTION 2
Assignment #7--1. Pediatric Patients   2. Geriatric Patients   3. Psychiatric
        Patients   4. Obstetrical Patient   5. Medical/Surgical Patients

Assignment #8--1. Chronic   2. Acute   3. a. Acute b. Chronic   4. Surgical
        5. a. Preoperative b. Operation   c. Postoperative

Assignment #9--1. Emergency Dept.   2. Coronary/Cardiac Care   3. Labor and
        Delivery   4. Newborn Nursery   5. Postoperative Recovery Room
        6. Premature Nursery   7. Intensive Care/Critical Care Unit
        8. Intensive Care/Critical Care Unit   9. Postoperative Recovery
        Room   10. Postoperative Recovery Room   11. Emergency Dept.
        12. Coronary Cardiac Care Unit   13. Emergency Dept.   14. Newborn
        Nursery

CHAPTER 1, SECTION 3
Assignment #12--1. B   2. C   3. D   4. A   5. F   6. E

Assignment #13--1. E   2. A   3. D   4. B   5. F   6. C

Assignment #14--1. E   2. C   3. C   4. F

Assignment #15--1. T   2. T   3. T   4. T

CHAPTER 1, WORDS TO REMEMBER/GLOSSARY

Assignment #16--1. Accuracy   2. Cooperate   3. Dependability   4. Ethical
        Behavior   5. Hygiene   6. Incident   7. Job Description

Chapter 1 Quiz--1. C   2. C   3. E   4. E   5. E   6. E   7. E   8. A   9. B
        10. E

CHAPTER 2, Section 1

Assignment #2--1. E (Note: This is the most desirable response. It makes hospital policy meet the patient's needs.)
2. D (Note: This is the most acceptable response. It tells the patient what is going to be done and when it is going to be done.)
3. D (Note: Many times the patient is trying to tell us something without really saying it. The head nurse or team leader will assess the patient to determine what is really wrong.)
4. C (Note: All members of the nursing health care team must cooperate with each other and the team leader.)
5. A (Note: The head nurse or team leader is a teacher, and you should be willing to learn new things all the time, to be able to do the best job possible and to give the patients the best care possible.)
6. B (Note: When you greet a patient, you should call the patient by name, introduce yourself by name and title, check the identification bracelet to be sure this is indeed the correct patient, and then deliver the message. Each patient is a person, with a name that should be used at all times.)

Assignment #3--1. Don't   2. Do   3. Don't   4. Don't   5. Do   6. Don't   7. Do   8. Do   9. Don't   10. Do

CHAPTER 2, SECTION 2

Assignment #5--1. B (Note: By reporting a change in the patient's condition to your head nurse or team leader, you are helping the patient.)
2. B (A severe change in bowel habits is a significant change in the patient's condition. By reporting this immediately, the head nurse or team leader can notify the physician.)
3. D (Note: When an emergency arises, the emergency signal is the correct signal to use. It gets the head nurse or team leader to the patient's room immediately. Itching is a very serious side effect of a blood transfusion and should be reported immediately.)

Assignment #6--1. O   2. O   3. S   4. S   5. O

CHAPTER 2, WORDS TO REMEMBER/GLOSSARY

Assignment #7--1. Chronic   2. Congenital   3. Cyanosis   4. Edema   5. Hereditary   6. Observation

Chapter 2 Quiz--1. a. F   b. F   c. T   d. T   e. T   2. C   3. E   4. C   5. B   6. B   7. C   8. C   9. D   10. D

CHAPTER 3

Chapter 3 Quiz--1. N.P.O.   2. O$_2$ 3. I.V.   4. Pre op   5. q2h
6. Registered Nurse   7. Specimen   8. Activities of daily living
9. Temperature, Pulse, Respirations   10. Central Supply Room

CHAPTER 4

CHAPTER 4, SECTION 1
Assignment #2--1. Spilled water on floor
2. C (Note: Spilled water could cause someone to slip or fall.)
3. The side rail on the far side of the bed is not raised.
4. A (Note: The patient could fall out of bed and be injured.)
5. Mr. Falcon
6. B (Note: Because he is receiving oxygen.)
7. Frayed razor cord
8. B (Note: Frayed cord could cause a fire or shock to someone trying to unplug it.)
9. The waste paper basket
10. D

CHAPTER 4, WORDS TO REMEMBER/GLOSSARY
Assignment #3--1. Cannula   2. Oxygen   3. Oxygen tent

Chapter 4 Quiz--1. F   2. F   3. T   4. T   5. T

CHAPTER 5

CHAPTER 5, SECTION 1
Assignment #2--P. All of the above

Assignment #3--1. T   2. F   3. T   4. T   5. F

Assignment #4--1. B   2. D   3. E

Assignment #5--A, B, C, E, F, H, J

Assignment #6--The nursing assistant should be using a paper towel to turn the faucet on or off.

CHAPTER 5, SECTION 2
Assignment #8--1. Dirty   2. Clean   3. Clean   4. Dirty   5. Dirty   6. Clean

Assignment #9--1. C   2. C   3. B

Assignment #10--B

Assignment #11--1. T   2. T   3. T   4. T   5. T

Assignment #12--1. C   2. E   3. A   4. D

Assignment #13--A. 1   B. 2   C. 5   D. 3   E. 4

CHAPTER 5, WORDS TO REMEMBER/GLOSSARY
Assignment #14--1. Autoclave   2. Communicable Infectious Disease   3. Friction
4. Infection   5. Medical Asepsis   6. Microorganism
7. Pathogens   8. Sterilization   9. Nosocomial   10. Asepsis
11. Bacteria   12. Clean   13. Dirty   14. Isolation
15. Isolation techniques 16. Spores   17. Virus

Chapter 5 Quiz--1. T   2. T   3. T   4. T   5. T   6. T   7. T   8. T   9. T 10. T
10. T

CHAPTER 6, SECTION 1
Assignment #2--Equipment missing: Bedpan

Assignment #3--A) Specimen containers   B) Tongue depressors   C) Urinal
              D) Tissues   E) Water pitcher   F) Plastic gloves
              G) Cups   H) Bedpan   I) Emesis basin

Assignment #4--A) Folding screen   B) Patient lift   C) Stretcher
              D) Supply table   E) Bed cradle   F) Walker
              G) Intravenous pole   H) Wheelchair

CHAPTER 6, SECTION 2
Assignment #6--1. Closed bed   2. Open bed   3. Postoperative bed
              4. Occupied bed

Assignment #7--1. Closed bed   2. Open bed   3. Occupied bed
              4. Postoperative bed

Assignment #8--See page 265.

Assignment #9--1. Do   2. Don't   3. Don't   4. Don't   5. Do   6. Don't
              7. Don't   8. Don't

Crossword puzzle (Chapter 6 — Words to Remember/Glossary)

Filled answers:

Across:
1. FANFOLD
3. BOTTOM
7. HAMPER
8. BEDSPREAD
9. SHAKE
11. UNIFORM
12. COTTON
17. SIDE
18. CBR
19. PIN
20. MATTRESS
23. MITERED
25. BAGS
26. HEMS

Down:
- FLOOR
- FITTED
- BLANKET
- LOOM
- REED
- CHAIR
- BEDSIDE
- LINEN
- ULCERS
- AIRBOX
- CONTAMINATED
- CORNERS
- PLASTIC
- REMOVE
- WRINKLED
- DRAW

CHAPTER 6, WORDS TO REMEMBER/GLOSSARY

Assignment #10--1. Bed cradle   2. Draw sheet   3. Emesis basin

Chapter 6 Quiz-- 1. T   2. F   3. F   4. T   5. F

CHAPTER 7

CHAPTER 7, Section 1
Assignment #2--1. C   2. A   3. D   4. B

Assignment #3--1. Oral hygiene   2. Make the bed   3. Pass fresh drinking water
4. Wash the patient's hands and face

Assignment #4--A. Teeth   B. Sick   C. Oral hygiene   D. Taste   E. Mouth
F. Fuzzy   G. Tongue   H. Coating   I. Appetite   J. Care
K. Mouth   L. Clean   M. Oral hygiene   N. Daily

Assignment #5--1. T   2. T   3. F   4. F   5. F   6. T

Assignment #6--1. B   2. C   3. A

Assignment #7--1. Complete bed bath   2. Tub bath   3. Partial bed bath
4. Shower   5. Complete bed bath   6. Shower   7. Partial bed bath
8. Complete bed bath

Assignment #8--1. F   2. T   3. F   4. T   5. T   6. F   7. T   8. T

Assignment #9--1. C   2. A   3. A   4. C   5. A

Assignment #10--1. T   2. F   3. T   4. T   5. F   6. F   7. T   8. F

Assignment #11--1. T   2. F   3. T   4. F   5. T   6. T   7. T   8. F   9. T
10. T   11. T   12. T

Assignment #12--1. Plastic   2. Three   3. Channel   4. Head   5. Open
6. Basin   7. Chair

CHAPTER 7, SECTION 2

Assignment #14--1. Bedpan   2. Bedpan cover   3. Toilet tissue   4. Towel
5. Wash basin with soap and water

Assignment #15--1. B   2. B   3. A   4. B   5. A   6. A   7. A   8. B

Assignment #16--1. Before   2. After   3. After   4. Before   5. Before

Assignment #17--1. F   2. T   3. T   4. F   5. F

CHAPTER 7, WORDS TO REMEMBER/GLOSSARY
Assignment #18--1. Dentures   2. Oral   3. Oral hygiene

Chapter 7, Quiz--1. I 2. G 3. A 4. H 5. D 6. B 7. J 8. E 9. C 10. F

CHAPTER 8

CHAPTER 8, SECTION 1
Assignment #2--1. Structure   2. Bodily   3. Microscopic   4. Cytoplasm, nucleus,
cell membrane   5. Division   6. Tissues   7. Organs   8. Systems

Assignment #3--1. Systems   2. Cell   3. Organs   4. Tissues

Assignment #4--1. g-h   2. c-h   3. c-e-g-h-j   4. d

Assignment #5--1. G   2. A   3. F   4. J   5. G   6. A   7. I   8. F 9. G
          10. J   11. F   12. A   13. A   14. H   15. C   16. I   17. F
          18. B   19. C   20. F   21. E   22. H   23. F   24. C   25. F
          26. B   27. E   28. F   29. H   30. C   31. F   32. B   33. C
          34. H   35. F   36. C   37. D   38. E   39. B   40. D   41. F
          42. D   43. E   44. D   45. C   46. F   47. B   48. D   49. E
          50. F   51. B   52. C   53. D   54. E   55. E   56. I   57. E

Assignment #6--1. E   2. F   3. A   4. G   5. H   6. D   7. C   8. B

CHAPTER 8, WORDS TO REMEMBER/GLOSSARY
Assignment #7--1. Abdomen   2. Anatomy   3. Cells   4. Connective tissue
          5. Epithelium   6. Organ   7. Tendons   8. Tissue   9. Tissue
          fluid   10. Tumor   11. Physiology

Chapter 8 Quiz--1. B   2. C   3. A   4. E   5. G   6. D   7. F   8. H   9. I
          10. J

CHAPTER 9

CHAPTER 9, SECTION 1
Assignment #1--

SKELETON AND SURFACE MUSCLES

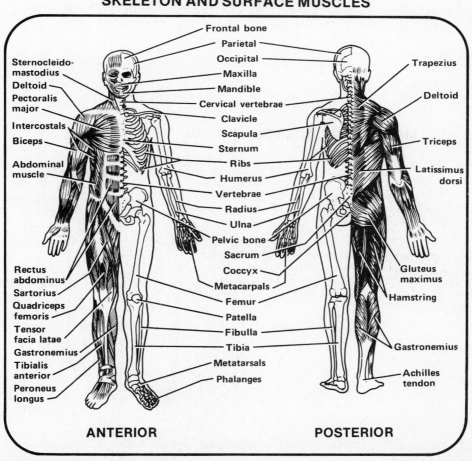

ANTERIOR   POSTERIOR

CHAPTER 9, SECTION 2
Assignment #3--1. B   2. B-A   3. D   4. With both hands   5. F

267

Assignment #4--1. C   2. B   3. E   4. A   5. E   6. B

Assignment #5--1. Bed   2. Folded   3. Under   4. Draw sheet   5. Roll   6. Grip
                7. Slide   8. Position   9. Friction   10. Irritation

Assignment #7--1. C   2. A   3. B   4. E   5. D   6. F   7. G

CHAPTER 9, SECTION 3

Assignment #9--1. F   2. T   3. F   4. T   5. T   6. F   7. T   8. T   9. T

Assignment #10--1. T   2. T   3. T   4. F   5. T

CHAPTER 9, SECTION 4
Assignment #12--1. Support   2. Weakness   3. Skin   4. Casts   5. Positions

Assignment #13--1. Never   2. Always   3. Always   4. Never   5. Always
                6. Always   7. Always   8. Always   9. Never   10. Always

CHAPTER 9, WORDS TO REMEMBER/GLOSSARY
Assignment #14--1. Ambulatory   2. Body alignment   3. Joint   4. Fracture
                5. Traction   6. Trapeze   7. Turning frames

Chapter 9 Quiz--1. D   2. B   3. E   4. D   5. E   6. B   7. A   8. B   9. B
                10. B

CHAPTER 10

CHAPTER 10, SECTION 1
Assignment #1--

MAGNIFIED CROSS SECTION OF THE SKIN

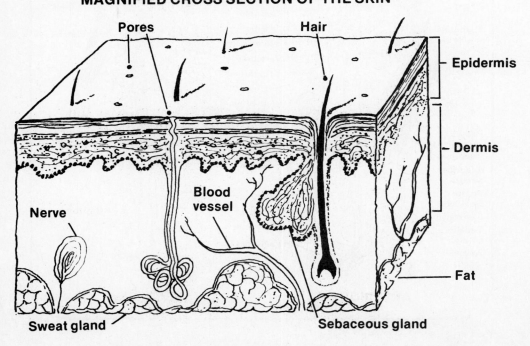

268

CHAPTER 10, SECTION 2
Assignment #3--1. Wrinkles   2. Bony   3. Friction   4. Redness   5. Two
           6. Bedpan   7. Rim   8. Dry   9. Rub   10. Plastic

Assignment #4--1. Assemble   2. Wash   3. Identify   4. Ask   5. Tell   6. Pull
           7. Put   8. Wipe, wash, removing   9. Rinse   10. Dry   11. Apply,
           massaging   12. Wipe   13. Apply   14. Leave   15. Turn
           16. Keep, remake   17. Make   18. Discard   19. Place
           20. Remove, Discard   21. Wash   22. Report

CHAPTER 10, WORDS TO REMEMBER/GLOSSARY
Assignment #5--1. Decubitus ulcers   2. Incontinence   3. Dermis   4. Epidermis

Chapter 10 Quiz--1. Yes   2. No   3. No   4. Yes   5. Yes   6. Yes   7. No
           8. Yes   9. A   10. C

CHAPTER 11

CHAPTER 11, SECTION 1
Assignment #1

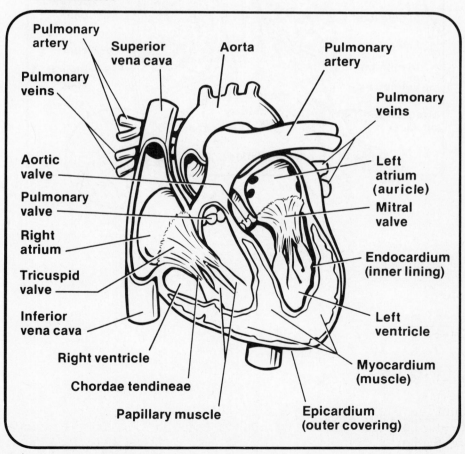

THE HEART

Pulmonary artery
Superior vena cava
Aorta
Pulmonary artery
Pulmonary veins
Pulmonary veins
Aortic valve
Left atrium (auricle)
Pulmonary valve
Mitral valve
Right atrium
Endocardium (inner lining)
Tricuspid valve
Inferior vena cava
Left ventricle
Right ventricle
Myocardium (muscle)
Chordae tendineae
Papillary muscle
Epicardium (outer covering)

THE RESPIRATORY SYSTEM

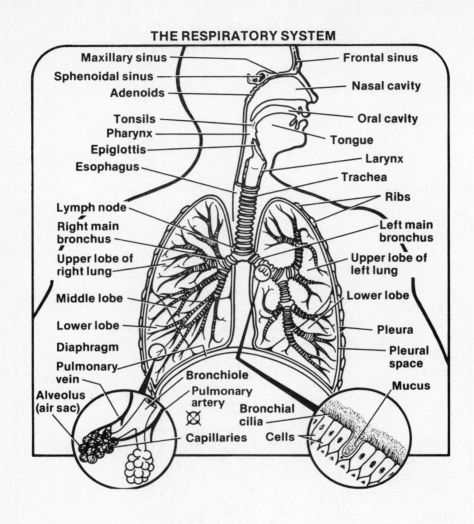

Maxillary sinus
Sphenoidal sinus
Adenoids
Tonsils
Pharynx
Epiglottis
Esophagus
Lymph node
Right main bronchus
Upper lobe of right lung
Middle lobe
Lower lobe
Diaphragm
Pulmonary vein
Alveolus (air sac)

Frontal sinus
Nasal cavity
Oral cavity
Tongue
Larynx
Trachea
Ribs
Left main bronchus
Upper lobe of left lung
Lower lobe
Pleura
Pleural space
Mucus

Bronchiole
Pulmonary artery
Bronchial cilia
Capillaries
Cells

Chapter 11, Section 2
Assignment #3--1. B.P.   2. T   3. R   4. R   5. B.P.   6. T   7. P   8. T
          9. R   10. P   11. B.P.   12. P

Assignment #4--1. A   2. C   3. B

Chapter 11, Section 3
Assignment #6--1. Do   2. Don't   3. Don't   4. Do   5. Do   6. Don't   7. Do
          8. Do

Assignment #7--

B.

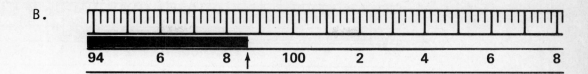

C.

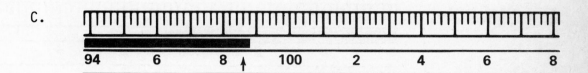

D.

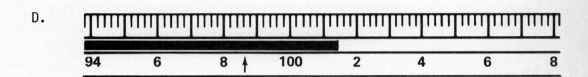

E.

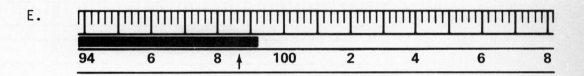

F.

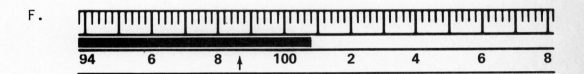

G.

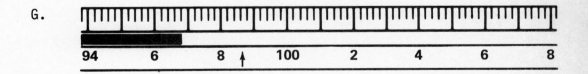

H.

I.

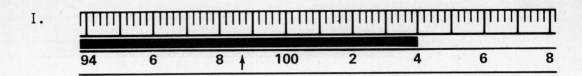

J.

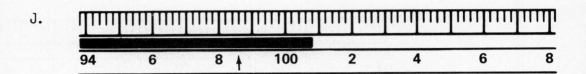

K.

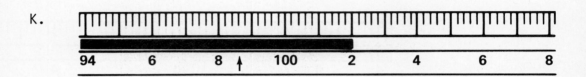

L.

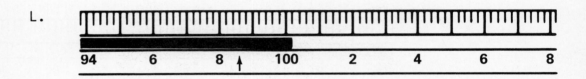

Assignment #8--1. C   2. B   3. A   4. A   5. B   6. B   7. A   8. C   9. A

Assignment #9--1. R   2. O   3. R   4. R   5. R   6. O   7. R   8. R

Assignment #10--1. Don't   2. Don't   3. Do   4. Don't   5. Do   6. Do   7. Do
                8. Don't   9. Do   10. Do

CHAPTER 11, SECTION 4
Assignment #12--

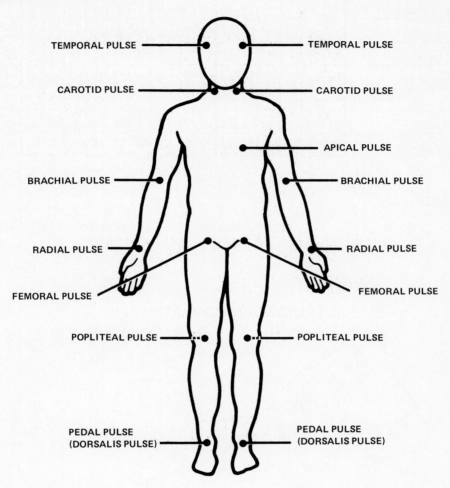

TEMPORAL PULSE — TEMPORAL PULSE

CAROTID PULSE — CAROTID PULSE

APICAL PULSE

BRACHIAL PULSE — BRACHIAL PULSE

RADIAL PULSE — RADIAL PULSE

FEMORAL PULSE — FEMORAL PULSE

POPLITEAL PULSE — POPLITEAL PULSE

PEDAL PULSE   PEDAL PULSE
(DORSALIS PULSE)   (DORSALIS PULSE)

Assignment #13--1. A   2. B   3. C   4. A   5. B

Assignment #14--A.

CHAPTER 11, SECTION 5
Assignment #16--1. T   2. T   3. T   4. T   5. T   6. F   7. F   8. T   9. T
                10. F

Assignment #17--1. C   2. B   3. E   4. A   5. D

Assignment #18--1. B   2. A   3. B   4. C   5. A

273

TEMPERATURE · PULSE · RESPIRATION FORM

Rm. #	Patient Name	12M T	P	R	4AM T	P	R	8AM T	P	R	12N T	P	R	4PM T	P	R	8PM T	P	R	
404A	Mary Jones	99⁶	88	20	99⁶	92	16	98³	80	16	98³	80	16	97⁴²	68	16	98²	80	18	
	Lil Carrie	98²	72	14	98²	74	20	97³	88	16	98	76	18	98	68	16	98⁴	72	16	
405A	Wm. Smith	97⁴	96	16	98²	78	18	99	86	18	99	72	14	(100²)	88	18	(105²)	88	20	
405B																				
406A	Pat Shiff	(101²)	104	22	(102²)	112	24	(101⁶)	96	22	(103)	96	24	(104²³)	104	26	(102⁴)	88	22	
406B	Gale Joseph	99³	92	20	100	88	22	99⁶	82	18	98⁸	72	18	(101²)	92	16	99⁶	86	18	

CHAPTER 11, SECTION 6
Assignment #21-- 1. C   2. C   3. A   4. B   5. E   6. B   7. D   8. (See below)
9. A   10. B   11. A. Mercury   B. Aneroid   12. A-C
13. A. Diaphragm   B. Bell   14. A   15. B

ANEROID SPHYGMOMANOMETER

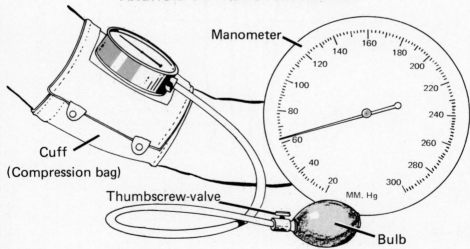

Manometer

Cuff
(Compression bag)

Thumbscrew-valve

Bulb

MM. Hg

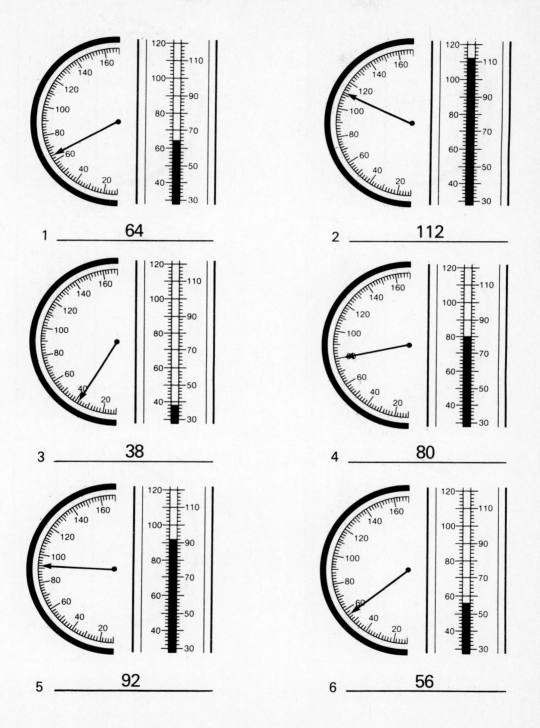

1 _____64_____

2 _____112_____

3 _____38_____

4 _____80_____

5 _____92_____

6 _____56_____

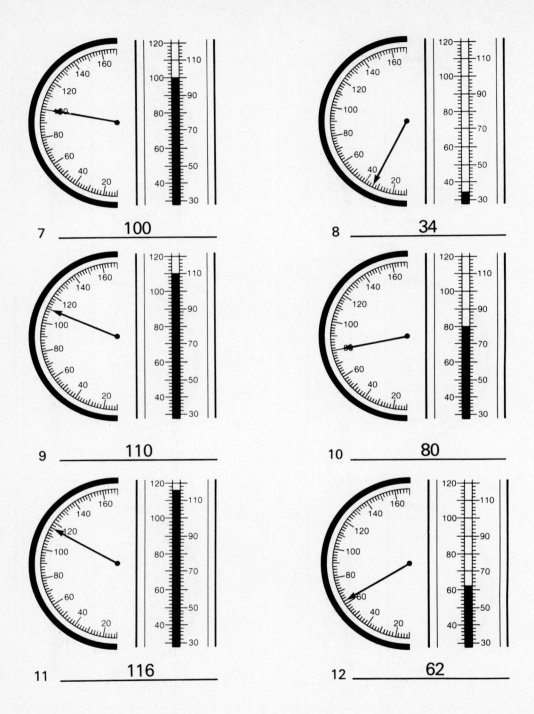

7 _____ **100**

8 _____ **34**

9 _____ **110**

10 _____ **80**

11 _____ **116**

12 _____ **62**

CHAPTER 11, WORDS TO REMEMBER/GLOSSARY
Assignment #23--1. Axillary   2. Blood pressure   3. Centigrade   4. Diastolic
            5. Fahrenheit   6. Pulse   7. Respiration   8. Systolic
            9. Vital signs   10. Blood   11. Pulmonary

Chapter 11 Quiz--1. N   2. A-B-C-D-E-F   3. E-H   4. J-K-L   5. K-L-N   6. M
            7. L   8. B   9. J-M-N   10. E-H

CHAPTER 12

CHAPTER 12, SECTION 1
Assignment #1--

THE DIGESTIVE SYSTEM

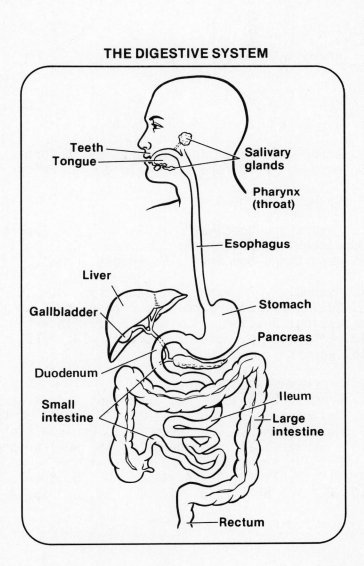

CHAPTER 12, SECTION 2
Assignment #3--1. C   2. B   3. A   4. D   5. B   6. D   7. D   8. C   9. A
            10. D   11. C   12. B   13. D   14. A

CHAPTER 12, SECTION 3
Assignment #6--1. T   2. F   3. T   4. T   5. T

Assignment #7--1. Do   2. Don't   3. Do   4. Do   5. Do   6. Do

Assignment #8--1. A   2. B   3. C   4. A   5. D   6. B   7. D   8. E   9. C
            10. E   11. E   12. A   13. C   14. D   15. E

CHAPTER 12, SECTION 4
Assignment #10--1. C   2. H   3. F   4. A   5. G   6. D   7. B   8. E

Assignment #11--1. F   2. T   3. F   4. T   5. F

Assignment #12--1. B   2. D   3. C   4. A

CHAPTER 12, SECTION 5
Assignment #14--1. B   2. E   3. D   4. B   5. A

Assignment #15--1. After   2. After   3. Before   4. Before   5. After
            6. Before   7. Before   8. Before   9. Before   10. After

Assignment #16--A, C, D, F, G, H, J

Assignment #17--1. Report and Specimen   2. Report   3. Report   4. Report and
            Specimen   5. Report and Specimen   6. Report   7. Report
            8. Report and Specimen   9. Report

Assignment #18--1. Assemble   2. Wash   3. Identify   4. Ask   5. Explain
            6. Pull   7. Turn, bend   8. Expose, raising   9. Lubricate,
            squeezing, rubbing   10. Raise   11. Insert   12. Use, attach
            13. Let, remain, remove, discard   14. Make   15. Wash
            16. Report

CHAPTER 12, WORDS TO REMEMBER/GLOSSARY
Assignment #19--1. Enema   2. Flatus   3. Lubricant   4. Rectal irrigation
            5. Calories   6. Nourishment   7. Anus   8. Colon
            9. Metabolism   10. Perineum   11. Peristalsis   12. Saliva
            13. Stomach   14. Therapeutic   15. Well-balanced diet

Chapter 12 Quiz--1. 1   2. 2   3. 3   4. 4   5. D   6. B   7. C   8. D   9. C
            10. E   11. B   12. D   13. E   14. C   15. A

THE URINARY SYSTEM

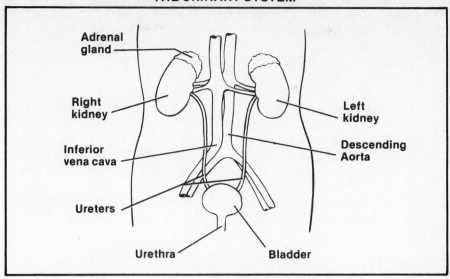

Assignment #3--1. T 2. T 3. T 4. T 5. T 6. F 7. T 8. F
Assignment #4--1. Imbalance   2. Imbalance   3. Balance   4. Imbalance 5. Imbalance
CHAPTER 13, SECTION 3
Assignment #6--

INTAKE AND OUTPUT SHEET						
Hospital # _____			Patient Name _____			
Date _____			Room # _____			
INTAKE			OUTPUT			
			URINE		GASTRIC	
Time 7-3	BY MOUTH	TUBE	PARENTERAL	VOIDED	CATHETER	EMESIS	SUCTION
	2	9		3			7
TOTAL	4	4	4		8		
Time 3-11	1	1	1	1	1	1	1
	2	9	,	3			
TOTAL					8		
Time 11-7	2	9	6	3			7
TOTAL					8		
24 HOUR TOTAL				5	5	5	5
24 Hour Grand Total ● Intake	10		24 Hour Grand Total ● Output			

279

Assignment #7--1. No   2. Fluid   3. Fluid   4. No   5. No   6. Fluid   7. No
            8. Fluid   9. Fluid   10. Fluid   11. Fluid   12. No   13. Fluid
            14. Fluid   15. Fluid   16. No   17. Fluid   18. No   19. Fluid
            20. No

Assignment #8--1. T   2. T   3. T   4. T   5. T

Assignment #9--1. 500cc   2. 100cc   3. 300cc   4. 650cc   5. 240cc   6. 300cc
            7. 900cc   8. 120cc   9. 400cc   10. 700cc

Assignment #10--1. Bedside   C) Tea   2. Graduate   3. Amount   4. Full
            5. A) Subtract   B) 100cc   C) Drank   D) Record   E) Intake
            6. A) 120cc   B) 120cc   C) Intake   7. A) 30cc   B) 30cc
            8. A) 240cc   B) 180cc   C) Consumed   D) 180cc   9. A) 90cc
            B) 90cc   10. A) Record   B) Intake   C) Intake   D) Sheet

Assignment #11--1. C) Water   2. Water   3. Graduate   4. Level - Cubic
            Centimeters   5. Paper   6. cc's

CHAPTER 13, SECTION 4
Assignment #13--1. A   2. D   3. C   4. E   5. E

CHAPTER 13, SECTION 5
Assignment #15--1. C   2. D   3. A   4. B   5. F   6. E   7. I   8. G   9. H

Assignment #16--1. Assemble   2. Wash   3. Pour   4. Place   5. Look   6. Record
            7. Write, record   8. Rinse, record   9. Rinse, return
            10. Wash   11. Report

Assignment #17--1. B   2. A   3. A   4. C   5. B   6. B   7. A

Assignment #18--1. B   2. C   3. A   4. D   5. B

Assignment #19--1. F   2. T   3. T   4. T   5. F

CHAPTER 13, SECTION 6
Assignment #21--1. Waste   2. Feces   3. Spit   4. Sputum   5. Laboratory
            6. Tests   7. Samples   8. Specimens   9. Collecting
            10. Accurate

Assignment #22--1. C   2. G   3. I   4. D   5. J   6. B   7. F   8. H   9. E
            10. A

Assignment #23--1. A   2. C   3. B

Assignment #24--1. Do   2. Don't   3. Don't   4. Don't   5. Do   6. Do   7. Don't
            8. Do   9. Do   10. Don't

Assignment #25--1. Sputum   2. Stool   3. Both   4. Sputum   5. Stool   6. Stool
            7. Stool   8. None   9. Sputum   10. Both

CHAPTER 13, WORDS TO REMEMBER/GLOSSARY
Assignment #26--1. Expectoration   2. Feces   3. Sputum   4. Urinalysis
                 5. Dehydration   6. Evaporate   7. Fluid   8. Fluid balance
                 9. Urinate   10. Catheter   11. Bladder   12. Urethra
Chapter 13 Quiz--1. B   2. C   3. A   4. D   5. A   6. B   7. C   8. B   9. D
                 10. C   11. D   12. B   13. B   14. F   15. C   16. D   17. B   18. A
                 19. G   20. E

CHAPTER 14

CHAPTER 14, SECTION 1
Assignment #1--

ENDOCRINE GLANDS

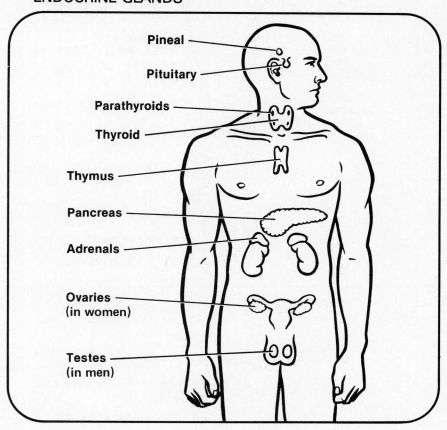

CHAPTER 14, SECTION 2
Assignment #3--1. B   2. A   3. C   4. C   5. B   6. C   7. C   8. B   9. B
               10. C   11. C   12. A   13. C   14. B   15. C   16. A   17. B   18. C
               19. A   20. B   21. B   22. A   23. C   24. C   25. A   26. C   27. B
               28. B   29. C   30. B
Assignment #4--1. T   2. F   3. F   4. F   5. T
Assignment #5--1. Don't   2. Don't   3. Do   4. Don't   5. Don't   6. Do
Assignment #6--1. F   2. F   3. T   4. T   5. F   6. T

CHAPTER 14, WORDS TO REMEMBER/GLOSSARY
1. Diabetes   2. Insulin   3. Pancreas
Chapter 14 Quiz--1. D   2. A   3. B-C   4. C-E   5. B-D

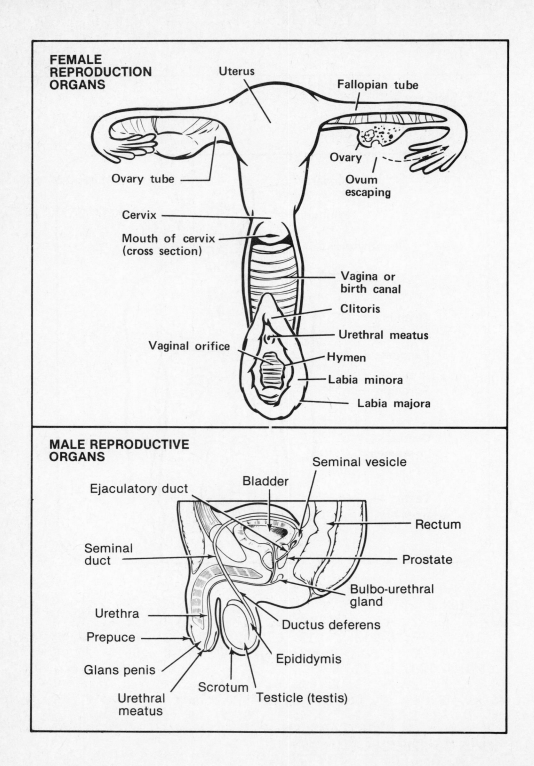

FEMALE REPRODUCTION ORGANS

Uterus

Fallopian tube

Ovary

Ovum escaping

Ovary tube

Cervix

Mouth of cervix (cross section)

Vagina or birth canal

Clitoris

Urethral meatus

Vaginal orifice

Hymen

Labia minora

Labia majora

MALE REPRODUCTIVE ORGANS

Ejaculatory duct

Bladder

Seminal vesicle

Rectum

Seminal duct

Prostate

Bulbo-urethral gland

Urethra

Ductus deferens

Prepuce

Glans penis

Epididymis

Urethral meatus

Scrotum

Testicle (testis)

CHAPTER 15, SECTION 2

Assignment #3--1. Do   2. Don't   3. Don't   4. Do   5. Do   6. Don't   7. Do
8. Do   9. Don't 10. Do

Assignment #4--<u>Segment 1</u>:   Poor, step 1, She forgot the bath thermometer, bedpan and cover, bath blanket, cotton balls and cleansing solution.

<u>Segment 2</u>:   Good

<u>Segment 3</u>:   Poor, step 15, She should have used 1,000 cc of water or solution. The water should be 105°F.

<u>Segment 4</u>:   Poor, step 19, She should have placed an emesis basin on the bed to receive the used cotton balls.

<u>Segment 5</u>:   Good.

<u>Segment 6</u>:   Poor, step 22, She should not touch the vulva with the nozzle.

<u>Segment 7</u>:   Poor, step 27, She forgot to help the patient sit up on the bedpan.

<u>Segment 8</u>:   Poor, steps 32 and 33, She forgot to lower the bed and she also forgot to change any linen that had become damp.

<u>Segment 9</u>:   Poor, step 36, She forgot to observe the contents of the bedpan.

<u>Segment 10</u>: Good.

CHAPTER 15, WORDS TO REMEMBER/GLOSSARY

1. Scrotom   2. Umbilicus   3. Vagina   4. Vaginal Douche

Chapter 15 Quiz--1. B   2. A   3. Malignant   4. A.I.D.S.   5. Comfort

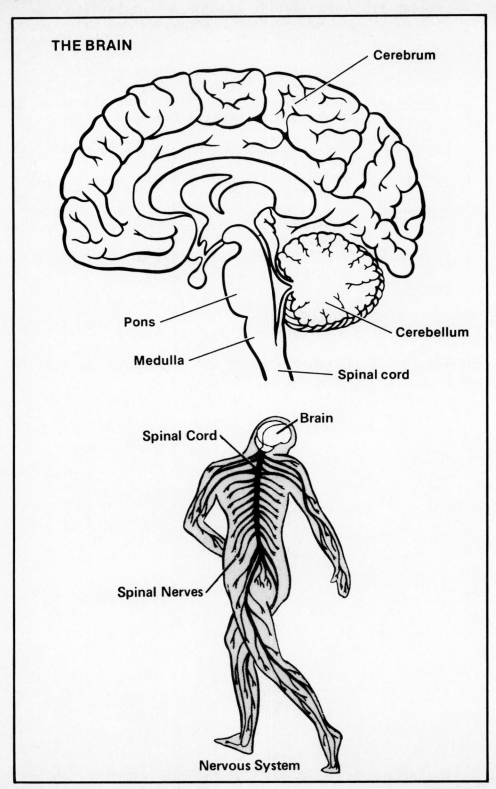

THE BRAIN

Cerebrum

Pons

Cerebellum

Medulla

Spinal cord

Brain

Spinal Cord

Spinal Nerves

Nervous System

SENSORY AND MOTOR PROCESSES IN OPERATION

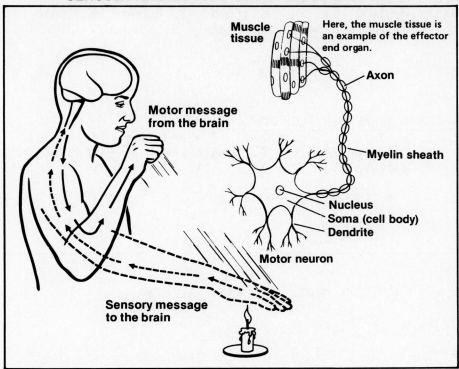

285

CHAPTER 16, SECTION 2
Assignment #3--1. D   2. A   3. C   4. D

Assignment #4--1. F   2. T   3. F   4. T   5. F   6. T   7. T   8. F   9. F

CHAPTER 16, SECTION 3
Assignment #6--1. Hygiene   2. Encrustation   3. Upper   4. Inner   5. Depress
            6. Gauze   7. Nose   8. Drain   9. Solution   10. Insert

CHAPTER 16, SECTION 4
Assignment #8--1. T   2. F   3. T   4. T   5. F   6. F   7. T   8. F   9. T
            10. T

CHAPTER 16, WORDS TO REMEMBER/GLOSSARY
Assignment #9--1. Seizure   2. Cerebral   3. Paralysis   4. Aphasia
            5. Cerebrovascular   6. Hemisphere   7. Encrustation   8. Plaque
            9. Rupture   10. Thrombus   11. Circulatory

Chapter 16 Quiz--1. 4   2. 1   3. 3   4. 2   5. 4   6. 3   7. 4   8. 3   9. 4
            10. 1

CHAPTER 17

CHAPTER 17, SECTION 1
Assignment #2--1. Cold   2. Heat   3. Heat   4. Heat   5. Cold   6. Cold

Assignment #3--1. G   2. L   3. L   4. L   5. G

Assignment #4--1. M   2. M   3. D   4. M   5. D   6. D   7. M   8. D   9. D
            10. D

Assignment #5--1. E   2. E   3. E   4. C   5. A

Assignment #6--1. Do   2. Do   3. Do   4. Don't   5. Don't   6. Do   7. Do
            8. Do   9. Don't   10. Don't

Assignment #7--A. 4   B. 8   C. 1   D. 12   E. 16   F. 13   G. 10   H. 2
            I. 7   J. 14   K. 5   L. 18   M. 11   N. 20   O. 9-B   P. 6
            Q. 19   R. 3   S. 17   T. 9-A   U. 15

Assignment #8--1. C   2. A   3. C   4. D   5. E

Assignment #9--1. Assemble   2. Wash   3. Identify   4. Ask   5. Tell
            6. Pull   7. Inspect   8. Plug   9. Place   10. Place, arrange
            11. Apply   12. Check   13. Return   14. Make   15. Wash
            16. Report

Assignment #10--1. F   2. T   3. T   4. T   5. F

CHAPTER 17, WORDS TO REMEMBER/GLOSSARY
Assignment #11--1. Cyanosis   2. Dry   3. Generalized   4. Localized   5. Moist

Chapter 17 Quiz--1. A-D-H-L-M   2. E-I-J-K   3. B-C-N   4. F-G   5. C   6. A
            7. C   8. A   9. A   10. B

CHAPTER 18

CHAPTER 18, SECTION 1
Assignment #2--1. B   2. A-B-E   3. C-D-E   4. A-B-C-D-E   5. A-B-C

Assignment #3--1. T   2. F   3. F   4. F   5. T

Assignment #4--1. T   2. F   3. F   4. T   5. T

CHAPTER 18, SECTION 2
Assignment #6--1. Ready   2. Transport   3. After   4. Number   5. Introduce

CHAPTER 18, SECTION 3
Assignment #8--1. After   2. Before   3. After   4. Before   5. Before

CHAPTER 18, WORDS TO REMEMBER/GLOSSARY
Assignment #9--1. Admission   2. Convalescent   3. Discharge

Chapter 18 Quiz--1. A   2. D   3. C   4. E   5. B   6. D   7. D and E   8. A
9. B   10. E

CHAPTER 19

CHAPTER 19, SECTION 1
Assignment #2--1. Don't   2. Do   3. Do   4. Do   5. Do   6. Do   7. Don't
8. Don't   9. Don't   10. Don't

CHAPTER 19, SECTION 2
Assignment #4--1. A   2. D   3. F   4. B   5. E   6. G   7. C   8. H   9. J
10. I   11. K

CHAPTER 19, WORDS TO REMEMBER/GLOSSARY

Assignment #5--1. Draping   2. Drape   3. Fowler's position   4. Lithotomy
5. Prone   6. Recumbent   7. Side   8. Sims'   9. Supine

Chapter 19 Quiz--1. During   2. Prepare   3. Prepare   4. During   5. T   6. T

CHAPTER 20

CHAPTER 20, SECTION 1
Assignment #2--1. C   2. E   3. A   4. D   5. B

Assignment #4--A, C, D, F, H

Assignment #5--1. B   2. C   3. C   4. A   5. A   6. B   7. A   8. C   9. C
10. B   11. C   12. C

CHAPTER 20, SECTION 2
Assignment #7--1. A   2. B   3. C   4. A   5. A   6. A

Assignment #8--1. B   2. A   3. C

CHAPTER 20, SECTION 3
Assignment #10--1. B   2. C   3. A   4. C   5. B   6. A   7. C

CHAPTER 20, SECTION 4
Assignment #12--1. 8   2. 13   3. 16   4. 25

Assignment #13--1. Operation   2. Abdomen   3. Feces   4. Stoma   5. Rectum
6. Ostomy appliance   7. Bag   8. Belt

CHAPTER 20, SECTION 5
Assignment #15--1. Support   2. Bandages   3. Pressure   4. Smooth   5. Bedsores
6. Reddened

Assignment #16--1. F   2. T   3. F   4. T

CHAPTER 20, WORDS TO REMEMBER/GLOSSARY
Assignment #17--1. Prep   2. Intravenous infusion   3. Anesthesia   4. Vomiting

Chapter 19 Quiz--1. A-B-C   2. C   3. B   4. A   5. C   6. D   7. B   8. E
9. A-D   10. C   11. T   12. F   13. F   14. T

CHAPTER 21

CHAPTER 21, SECTION 1
Assignment #2--1. C   2. B   3. D   4. F   5. E   6. A

Assignment #3--1. C   2. E   3. D   4. H   5. A   6. I   7. B   8. J   9. F
10. G

Assignment #4--1. B-D   2. E   3. E   4. E   5. D

Assignment #5--1. E   2. B   3. G   4. A   5. C   6. D   7. F

CHAPTER 21, WORDS TO REMEMBER/GLOSSARY
Assignment #6--1. Geriatric   2. Emotional   3. Relations   4. Ambulatory
5. Bed   6. Older

Chapter 21 Quiz--1. Always   2. Never   3. Always   4. Always   5. Sometimes
6. Always   7. Never   8. Never   9. Always   10. Sometimes

CHAPTER 22

CHAPTER 22, SECTION 1
Assignment #2--1. A   2. C   3. B   4. D   5. G   6. E   7. F   8. J   9. H
10. I

CHAPTER 22, SECTION 2
Assignment #4--1. F   2. T   3. T   4. F   5. F   6. T   7. T   8. T   9. F
10. F

Assignment #5--1. B   2. D

CHAPTER 22, SECTION 3
Assignment #7--1. Do   2. Don't   3. Do   4. Do   5. Don't   6. Do   7. Don't
8. Do   9. Do   10. Don't

Assignment #8--1. D   2. C   3. C

Assignment #9--1. Thumb   2. Rectum   3. Finger   4. Press   5. Gloves
6. Sheets   7. Position   8. Signal   9. Bedpan   10. Training

CHAPTER 22, WORDS TO REMEMBER/GLOSSARY
Assignment #10--1. Psychological   2. Psychosocial   3. Depression
                4. Suppository   5. Physical therapist   6. Occupational
                therapist   7. Flex   8. Range of motion   9. Incontinence
                10. Rehabilitation

Chapter 22 Quiz--1. E   2. C   3. D   4. E   5. D

CHAPTER 23 _____

CHAPTER 23, SECTION 1
Assignment #2--1. T   2. T   3. T   4. T   5. T

Assignment #3--1. No   2. Yes   3. No   4. Yes   5. Yes   6. No

CHAPTER 23, SECTION 2
Assignment #5--1. C   2. B   3. B   4. A   5. B

CHAPTER 23, WORDS TO REMEMBER/GLOSSARY
Assignment #6--1. Postmortem   2. Rigor mortis   3. Hospice   4. Deceased

Chapter 23 Quiz--1. B   2. D   3. C   4. A   5. A   6. C   7. F   8. T   9. T
                10. F

CHAPTER 24 _____

CHAPTER 24, SECTION 1
Assignment #2--A, B, C, E, F, H, I, J, L, M, O

Assignment #3--1. B   2. A   3. C   4. A   5. C   6. B

CHAPTER 24, SECTION 2
Assignment #5--1. T   2. F   3. T   4. F   5. T   6. T   7. F

Assignment #6--1. D   2. C

Assignment #7--1. Air   2. Vomiting, abdominal   3. Slowly   4. Two   5. Rub, pat
                6. Full   7. Held   8. Temperature

Assignment #8--1. D   2. C   3. A   4. D   5. C   6. C

Assignment #9--1. F   2. T   3. T   4. F   5. T

Assignment #10--1. Sponge   2. Once   3. Mild, water   4. Safety   5. Dry
                6. Cover

Assignment #11--1. B   2. A   3. E   4. E

Assignment #12--1. T   2. F   3. T   4. T   5. F   6. T

CHAPTER 24, SECTION 3
Assignment #14--1. B   2. E   3. D

Assignment #15--1. No   2. No   3. Yes   4. No   5. No   6. Yes

CHAPTER 24, WORDS TO REMEMBER/GLOSSARY
Assignment #16--1. Diarrhea   2. Stool   3. Umbilical   4. Well-balanced

Chapter 24 Quiz--1. C   2. A-B-C   3. A   4. D   5. B   6. B-D   7. A-B-D
                8. A-B

FINAL TEST ANSWER SHEET

 1. E   2. C   3. B   4. B   5. B   6. A   7. B   8. B   9. C   10. B   11. E
12. B   13. B   14. C   15. E   16. C   17. C   18. C   19. A   20. C   21. A   22. B
23. C   24. D   25. B   26. E   27. B   28. B   29. B   30. C   31. E   32. A   33. C
34. C   35. B   36. C   37. A   38. A   39. C   40. B   41. B   42. C   43. A   44. A
45. E   46. E   47. E   48. E   49. E   50. D